ALICE DOESN'T

ALICE

INDIANA UNIVERSITY PRESS • BLOOMINGTON

Chapters 3 and 4 are revised versions of articles published originally in *Screen* 22, no. 3 (1981) and *Discourse*, no. 5 (1983). Portions of chapters 1 and 2 have appeared in somewhat different form in *Yale Italian Studies*, no. 2 (1980) and *Cine-Tracts*, no. 11 (1980). The title and a few paragraphs of chapter 1 were also used for the concluding essay of Teresa de Lauretis and Stephen Heath, eds., *The Cinematic Apparatus* (London: Macmillan, and New York: St. Martin's Press, 1980).

Manufactured in the United States of America

Library of Congress Cataloging in Publication Data

De Lauretis, Teresa.
  Alice doesn't.

  "November 1982."
  Includes bibliographical references and index.
  1. Feminism and motion pictures—Addresses, essays, lectures.   2. Moving-pictures—Psychological aspects—Addresses, essays, lectures.   3. Moving-pictures—Philosophy—Addresses, essays, lectures.   4. Moving-picture plays—History and criticism—Addresses, essays, lectures.   5. Semiotics—Addresses, essays, lectures.
  I. Title.
PN1995.9.W6D4   1984   791.43′0141   83-48189
ISBN 0-253-30467-9
ISBN 0-253-20316-3 (pbk.)
7 8 9 10 99 98 97 96 95

CONTENTS

PREFACE

The essays collected in this book have been conceived and written over the past four years. On or very near my writing desk, in whatever city I happened to be during that time, there was always this sign:

I'd picked it up at a demonstration or a meeting—I don't remember exactly—and have kept it with me ever since. It seems appropriate to name the book after it, for not only is the book intended in the same sense as the placard, but both are signs of the same struggle, both are texts of the women's movement. The images or references suggested by the name "Alice" are many and will probably vary with each reader. Whether you think of Alice in Wonderland or Radio Alice in Bologna; of Alice B. Toklas, who "wrote" an autobiography as well as other things; or of Alice James, who produced an illness while her brothers did the writing; of Alice Sheldon, who writes science fiction, but with a male pseudonym; or of any other Alice, is entirely up to you, reader. For me it is important to acknowledge, in this title, the unqualified opposition of feminism to existing social relations, its refusal of given definitions and cultural values; and at the same time to affirm the political and personal ties of shared experience that join women in the movement and are the condition of feminist work, theory and practice.

March 1983

ACKNOWLEDGMENTS

My first thanks go to those women from and with whom I have learned what feminist practice is, what feminist theory should be, and, more rarely but far more delightfully, what the two can be together. I thank Tania Modleski, Catherine McClenahan, and Mary Russo for reading portions of the manuscript in draft form and rejoicing in my small victories. I thank all those who offered me their knowledges and skills, friendship or love during the writing of the essays, the hard times, and the difficulties; in particular, Elizabeth Elkins, Andreas Huyssen, Stephanie Jed, Patricia Mellencamp, Franco Mollia, Sondra O'Neale, Kaja Silverman, Michael Silverman, William Tay, Patrizia Violi. And Paul Loeffler. I thank the colleagues who welcomed me as Visiting Professor in the Literature Department of the University of California, San Diego, where I began to put the book together; and all my students, past and present, for the encouragement they gave by their seldom less than excited response.

Last but not least I thank the University of Wisconsin-Milwaukee Center for Twentieth Century Studies, its Director, Kathleen Woodward, its staff, Jean Lile and Carol Tennessen, for their magnificent hospitality during my tenure as a Fellow of the Center, where over a third of this book was written; and Ginny Schauble for her patience and virtuosity in typing it. I also want to acknowledge a special debt of gratitude to Dean William Halloran and former Associate Dean G. Micheal Riley of the College of Letters and Science for their continuous and generous support of my work.

ix

ALICE DOESN'T

Feminism, Semiotics, Cinema: An Introduction

IN THE HEART OF LOOKING-GLASS COUNTRY, between her fifth and sixth moves across the chessboard, Alice comes to the center of the labyrinth of language. This is also the center of her journey, of her dream, and of the game in which she as a white pawn plays and wins in eleven moves. On the wall of the labyrinth sits Humpty Dumpty, poised over the abyss of meaning; he thinks himself the master of language.

> "When *I* use a word," Humpty Dumpty said, in a rather scornful tone, "it means just what I choose it to mean—neither more nor less."
> "The question is," said Alice, "whether you *can* make words mean so many different things."
> "The question is," said Humpty Dumpty, "which is to be master—that's all."[1]

Like all masters, Humpty Dumpty is arrogant and very rude to Alice, tells her she's indistinguishable from all the others, and darkly intimates that she "might have left off at seven" (died or, more likely, stopped growing before puberty and adult womanhood). Yet she feels obliged to be polite, as she has been taught, and tries to make conversation with no idea that her simple questions are taken by him as riddles: riddles, however, to which he has all the answers, for precisely conversation, speech and language, is the terrain in which his mastery is exercised. ("It wasn't at all like conversation, she thought, as he never said anything to *her;* in fact, his last remark was evidently addressed to a tree.")

But of the two, it is Alice who wins in the long run because she knows that language, as Bakhtin put it, is "populated—over-populated—with the intentions of others"; and thus she knows ("I'm

1

certain of it, as if his name were written all over his face!") that his crash is imminent and irreparable.[2] The Looking-Glass world which the brave and sensible Alice enters, refusing to be caught up in her own reflection on the mantelpiece, is not a place of symmetrical reversal, of anti-matter, or a mirror-image inversion of the one she comes from. It is the world of discourse and of asymmetry, whose arbitrary rules work to displace the subject, Alice, from any possibility of naturalistic identification. Although in the transit Alice is divested of many a smug, self-righteous certainty, still she keeps on asking questions and sensibly wanting to know, who "dreamed it all?" However inextricably caught up she and the Red King may be in each other's dream and discursive universe, they are not one and the same; and her question is asked, as it should be, not metaphysically but practically.

If I have chosen this text to introduce a series of considerations on feminism, semiotics, and cinema, it is in part because it prevents an easy or natural identification. Lewis Carroll's Alice is hardly a feminist heroine; and the well-known biographical fact of the author's erotic interest in the seven-year old girl for whom the book was written would suffice to discourage a sentimental reading of the character. Far from proposing this Alice (or any other) as yet another "image" of woman or as the symbol of a struggle too real and too diversified to be even minimally "represented" in a single text, character, or person, I like to think of her tale as a parable suggesting—merely suggesting—the situation, the predicament, and the adventure of critical feminism. Like Alice with her ball of worsted, an unheroic Ariadne's thread which the kitten keeps unraveling, feminism has dared the labyrinth of language, has dreamed and been dreamed by the Red King, has met its Humpty Dumpty and its benevolent White Knight.[3] We too have been told we are all alike and should "have left off at seven"; we too have been polite, as we were taught, and have paid compliments and tried to make conversation only to be told we "have no more sense than a baby"; we too have been puzzled to see our simplest questions taken as riddles, and acquiesced to the answers given, "not wishing to begin an argument." We also know that language, of which we have no mastery, for it is indeed populated with the intentions of others, is finally much more than a game. And just as Alice actually gets the stuffy Humpty Dumpty to explain to her "the meaning" of Jabberwocky ("You seem very clever at explaining words, Sir," said Alice. "Would you kindly tell me . . ."), I like to imagine that feminism now interrogates semiotic and film theory, then moves on to the next square, where the echo eventually will reach us of Humpty Dumpty's great fall.

Now there is another example of how language means more than one wants it to mean. My comparison of the feminist critical journey with Alice's beyond the looking-glass is mediated by the textual metaphor of the game of chess which, long after Carroll, was to appeal to the (fore)fathers of structuralism, Saussure and Lévi-Strauss. They used it to illustrate the concept of system, Saussure's *langue* and Lévi-Strauss's structure, systems of rules that cannot but be obeyed if one is to communicate, speak, or participate in the social symbolic exchange; and precisely for this reason their theories have been considered pernicious or at least of little value to those eager to dismantle all systems (of power, oppression, or philosophy) and to theorize instead ideas of individual, class, race, gender, or group freedom. Even though I may not find the idea of freedom particularly useful and prefer to think in terms of resistance or contradiction, I admit to a certain instinctive annoyance at having to use, at having used unintentionally, the language of the masters. Yet I remind myself that language and metaphors, especially, need not be thought of as *belonging* to anyone; that in fact masters are made as we, like Alice, "make conversation" and, not wishing to begin an argument, accept their answers or their metaphors. "Whoever defines the code or the context, has control . . . and all answers which accept that context abdicate the possibility of redefining it."[4]

The point seems to be, one must be willing "to begin an argument," and so formulate questions that will redefine the context, displace the terms of the metaphors, and make up new ones. But language, I said, is more than a game. The argument begun by feminism is not only an academic debate on logic and rhetoric—though it is that too, and necessarily, if we think of the length and influence that formal schooling has on a person's life from pre-school to secondary and/or higher education, and how it determines their social place. That argument is also a confrontation, a struggle, a political intervention in institutions and in the practices of everyday life. That the confrontation is itself discursive in nature—in the sense that language and metaphors are always embedded in practices, in real life, where meaning ultimately resides—is implicit in one of the first metaphors of feminism: the personal is political. For how else would social values and symbolic systems be mapped into subjectivity if not by the agency of the codes (the relations of the subject in meaning, language, cinema, etc.) which make possible both representation and self-representation?

The unholy alliance of feminism, semiotics, and film is of long standing. In cinema the stakes for women are especially high. The representation of woman as spectacle—body to be looked at, place of sexuality, and object of desire—so pervasive in our culture, finds in narrative cinema its most complex expression and widest circulation. As it set about to demystify the sexist stereotyping of women, in the late sixties and early seventies, feminist film criticism first availed itself of the marxian critique of ideology and pointed to the sizable profits accruing to patriarchy from the accepted view of woman as the possessor of an ahistorical, eternal feminine essence, a closeness to nature that served to keep women in "their" place. The semiotic notion that language and other systems of signification (e.g., visual or iconic systems) produce signs, whose meanings are established by specific codes, was quickly seen as relevant to cinema and, in particular, capable of explaining how the image of woman was constructed by the codes of cinematic representation. How the two theoretical frameworks, marxism and semiotics, were integrated into the early feminist critique of Hollywood cinema is brilliantly evident in Claire Johnston's 1974 paper, "Women's Cinema as Counter-Cinema." For example:

> The idea that art is universal and thus potentially androgynous is basically an idealist notion: art can only be defined as a discourse within a particular conjuncture—for the purpose of women's cinema, the bourgeois, sexist ideology of male dominated capitalism. It is important to point out that the workings of ideology do not involve a process of deception/intentionality. For Marx, ideology is a reality, it is not a lie. . . . Clearly, if we accept that cinema involves the production of signs, the idea of non-intervention is pure mystification. The sign is always a product. What the camera in fact grasps is the "natural" world of the dominant ideology. Women's cinema cannot afford such idealism; the "truth" of our oppression cannot be "captured" on celluloid with the "innocence" of the camera: it has to be constructed/manufactured. New meanings have to be created by disrupting the fabric of the male bourgeois cinema within the text of the film.[5]

The reference to nonintervention signals a debate with the other major position within feminist filmmaking and criticism, a stance against theory and based on the idea of a feminine creativity buried deep in individual women-artists and waiting to be released or expressed through women's cinema. Thus the early work in what was called feminist film culture shows the trends that were to be pursued over the next decade and sets out the terms of an "argument," against mainstream culture and within feminism itself, which would be carried into other areas of critical writing and develop into current feminist theory.

The essays in this book continue and extend that argument. Each essay may be seen as an eccentric reading, a confrontation with theoretical discourses and expressive practices (cinema, language, narrative, imaging) which construct and effect a certain representation of "woman." By "woman" I mean a fictional construct, a distillate from diverse but congruent discourses dominant in Western cultures (critical and scientific, literary or juridical discourses), which works as both their vanishing point and their specific condition of existence. An example might be helpful. Let's say that this book is about woman in the same manner as science fiction is about the future—a speculation on present social reality cast in a particular perspective whose vanishing point is "the future," be it "1984," "2001," or "a year ago tomorrow." From the present state of scientific theory and research, the science fiction writer extrapolates and projects the possibilities that, were they to be realized and concretized into a social technology, would effect an alternate world; that future, then, being at once the vanishing point of the fictional construct and its specific, textual condition of existence, i.e., the world in which the fictional characters and events exist. Similarly here *woman,* the other-from-man (nature and Mother, site of sexuality and masculine desire, sign and object of men's social exchange) is the term that designates at once the vanishing point of our culture's fictions of itself and the condition of the discourses in which the fictions are represented. For there would be no myth without a princess to be wedded or a sorceress to be vanquished, no cinema without the attraction of the image to be looked at, no desire without an object, no kinship without incest, no science without nature, no society without sexual difference.

By *women,* on the other hand, I will mean the real historical beings who cannot as yet be defined outside of those discursive formations, but whose material existence is nonetheless certain, and the very condition of this book. The relation between women as historical subjects and the notion of woman as it is produced by hegemonic discourses is neither a direct relation of identity, a one-to-one correspondence, nor a relation of simple implication. Like all other relations expressed in language, it is an arbitrary and symbolic one, that is to say, culturally set up. The manner and the effects of that set-up are what the book intends to explore. And since one of its rhetorical strategies is questioning the terms in which the relation between *women* and *woman* has been cast, the two terms will be kept distinct.

The concerns of the essays are theoretical insofar as each avails itself of current work in several theoretical domains from semiotics and psychoanalysis to anthropology and visual perception. The book does not, however, align itself fully with any one theory or fit snugly within disciplinary boundaries; nor will it constitute itself as outline of a disciplinary field, least of all a discipline of feminism. In conducting my "argument" with those critical discourses and textual practices, whether by reading between the signs or by rereading a text against the grain, my purpose is twofold. One objective is to question the ways in which the relation between woman and women is set up, and to uncover/discover/track down the epistemological models, the presuppositions and the implicit hierarchies of value that are at work in each discourse and each representation of woman. At times the representation is sharply focused and clearly articulated: in Freud's and Lacan's theories of psychoanalysis, in the writings of Lévi-Strauss or Calvino, in Hitchcock's or Snow's films. In other cases, such as the films of Nicolas Roeg, Foucault's "history of sexuality," Eco's or Lotman's semiotics, the representation is excessive, ambiguous, obfuscated, or repressed.

The second project of this work is to confront those texts and discourses with feminist theory and *its* articulation of what is at issue in cultural notions of femininity, the working of desire in narrative, the configurations of affective investment in cinematic identification and spectatorship, or the mutual overdetermination of meaning, perception, and experience. For example, Virginia Woolf's metaphor of woman as the looking-glass held up to man ("Women have served all these centuries as looking-glasses possessing the magic and delicious power of reflecting the figure of man at twice his natural size") is recast in Laura Mulvey's film-theoretical metaphor of woman as image and bearer of the look, and followed through in its implications for female spectators.[6] What happens, I will ask, when woman serves as the looking-glass held up to women? Or further, with another metaphor, when women look into Perseus' shield while Medusa is being slain?

When Luce Irigaray rewrites Freud's essay on "Femininity," inscribing her own critical voice into his tightly woven argumentation and creating an effect of distance, like a discordant echo, which ruptures the coherence of address and dislocates meaning, she is performing, enacting, the division of women in discourse.[7] When others after her—writers, critics, filmmakers—turn back the question on itself and remake the story of Dora, *Bohème*, Rebecca, or Oedipus, opening up a space of contradiction in which to demonstrate the non-coincidence of woman and women, they also destabilize and finally alter the meaning of those representations.

Strategies of writing *and* of reading are forms of cultural resistance. Not only can they work to turn dominant discourses inside out (and show that it can be done), to undercut their enunciation and address, to unearth the archaeological stratifications on which they are built; but in affirming the historical existence of irreducible contradictions for women in discourse, they also challenge theory in its own terms, the terms of a semiotic space constructed in language, its power based on social validation and well-established modes of enunciation and address. So well-established that, paradoxically, the only way to position oneself outside of that discourse is to displace oneself within it—to refuse the question as formulated, or to answer deviously (though in its words), even to quote (but against the grain). The limit posed but not worked through in this book is thus the contradiction of feminist theory itself, at once excluded from discourse and imprisoned within it. The horizon of the present work is the question, scarcely broached as yet within feminist theory, of the politics of self-representation.

The first essay, "Through the Looking-Glass," examines the position of the subject in recent film theories developed from semiotics and psychoanalysis. Starting from a short fiction by Italo Calvino and using it as a parable, the essay retraces the assumptions of classical semiology and Lacanian psychoanalysis to their common heritage in structural linguistics, to Claude Lévi-Strauss's concept of the symbolic function and his hypothesis concerning kinship structures. It argues that, while semiology disregards the questions of sexual difference and subjectivity as non-pertinent to its theoretical field, and while psychoanalysis assumes them as its primary focus, both theories deny women the status of subjects and producers of culture. Like cinema, they posit woman as at once the object and the foundation of representation, at once telos and origin of man's desire and of his drive to represent it, at once object and sign of (his) culture and creativity. In this context subjectivity, or subjective processes, are inevitably defined in relation to a male subject, that is to say, with man as the sole term of reference. Hence the position of woman in language and in cinema is one of non-coherence; she finds herself only in a void of meaning, the empty space between the signs—the place of women spectators in the cinema between the look of the camera and the image on the screen, a place not represented, not symbolized, and thus preempted to subject (or self) representation.

"Imaging," the title of the second essay, initially designates in general terms the ways in which meanings are attached to images. But a discussion of the theoretical accounts of the image given by semiotics and recent studies of perception, and a reconsideration of the problem of cinematic articulation in the light of Pasolini's controversial critical statements, leads to another conception of the process of imaging. Because the spectator is personally addressed by the film and subjectively engaged in the viewing process, not only semantic and social values, but affect and fantasy as well, are bound to images. Cinematic representation can then be understood more specifically as a kind of mapping of social vision into subjectivity. In other words, cinema's binding of fantasy to significant images affects the spectator as a subjective production, and so the movement of the film actually inscribes and orients desire. In this manner cinema powerfully participates in the production of forms of subjectivity that are individually shaped yet unequivocally social. The second part of this chapter takes up one of the basic issues in women's cinema, the debate about the role of narrative within alternative and avant-garde film practices that has been central to film theory since Laura Mulvey set out its terms in "Visual Pleasure and Narrative Cinema." In view of the redefinition of the notion of imaging, the essay proposes that the present task of women's cinema may be not the destruction of narrative and visual pleasure, but rather the construction of another frame of reference, one in which the measure of desire is no longer just the male subject. For what is finally at stake is not so much how "to make visible the invisible" as how to produce the conditions of visibility for a different social subject.

The next two chapters look at two very recent films and make the previous arguments more concrete by bouncing them off or supporting them on specific texts. The analysis of each film is set in the context of issues that are currently being addressed in film criticism and independent filmmaking, in particular the issues of narrative, identification, and spectatorship. However different from one another, both films rely heavily on montage as the specific code by which narrativity is achieved or subverted. In "Snow on the Oedipal Stage," my reading of Michael Snow's *Presents* (1981) confronts the avant-garde project of breaking the nexus of look and identification in order to foreground the illusionist, naturalizing, and suturing operations of narrative cinema. Without denying the artistic excellence of Snow's films or the critical importance of his sustained work on the codes of cinematic perception, I will contend that *Presents* investigates the problem of seeing as one of enunciation or expressive modalities, a problem of "art," which as such does not pose the question of address, or how the spectator may be engaged in the film's imaging; thus, if female spectators find themselves placed in virtually the same position here as they are in classical cinema, it is because the inscription of sexual difference in the image(s) is not questioned but taken for granted. I will then argue that even in non-narrative films, such as *Presents,* narrativity is what overdetermines identification, the spectator's relations to the film, and therefore the very reading of the images.

Nicolas Roeg's *Bad Timing* (1980) is a narrative film, though one that works against narrative or seeks to disrupt its movement. My analysis will start from certain notions contained in the writings of Michel Foucault, which have become increasingly influential in film theory, and engage them from a feminist critical position. The reading is again eccentric: it argues both with and against Foucault's concepts of (1) sexuality as a technology of sex, (2) the social as a practical field in which technologies—cinema here—are deployed, and (3) the relation of "resistance" to the apparati of "power/knowledge." Finally it suggests other terms in which the figures of resistance, difference, and spectatorship (the relation of viewers to the film text and to cinematic representation) may be articulated, theoretically as well as cinematically.

An especial concern with narrative has developed in the last few chapters, and not by chance. Narrative and narrativity (by "narrativity" I mean both the making and the working of narrative, its construction and its effects of meaning) are fundamental issues in semiotics and cinema. And if film studies cannot do without narrative theory, any theory of narrative should be informed by the critical discourse on narrative that has been elaborated within film theory. As for feminist criticism, a theoretical return to narrative also means the opportunity to reread certain sacred texts and to pose questions long postponed, preempted, or displaced by other interests. Thus the fifth chapter, "Desire in Narrative," covers a wide range. It starts from the structural analysis of narrative in the early writings of Propp and Barthes, and compares it with subsequent semiotic views such as Lotman's on plot typology; it measures the semiotic postulate that narrative is universal and transhistorical with recent studies of its presence in various genres—from myth and folktale to scientific narrative or to what Victor Turner calls "social drama," from literature to film and from historical narration to the case history; it takes issue with literary critics, anthropologists, psychoanalysts, film theorists, and directors. The overriding question is: in what ways does narrative work to engender the subject in the movement of its discourse, as it defines positions of meaning, identification, and desire? Freud's story of femininity, Heath's account of narrative cinema as Oedipal drama, and Metz's notion of identification are points of departure for a more adequate and specific understanding of the subjective processes involved in female spectatorship: that is to say, the operations by which narrative and cinema solicit women's consent and by a surplus of pleasure hope to seduce women into femininity.

The last chapter, "Semiotics and Experience," picks up several strands of an "argument" begun in the first essay in the form of a question and disseminated across the book: how does one write or speak as a woman? How can we think of women outside of the man/non-man dichotomy, the "sexual difference" on which all discourse is based? How do we envision women as subjects in a culture that objectifies, imprisons and excludes, woman? Semiotics and psychoanalysis have given different accounts of the subject, but neither is capable of answering these questions. In re-examining Eco's reading of Peirce, and the debate in film theory around the Lacanian notion of the subject, the essay attempts to locate their limits in their failure or refusal to link subjectivity to practices and to theorize the notion of experience. This, it claims, remains one of the most important projects of feminist theory.

The format of this book does not follow a narrative, beginning-middle-and-end pattern. It is not, of course, a work of fiction. Nor does it set out to formulate a hypothesis, present supportive evidence, and conclude by confirming the hypothesis. It is not a theorem, a philosophical treatise, or a court brief. Curiously enough, however, the reader may catch it playing devil's advocate to Freud and public prosecutor against more innocuous personages; setting up Oedipus and restaging the encounter with the Sphinx; in sum, drawing its own allegories and maps of misreadings. It will tell some stories and retell others. It will look back at some movies with an evil eye. It will ask questions, interrupt, contend, suppose. And time and time again the same concerns, issues, and themes will return throughout the essays, each time diffracted by a different textual prism, seen through a critical lens with variable focus. There are, needless to say, no final answers.

Through the
Looking-Glass: Woman,
Cinema, and Language
1

From there, after six days and seven nights, you arrive at Zobeide, the white city, well exposed to the moon, with streets wound about themselves as in a skein. They tell this tale of its foundation: men of various nations had an identical dream. They saw a woman running at night through an unknown city; she was seen from behind, with long hair, and she was naked. They dreamed of pursuing her. As they twisted and turned, each of them lost her. After the dream they set out in search of that city; they never found it, but they found one another; they decided to build a city like the one in the dream. In laying out the streets, each followed the course of his pursuit; at the spot where they had lost the fugitive's trail, they arranged spaces and walls differently from the dream, so she would be unable to escape again.

This was the city of Zobeide, where they settled, waiting for that scene to be repeated one night. None of them, asleep or awake, ever saw the woman again. The city's streets were streets where they went to work every day, with no link any more to the dreamed chase. Which, for that matter, had long been forgotten.

New men arrived from other lands, having had a dream like theirs, and in the city of Zobeide, they recognized something of the streets of the dream, and they changed the positions of arcades and stairways to resemble more closely the path of the pursued woman and so, at the spot where she had vanished, there would remain no avenue of escape.

Those who had arrived first could not understand what drew these people to Zobeide, this ugly city, this trap.

ITALO CALVINO, *Invisible Cities*

ZOBEIDE, A CITY BUILT FROM A DREAM OF WOMAN, must be constantly rebuilt to keep woman captive. The city is a representation of woman; woman, the ground of that representation. In endless circularity ("streets wound about themselves as in a skein"), the woman is at

12

once the dream's object of desire and the reason for its objectification: the construction of the city. She is both the source of the drive to represent and its ultimate, unattainable goal. Thus the city, which is built to capture men's dream, finally only inscribes woman's absence. The founding tale of Zobeide, fifth of the category "Cities and Desire" in Calvino's *Invisible Cities,* tells the story of the production of woman as text.

Invisible Cities is a sort of historical fiction, a postmodern *Decameron* in which Marco Polo, eternal exile and trader in symbols, recounts to Kublai Khan, emperor of the Tartars, the cities he has seen.[1] As the voices of Marco Polo and Kublai Khan in dialogue across continents and centuries outline a vision of historical process sustained by a dialectic of desire, the whole text reproposes and reduplicates open-endedly the image of woman inscribed in the city of Zobeide. All the invisible cities described by Marco Polo to the Hegelian Khan have names of women, and, significantly, Zobeide is mentioned in *The Arabian Nights* as the name of a wife of the Caliph Harún-al-Rashid.

Woman is then the very ground of representation, both object and support of a desire which, intimately bound up with power and creativity, is the moving force of culture and history. The work of building and rebuilding the city, in a continuing movement of objectification and alienation, is Calvino's metaphor for human history as semiotic productivity; desire provides the impulse, the drive to represent, and dream, the modes of representing.[2] Of that semiotic productivity, woman—the dream woman—is both telos and origin. Yet that woman, because of whom the city is built, who is the foundation and the very condition of representation, is nowhere in the city, stage of its performance. ("This was the city of Zobeide, where they settled, waiting for that *scene* to be repeated *one night*. None of them, asleep or awake, ever saw the woman again.")

The city is a text which tells the story of male desire by performing the absence of woman and by producing woman as text, as pure representation. Calvino's text is thus an accurate representation of the paradoxical status of women in Western discourse: while culture originates from woman and is founded on the dream of her captivity, women are all but absent from history and cultural process. This is probably why we are not surprised that in that primal city built by men there are no women, or that in Calvino's seductive parable of "human" history, women are absent as historical subjects. This is also why I chose this text as a pre-text, a subterfuge, a lure, and an expedient with which to pose, from the impossible position of woman, the question of the representation of woman in cinema and language. Like cinema, the city of Zobeide is an imaginary signifier, a practice of language, a continuous movement of representations built from a dream of woman, built to keep woman captive. In the discursive space of the city, as in the constructs of cinematic discourse, woman is both absent and captive: absent as theoretical subject, captive as historical subject. The story of Zobeide therefore is a pretext to dramatize and to perform on my part the contradiction of feminist discourse itself: what does it mean to speak, to write, to make films *as* a woman? The following essay, then, is written on the wind, through the silence that discourse prescribes for me, woman writer, and across the chasm of its paradox that would have me at once captive and absent.

Recent critical speculation has been elaborating a theory of cinema as a social technology. Considering the cinematic apparatus as a historical and ideological form, it has proposed that the facts of cinema, and its conditions of possibility, should be understood as "a relation of the technical and the social."[3] Ironically, in view of the absence/captivity of woman as subject, and of the alleged feminine discomfort with technology, it has become apparent that such a relation cannot be effectively articulated without reference to a third term—subjectivity, or the construction of sexual difference—and that the questions of women, therefore, not only occupy a critical space within a historical materialist theory of the cinema, but directly concern its basic premises.

As social beings, women are constructed through effects of language and representation. Just as the spectator, the term of the moving series of filmic images, is taken up and moved along successive positions of meaning, a woman (or a man) is not an undivided identity, a stable unity of "consciousness," but the term of a shifting series of ideological positions. Put another way, the social being is constructed day by day as the point of articulation of ideological formations, an always provisional encounter of subject and codes at the historical (therefore changing) intersection of social formations and her or his personal history. While codes and social formations define positions of meaning, the individual reworks those positions into a personal, subjective construction. A social technology—cinema, for example—is the semiotic apparatus in which the encounter takes place and the individual is addressed as subject. Cinema is at once a material apparatus and a signifying practice in which the subject is implicated, constructed, but not exhausted. Obviously, women are addressed by cinema and by film, as are men. Yet what distinguishes the forms of that address is far from obvious (and to articulate the different modes of address, to describe their functioning as ideological effects in subject construction, is perhaps the main critical task confronting cinematic and semiotic theory).

Whether we think of cinema as the sum of one's experiences as spectator in the socially determined situations of viewing, or as a series of relations linking the economics of film production to ideological and institutional reproduction, the dominant cinema specifies woman in a particular social and natural order, sets her up in certain positions of meaning, fixes her in a certain identification. Represented as the negative term of sexual differentiation, spectacle-fetish or specular image, in any case ob-scene, woman is constituted as the ground of representation, the looking-glass held up to man. But, as historical individual, the female viewer is also positioned in the films of classical cinema as spectator-subject; she is thus doubly bound to that very representation which calls on her directly, engages her desire, elicits her pleasure, frames her identification, and makes her complicit in the production of (her) woman-ness. On this crucial relation of woman as constituted in representation to women as historical subjects depend at once the development of a feminist critique and the possibility of a materialist, semiotic theory of culture. For the feminist critique is a critique of culture at once from within and from without, in the same way in which women are both *in* the cinema as representation and *outside* the cinema as subjects of practices. It is therefore not simple numerical evidence (women hold up half of the sky) that forces any theoretical speculation on culture to hear the questions of women, but their direct critical incidence on its conditions of possibility.

Two major conceptual models are involved in the current development of film theory, from classical semiology to the more recent metapsychological studies, and in its formulation of concepts of signification, symbolic exchange, language, the unconscious, and the subject: a structural-linguistic model and a dynamic, psychoanalytic model. In both cases, cinema being an apparatus of social representation, the relations of subjectivity, gender, and sexual difference to meaning and ideology are central to cinematic theory. The structural-linguistic model, which excludes any consideration of address and of the social differentiation of spectators (that is to say, it excludes the whole issue of ideology and the subject's construction in it), assumes sexual difference as simple complementarity within a "species," as biological fact rather than sociocultural process. The psychoanalytic model, on the other hand, does acknowledge subjectivity as a construction in language, but articulates it in processes (drive, desire, symbolization) which depend on the crucial instance of castration, and are thus predicated exclusively on a male or masculine subject.

In the two models under consideration, then, the relation of woman to sexuality is either reduced and assimilated to, or contained within, masculine sexuality. But whereas the structural-linguistic model, whose theoretical object is the formal organization of signifiers, assumes sexual difference as a preestablished, stable semantic content (the signified in the cinematic sign), the psychoanalytic model theorizes it in an ambiguous and circular way: on the one hand, sexual difference is a meaning-effect produced in representation; on the other, paradoxically, it is the very support of representation. Both models, however, contain certain contradictions which are produced textually and are thus historically verifiable, for they can be located in the theoretical discourses and in the practices that motivate them.[4] For example, as we shall see, the equation

woman : representation :: sexual difference : value in nature

(where woman as sign or woman as the phallus equals woman as object of exchange or woman as the real, as Truth) is not the formula of a naively or malignantly posited equivalence, but the end result of a series of ideological operations that run through an entire philosophical-discursive tradition. It is in these operations that a theory of the cinema must interrogate its models, as it interrogates the operations of the cinematic apparatus.

More and more frequently in the critical discourse on cinema the nexus representation/subject/ideology has been posed in terms of language, language thus becoming the site of their junction and articulation. Cinema *and* language. What relation does the *and* express? Classical semiology linked cinema and language in what could be called a metonymic relation: all sign systems are organized like language, which is the universal system of signs; and cinema is one system among others, a branch or sector of that multinational organization of signs. Recently, a theory of signifying practices based in psychoanalytic discourse has established between cinema and language something of a metaphoric relation: though realized in distinct practices and material apparati, both cinema and language are imaginary-symbolic productions of subjectivity, their differences being less relevant than their homologous functioning in/as subject processes.

I have used the words "metonymic" and "metaphoric" not inadvertently but as an ironic quotation, to underline the dependence on language common to the semiological and psychoanalytic reflections (evident in Metz's recent work), a dependence which heavily tilts the balance of the relation and instates an obvious hierarchy, the subordination of cinema to language. I would suggest, further, that just as metaphor and metonymy—in the linguistic framework—continually slide ("are projected," Jakobson says)[5] one onto the other, so are those discourses mutually implicated, convergent, and complicit; and insofar as they originate in a structural-linguistic model of language, they circumscribe a theoretical area of cinema *as* language, each representing one axis, one mode of discursive operation.

So I have set myself up to argue that the semiological and psychoanalytic discourses on cinema are, in some respect, similar; and from my rhetorical strategy (the pretext of a parable about woman as representation) the reader might correctly infer that my argument will have something to do with woman. Semiotics tells us that similarity and difference are relational categories, that they can only be established in relation to some term of reference, which is thus assumed as the point of theoretical articulation; and indeed *that* term de-termines the parameters and the conditions of comparison. Should another term of reference be assumed, the relation and the terms of the relation would be differently articulated; the first relation would be disturbed, displaced, or shifted toward another relation. The terms, and perhaps the parameters and conditions of the comparison, would change, and so would the *value* of the "and," which in our case expresses the relation of cinema to language.

My term of reference and my point of enunciation (both of which, reader, are performative fictions) will be the absent woman inscribed in Calvino's city. Not unlike the city, cinematic theory is built in history, inscribed in historically specific discourses and practices; and while those discourses have traditionally assigned to woman a position of non-subject, the latter determines, grounds, and supports the very concept of subject and thus the theoretical discourses which inscribe it. Like the city of Zobeide, then, cinematic theory cannot disengage itself from the trouble caused by woman, the problems she poses to *its* discursive operations.

The hypothesis of classical semiology that cinema, like language, is a formal organization of codes, specific and non-specific, but functioning according to a logic internal to the system (cinema or film), apparently does not address me, woman, spectator. It is a scientific hypothesis and as such addresses other "scientists" in a closed economy of discourse. In building the city, the semiologist wants to know how the stones are put together to make a wall, an arcade, a stairway; he pretends not to care why any of these is being built or for whom. However, if asked about woman, he would have no doubt as to what woman was, and he would admit to dreaming about her, during the breaks from his research. Woman, he would say, is a human being, like man (semiology, after all, is a human science), but her specific function is reproduction: the reproduction of the biological species and the maintenance of social cohesion. The assumption implicit in his answer—that sexual difference is ultimately a question of complementarity, a division of labor, within the human species—is fully explicit in Lévi-Strauss's theory of kinship, which, together with Saussurian linguistics, historically constitutes the conceptual basis for the development of semiology.

The semiologist, of course, has read Lévi-Strauss as well as Saussure, plus some Freud and probably Marx. He has heard that the incest prohibition, the "historical" event instituting culture and found in all human societies, requires that women be possessed and exchanged among men to ensure the social order; and that although marriage regulations, the rules of the game of exchange, vary greatly throughout world societies, they all ultimately depend on the same kinship structures, which are really quite like linguistic structures. This, emphasizes Lévi-Strauss, becomes apparent only by applying the analytical method of structural linguistics to the "vocabulary" of kinship, i.e., by "*treating* marriage regulations and kinship systems *as a kind of language*."[6] One then understands that women are not simply goods or objects exchanged by and among men but also signs or messages which circulate among "individuals" and groups, ensuring social communication. Words too, like women, once had the value of (magical) objects; and to the extent that words have become common property, "la chose de tous," losing their character as values, language "has helped to impoverish perception and to strip it of its affective, aesthetic and magical implications." However, "in contrast to words, which have wholly become signs, woman has remained at once a sign and a value. This explains why the relations between the sexes have preserved that affective richness, ardour and mystery which doubtless originally permeated the entire universe of human communications."[7]

In sum: women are objects whose value is founded in nature ("valuables *par excellence*" as bearers of children, food gatherers, etc.); at the same time they are signs in social communication established and guaranteed by kinship systems. But it so happens that in positing exchange as a theoretical abstraction, a structure, and therefore "not itself constitutive of the subordination of women," Lévi-Strauss overlooks or does not see a contradiction that lies at the base of his model: for women to have (or to be) exchange value, a previous symbolization of biological sexual difference must have taken place. Women's economic value must be "predicated on a pre-given *sexual division* which must already be social."[8] In other words, at the origin of society, at the (mythical) moment in which the incest taboo, exchange, and thus the social state are instituted, the terms and items of exchange are already constituted in a hierarchy of value, are already subject to the symbolic function.

How can such remarkable oversight have occurred? Only, I suggest, as ideological effect of the discourses in which Lévi-Strauss's discourse is inscribed (as an "effect of the code")[9] and of the different semiotic values of the term "value" in the theoretical models upstream of Lévi-Strauss's theory: on the one hand the Saussurian model, which defines value entirely as a differential, systemic relation; on the other the marxian notion of value, invoked to support the thesis— Lévi Strauss's humanistic appeal—that women contribute to the wealth of a culture both as objects of exchange and as persons, as both signs and "generators of signs." Hence the confusion, the double status of woman as bearer of economic, positive value, and woman as bearer of semiotic, negative value, of difference.

The assimilation of the notion of sign (which Lévi-Strauss takes from Saussure and transposes to the ethnological domain) with the notion of exchange (which he takes from Marx, collapsing use-value and exchange-value) is not a chance one: it comes from an epistemological tradition that for centuries has sought to unify cultural processes, to explain "economically" as many diverse phenomena as possible, to totalize the real and, either as humanism or as imperialism, to control it. But the point is this: the universalizing project of Lévi-Strauss—to collapse the economic and the semiotic orders into a unified theory of culture—depends on his positing woman as the functional opposite of subject (man), which logically excludes the possibility—the theoretical possibility—of women ever being subjects and producers of culture. More importantly, though perhaps less evidently, this construction is founded on a particular representation of sexual difference implicit in the discourse of Lévi-Strauss.

So it is not a matter of proving or disproving his ethnological "data," the "real" conditions of women, their being or not being chattels or signs of masculine exchange in the real world. It is in his theory, in his conceptualization of the social, in the very terms of his discourse that women are doubly negated as subjects: first, because they are defined as vehicles of men's communication—signs of their language, carriers of their children; second, because women's sexuality is reduced to the "natural" function of childbearing, somewhere in between the fertility of nature and the productivity of a machine. Desire, like symbolization, is a property of men, property in both senses of the word: something men own, possess, and something that inheres in men, like a quality. We read:

> The emergence of symbolic thought must have required that women, like words, should be things that were exchanged. In this new case, indeed, this was the only means of overcoming the contradiction by which the same woman was seen under two incompatible aspects: on the one hand, as the object of personal desire, thus exciting sexual and proprietorial instincts; and, on the other, as the subject [sic] of the desire of others, and seen as such, i.e., as the means of binding others through alliance with them.[10]

Who speaks in this text? The syntactic and logical subject throughout is an abstract noun, "l'émergence de la pensée symbolique," and the verbs are impersonal in form as if a pure language—scientifically hypothetical, value-free, and subject-less—were speaking. And yet a speaking subject, a *masculine* subject of enunciation, has left his footprints. Consider the sentence: "the same woman was seen . . . as the object of personal desire, thus exciting sexual and proprietorial instincts." Barring a homogeneously homosexual society (from which Lévi-Strauss could not have descended), the personal desire and the sexual and proprietorial instincts must be those of men, who are then the term of reference for desire, sexuality, property.

And so that woman, seen as "the subject of the desire of others," is, lo and behold, the very same character running naked through the city's streets. But if we asked the semiologist about the dream woman, he would now say that she is just that—a dream, an imaginary fantasy, a fetish, a screen memory, a movie. By now, years have passed, and the semiologist has been reading Jacques Lacan and has forgotten Lévi-Strauss.

The city, he begins to think, is where the unconscious speaks, where its walls, arcades, and stairways signify a subject appearing and disappearing in a dialectic of difference. Upon entering the city, the traveler is taken up and shifted in the symbolic order of its layout, the disposition of buildings and empty spaces through which the traveler pursues imaginary reflections, apparitions, ghosts from the past. Here and there the traveler seems to recognize a certain place, stops for a moment, sutured; but that place is already another place, unfamiliar, different. And so, moving through the city—made hundreds of years ago but always new to each entering traveler and in continuous metamorphosis like the ocean of Lem's *Solaris*—the newcomer becomes a subject.

This is an interesting city indeed, thinks the semiologist, as she continues to read. She wants to know whether the traveler, having become a resident, so to speak, a subject-in-process through the city, can do anything to change some of its blatantly oppressive aspects, for example to do away with ghettos. But she finds out that the city is ruled by an agency—The Name of the Father—which alone undergoes no metamorphosis and in fact oversees and determines in advance all urban planning.

At this point the semiotician goes back to reread Lévi-Strauss and realizes that Lacan's conception of language as the symbolic register is forged on the trace of Lévi-Strauss's formulation of the unconscious as the organ of the symbolic function:

The unconscious ceases to be the ultimate haven of individual pecu-
liarities—the repository of a unique history which makes each of us an
irreplaceable being. It is reducible to a function—the symbolic function, which no doubt is specifically human, and which is carried out
according to the same laws among all men, and actually corresponds to
the aggregate of these laws. . . . The preconscious, as a reservoir of
recollections and images amassed in the course of a lifetime, is merely
an aspect of memory. . . . The unconscious, on the other hand, is
always empty—or, more accurately, it is as alien to mental images as is
the stomach to the foods which pass through it. As the organ of a
specific function, the unconscious merely imposes structural laws upon
inarticulated elements which originate elsewhere—impulses, emotions,
representations, and memories. We might say, therefore, that the preconscious is the individual lexicon where each of us accumulates the
vocabulary of his personal history, but that this vocabulary becomes
significant, for us and for others, only to the extent that the unconscious structures it according to its laws and thus transforms it into
language.[11]

No longer located in the psyche, the Lévi-Straussian unconscious is a
structuring process, a universal articulatory mechanism of the human
mind, the structural condition of all symbolization. Similarly, the
Lacanian symbolic is the structure, the law which governs the distribu-
tion-circulation of signifiers, to which the individual, child or *infans*
accedes in language, becoming a subject. In shifting the focus on to
the subject, Lacan departs from Lévi-Strauss's structuralism, but the
incest prohibition and structure of exchange guaranteed by the name
(and the no) of the Father are still the condition—the structural condition—of the subject's rite of passage through culture. Thus, as
Gayle Rubin observed, the same conceptual set underlies both
theories:

In one sense, the Oedipal complex is an expression of the circulation of
the phallus in intrafamily exchange, an inversion of the circulation of
women in interfamily exchange. . . . The phallus passes through the
medium of women from one man to another—from father to son,
from mother's brother to sister's son, and so forth. In this family Kula
ring, women go one way, the phallus the other. It is where we aren't. In
this sense, the phallus is more than a feature which distinguishes the
sexes; it is the embodiment of the male status, to which men accede,
and in which certain rights inhere—among them, the right to a
woman. It is an expression of the transmission of male dominance. It
passes through women and settles upon men. The tracks which it
leaves include gender identity, the division of the sexes.[12]

It is that structure which Lacanian psychoanalysis holds responsible for the non-coherence or division of the subject in language, theorizing it as the function of castration. Again, as for Lévi-Strauss, the point of enunciation (and term of reference) of desire, drive, and symbolization is a masculine one. For, even though castration is to be understood as referring strictly to the symbolic dimension, its signifier—the phallus—can only be conceived as an extrapolation from the real body. When Lacan writes, for example, that "the interdiction against autoerotism, bearing on *a particular organ,* which for that reason *acquires the value of an ultimate (or first) symbol of lack (manque),* has the impact of pivotal experience," there is no doubt as to which particular organ is meant: the penis/phallus, symbol of lack and signifier of desire.[13] Despite repeated statements by Lacan(ians) that the phallus is not the penis, the context of the terms I have emphasized in the quotation makes it clear that desire and signification are defined ultimately as a process inscribed in the male body, since they are dependent on the initial—and *pivotal*—experiencing of one's penis, on having a penis. In his discussion of *Encore,* Lacan's 1972–73 seminar devoted to Freud's question "What does a woman want?", Stephen Heath criticizes Lacan's "certainty in a representation and its vision," his pointing to Bernini's statue of Saint Teresa as the visible evidence of the *jouissance* of the woman.[14] Against the effective implications of the psychoanalytic theory he himself developed, Lacan runs analysis back into biology and myth, reinstating sexual reality as nature, as origin and condition of the symbolic. "The constant limit of the theory is the phallus, the phallic function, and the theorisation of that limit is constantly eluded, held off, for example, by collapsing castration into a scenario of vision"; thus, in the supposedly crucial distinction between penis and phallus, Heath concludes, "Lacan is often no further than the limits of pure analogical rationalisation."[15]

In the psychoanalytic view of signification, subject processes are essentially phallic; that is to say, they are *subject* processes *insofar* as they are instituted in a fixed order of language—the symbolic—by the function of castration. Again female sexuality is negated, assimilated to the male's, with the phallus representing the autonomy of desire (of language) in respect to a matter which is the female body. "Desire, as it detaches itself from need to assume its universal norm in the phallus, is masculine sexuality, which defines its autonomy by relinquishing to women the task of guaranteeing survival (survival of the species as well as satisfaction of the need for love)."[16]

The semiotician is puzzled. First, sexual difference is supposed to be a meaning-effect produced in representation; then, paradoxically, it turns out to be the very support of representation. Once again, as in the theory of kinship, an equivalence is postulated for two inconsistent equations. To say that woman is a sign (Lévi-Strauss) or the phallus (Lacan) is to equate woman with representation; but to say that woman is an object of exchange (Lévi-Strauss) or that she is the real, or Truth (Lacan), implies that her sexual difference is a value founded in nature, that it preexists or exceeds symbolization and culture. That this inconsistency is a fundamental contradiction of both semiology and psychoanalysis, due to their common structural heritage, is confirmed by Metz's recent work.[17]

In *The Imaginary Signifier* Metz shifts his investigation from the semiological study of the cinematic signifier (its matter and form of expression), to the "psychoanalytic exploration of the signifier" (p. 46), to the signifier in cinema "as a *signifier effect*" (p. 42). The great divide, in this exploration, is the Lacanian concept of the mirror stage, which generates the ambiguous notion of "imaginary signifier." The term "signifier" has a double status in this text—which corresponds to the two sides of the inconsistency mentioned earlier—and thus covers up a gap, a solution of continuity in Metzian discourse from linguistics to psychoanalysis. In the first part of the essay, his use of the term is consonant with the Saussurian notion of signifier; he speaks in fact of signifiers as "coupled" to signifieds, of the script as "manifest signified," and of the "manifest filmic material as a whole," including signifieds and signifiers (pp. 38–40). Elsewhere, however, the cinema signifier is presented as a subject-effect, inaugurated in or instituted by the ego "as transcendental yet radically deluded subject" (p. 54): "At the cinema . . . I am the *all-perceiving* . . . a great eye and ear without which the perceived would have no one to perceive it, the *constitutive* instance, in other words, of the cinema signifier (it is I who make the film)" (p. 51). The filmic material as "really perceived imaginary," as already imaginary, and as object, becomes significant (becomes an imaginary signifier) to a perceiving subject in language. Metz thus abandons the signified as too naive a notion of meaning (with which Saussure himself was never concerned) only to include, to subsume meaning in the signifier. The problem with this notion of meaning is that, being coextensive with the signifier as a subject-effect, meaning can only be envisaged as always already given in that fixed order which is the symbolic. In this sense Laplanche and Pontalis can say that "the phallus turns out to be the meaning—i.e., what is *symbolized*—behind the most diverse ideas"; as the signifier of desire, the phallus must also be its meaning, in fact the only meaning.[18] And so, caught between the devil and the deep blue sea, Metz in the last instance goes back to the equation of cinematic code(s) and language, now called the symbolic. He speaks of the "mirror of the screen, a symbolic apparatus" (p. 59) and of "inflections peculiar to the work of the symbolic such as the order of 'shots' or the role of 'sound off' in some cinematic sub-code" (p. 29). He returns, that is, to a systemic and linear notion of signification as approached by linguistics.[19]

The double status of the Metzian signifier—as matter/form of expression and as subject-effect—covers but does not bridge a gap in which sits, temporarily eluded but not exorcised, the referent, the object, reality itself (the chair in the theatre "in the end" is a chair; Sarah Bernhardt "at any rate" is Sarah Bernhardt—not her photograph; the child sees in the mirror "its own body," a real object, thus, henceforth, *known* to be its own image as opposed to the "imaginary" images on the screen, and so on, pp. 47–49). In the linguistic model, that gap, that substantial discontinuity between discourse and reality, can not be bridged nor can its terrain be mapped. On the contrary, the project of semiotics should be precisely such mapping: how the physical properties of bodies are socially assumed as signs, as vehicles for social meaning, and how these signs are culturally generated by codes and subject to historical modes of sign production. Lévi-Strauss retained the linguistic conceptual framework in his analysis of kinship and myth as semantic structures, and Lacan reinscribed that structuration in subject processes. That is why, finally, the psychoanalytic vision of cinema, in spite of Metz's effort, still poses woman as telos and origin of a phallic desire, as dream woman forever pursued and forever held at a distance, seen and invisible on another scene.

Concepts such as voyeurism, fetishism, or the imaginary signifier, however appropriate they may seem to describe the operations of dominant cinema, however convergent—precisely because convergent?—with its historical development as an apparatus of social reproduction, are directly implicated in a discourse which circumscribes woman in the sexual, binds her (in) sexuality, makes her the absolute representation, the phallic scenario. It is then the case that the ideological effects produced in and by those concepts, that discourse, perform, as dominant cinema does, a political function in the service of cultural domination including, but not limited to, the sexual exploitation of women and the repression or containment of female sexuality.

Consider the following discussion of the pornographic film by Yann Lardeau. The pornographic film is said relentlessly to repropose sexuality as the field of knowledge and power, power in the uncovering of truth ("the naked woman has always been, in our society, the allegorical representation of Truth"). The close-up is its operation of truth, the camera constantly closing in on the woman's sex, exhibiting it as object of desire and definitive place of *jouissance* only in order to ward off castration, "to keep the subject from his own lack": "too heavily marked as a term—always susceptible of castration—the phallus is unrepresentable. . . . The porno film is constructed on the *disavowal of castration,* and *its operation of truth is a fetishistic operation.*"[20] Cinema, for Lardeau, is *pour cause* pornography's privileged mode of expression. The fragmentation and fabrication of the female body, the play of skin and make-up, nudity and dress, the constant recombination of organs as equivalent terms of a combinatory are but the repetition, inside the erotic scene, of the operations and techniques of the apparatus: fragmentation of the scene by camera movements, construction of the representational space by depth of field, diffraction of light, and color effects—in short, the process of fabrication of the film from découpage to montage. "It all happens as if the porno film were putting cinema on trial." Hence the final message of the film: "it is cinema itself, as a medium, which is pornographic."

> Dissociated, isolated (autonomized) from the body by the close-up, circumscribed in its genital materiality (reified), [the sex] can then freely circulate outside the subject—as commodities circulate in exchange independently of the producers or as the linguistic sign circulates as value independent of the speakers. Free circulation of goods, persons and messages in capitalism—this is the liberation effected by the close-up, sex delivered into pure abstraction.[21]

This indictment of cinema and sexuality in capitalism as apparati for the reproduction of alienated social relations is doubtless acceptable at first. But two objections eventually take shape, one from the other. First: as the explicit reference to the models discussed earlier is posed in terms critical of the linguistic model alone, while the Lacanian view of subject processes is simply assumed uncritically, Lardeau's analysis cannot but duplicate the single, masculine perspective inherent in a phallic conception of sexuality; consequently, it reaffirms woman as representation and reproposes woman as scene, rather than subject, of sexuality. Second: however acceptable it may have seemed, the proposition that cinema is pornographic and fetishistic resolves itself in the closure of syllogism; begging its question and unable to question its premise, such a critique is unable to engage social practice and historical change.

But, it may be counter-objected, the pornographic film is just *that* kind of social practice; it addresses, is made for, men only. Consider, then, the classical Hollywood narrative fiction film, even the sub-genre known as "the woman's film."

> Think again of *Letter from an Unknown Woman* and its arresting gaze on the illuminated body of Lisa/Joan Fontaine, the film the theatre of that. . . . With the apparatus securing its ground, the narrative plays, that is, on castration known and denied, a movement of difference in the symbolic, the lost object, and the conversion of that movement into the terms of a fixed memory, an invulnerable imaginary, the object—and with it the mastery, the unity of the subject—regained. Like fetishism, narrative film is the structure of a *memory-spectacle,* the perpetual story of a 'one time', a discovery perpetually remade with safe fictions.[22]

Again and again narrative film has been exposed as the production of a drama of vision, a memory spectacle, an image of woman as beauty—desired and untouchable, desired *as* remembered. And the operations of the apparatus deployed in that production—economy of repetition, rhymes, relay of looks, sound-image matches—aim toward the achieved coherence of a "narrative space" which holds, binds, entertains the spectator at the apex of the representational triangle as the subject of vision.[23] Not only in the pornographic film, then, but in the "woman's film" as well, is cinema's ob-scenity the form of its expression and of its content.

The paradox of this condition of cinema is nowhere more evident than in those films which openly pose the question of sexuality and representation in political terms, films like Pasolini's *Salò,* Cavani's *The Night Porter,* or Oshima's *In the Realm of the Senses.* It is in such films that the difficulties in current theorization appear most evident and a radical reformulation of the questions of enunciation, address, and subject processes most urgent. For example, in contrast with the classic narrative film and its production of a fixed subject-vision, Heath asks us to look at Oshima's film as the film of the uncertainty of vision. It is, he writes, "a film working on a problem . . . the problem of 'seeing' for the spectator."[24] By shifting to—and forcing on—the spectator the question of "the relations of the sexual and the political in cinema," by marking out the difficulties—perhaps the impossibility—posed by their articulation in representation, the film includes the spectator's view as divided, disturbs the coherence of identification, addressing a subject in division. Thus, it is compellingly argued, the struggle is still with representation—not outside or against it—a struggle in the discourse of the film and on the film.

It is not by chance that women's critical attention to cinema most often insists on the notions of representation and identification, the terms in which are articulated the social construction of sexual difference and the place of woman, at once image and viewer, spectacle and spectator, in that construction.

> One of the most basic connections between women's experience in this culture and women's experience in film is precisely the relationship of spectator and spectacle. Since women are spectacles in their everyday lives, there's something about coming to terms with film from the perspective of what it means to be an object of spectacle and what it means to be a spectator that is really a coming to terms with how that relationship exists both up on the screen and in everyday life.[25]

In the psychoanalytic view of film as imaginary signifier, representation and identification are processes referred to a masculine subject, predicated on and predicating a subject of phallic desire, dependent on castration as the constitutive instance of the subject. And woman, in a phallic order, is at once the mirror and the screen—image, ground, and support—of *this* subject's projection and identification: "the spectator *identifies with himself*, with himself as pure act of perception"; and, "as he identifies with himself as look, the spectator can do no other than identify with the camera."[26] Woman, here, cannot but be "cinema's object of desire," the sole imaginary of the film, " 'sole' in the sense that any difference is caught up in that structured disposition, that fixed relation in which the film is centered and held, to which the times and rhythms and excesses of its symbolic tissue and its narrative drama of vision are bound."[27]

Like the city of Zobeide, those discourses specify woman in a particular natural and social order: naked and absent, body and sign, image and representation. And the same tale is told of cinema and its foundation: "men of various nations had an identical dream. They saw a woman running at night through an unknown city; she was naked, with long hair, and she was seen from behind . . ." (for the female sex is invisible in psychoanalysis, and in semiology it does not exist at all). What this theory of the cinema cannot countenance, given its phallic premise, is the possibility of a different relation of the spectator-subject to the filmic image, of different meaning-effects being produced for and producing the subject in identification and representation—in short, the possibility of other subject processes obtaining in that relation. This very issue, the modalities of spectatorship, informs the debate, in avant-garde film practice and theory, around narrative and abstract representation, illusionist versus structural-materialist film; it also provides the context and a main focus of the feminist intervention.[28] As Ruby Rich puts it,

> According to Mulvey, the woman is not visible in the audience which is perceived as male; according to Johnston, the woman is not visible on the screen. . . . How does one formulate an understanding of a structure that insists on our absence even in the face of our presence? What is there in a film with which a woman viewer identifies? How can the contradictions be used as a critique? And how do all these factors influence what one makes as a woman filmmaker, or specifically as a feminist filmmaker?[29]

What one may make, as a feminist filmmaker, are films "working on a problem," in Heath's words. Such must be, provisionally, the task of the critical discourse as well: to oppose the simply totalizing closure of final statements (cinema is pornographic, cinema is voyeurist, cinema is the imaginary, the dream-machine in Plato's cave, and so on); to seek out contradictions, heterogeneity, ruptures in the fabric of representation so thinly stretched—if powerful—to contain excess, division, difference, resistance; to open up critical spaces in the seamless narrative space constructed by dominant cinema *and* by dominant discourses (psychoanalysis, certainly, but also the discourse on technology as autonomous instance, or the notion of a total manipulation of the public sphere, the exploitation of cinema, by purely economic interests); finally, to displace those discourses that obliterate the claims of other social instances and erase the agency of practice in history.

The importance of psychoanalysis for the study of cinema and of film is not to be denied. It has served to dislodge cinematic theory from the scientistic, even mechanistic enterprise of a structural semiology and urged upon it the instance of the subject, its construction and representations, in cinematic signification—just as the historical importance of semiology was to affirm the existence of coding rules and thus of a socially constructed reality there where a transcendental reality, nature (Bazin's "ontology of the image"), had been supposed to manifest itself. Yet nature does linger, if only as residue, in the semiological and psychoanalytic discourses; it lingers as nonculture, non-subject, non-man, as—in the last instance—base and support, mirror and screen of his representation. Thus Lea Melandri, in another context:

> Idealism, the oppositions of mind to body, of rationality to matter, originate in a twofold concealment: of the woman's body and of labor power. Chronologically, however, even prior to the commodity and the labor power that has produced it, the matter which was negated in its concreteness and particularity, in its "relative plural form," is the woman's body. Woman enters history having already lost concreteness and singularity: she is the economic machine that reproduces the human species, and she is the Mother, an equivalent more universal than money, the most abstract measure ever invented by patriarchal ideology.[30]

The hierarchical setting up of "language" as universal model, which was the error of classical semiology, is also the structural heritage of Lacanian theory. In the former the language of linguistics was the privileged model for all signification systems and their "internal" mechanisms; in the latter the symbolic as phallic structure is taken as the primary model of subject processes. If and when either of those models is immediately transferred to the cinema, certain problems are voided and avoided, excluded from the theoretical discourse or disposed of within it. For example, the problem of materiality: while the material heterogeneity of the cinema in relation to language is readily asserted, the possibility that diverse forms of semiotic productivity, or different modes of sign production, may entail other subject processes has not been seriously considered.[31] Then there is the problem of the historicity of language, of cinema, and of the other apparati of representation; their uneven ratios of development, their specific modes of address, their particular relations to practice, and their combined, perhaps even contradictory effects on social subjects.

As I walk invisible and captive through the city, I keep thinking that the questions of signification, representation, and subject processes in cinema must be reformulated from a less rigid view of meaning than is fixed by Lacanian psychoanalysis; and that a materialist theory of subjectivity cannot start out from a given notion of the subject, but must approach the subject through the apparati, the social technologies in which it is constructed. Those apparati are distinct, if not disparate, in their specificity and concrete historicity, which is why their co-participation, their combined effect, cannot be easily assessed. Thus, for instance, while the novel, the cinema, and television are all "family machines," they cannot simply be equated with one another. As social technologies aimed at reproducing, among other things, the institution family, they do overlap to a certain degree, but the amount of overlap or redundancy involved is offset, precisely, by their material and semiotic specificity (modes of production, modalities of enunciation, of inscription of the spectator/interlocutor, of address). The family that watches together is really another institution; or better, the subject produced in the family that watches TV is not the same social subject produced in families that only read novels. Another example: the reworking of visual perspective codes into a narrative space in sound films, admirably analyzed by Stephen Heath,[32] certainly recreates some of the subject-effects of perspectival painting, but no one would seriously think that Renaissance painting and Hollywood cinema, as social apparati, address one and the same subject in ideology.

Language, no doubt, is one such social apparatus, and perhaps a universally dominant one. But before we elect it as absolutely representative of subjective formations, we ought to ask: what language? The language of linguistics is not the language spoken in the theatre, and the language we speak outside the movie theatre cannot be quite the same language that was spoken on Plymouth Rock. The point is too obvious to belabor. To put it briefly, after all the work done on the forming influence of visual codes like perspective, the still and motion cameras, and so forth, can one really think that the various forms of mechanical reproduction of language (visual and sound) and its incorporation into practically all apparati of representation have no impact on its social and subjective effects? In this respect, we should consider not only the question of internal speech in the film but also, reciprocally, the possible question of an internal sight or vision in language ("visible speech," *visibile parlare,* is the term of Dante's imaging, the inscription on the gates of Hell), both of which invoke the problematic of the relation of language to sensory perception, of what Freud called word-presentation and thing-presentation in the interplay of primary and secondary processes.[33]

If cinema can be said to be "a language," it is precisely because "language" *is* not; language is not a unified field, outside of specific discourses like linguistics or *The Village Voice.* There are "languages," practices of language and discursive apparati that produce meanings; and there are different modes of semiotic production, ways in which labor is invested in the production of signs and meanings. The types of labor invested, and the modes of production involved, it seems to me, are directly, materially, relevant to the constitution of subjects in ideology—class subjects, race subjects, sexed subjects, and any other differential category that may have political use-value for particular situations of practice at particular historical moments.

It has been said that, if language can be considered an apparatus, like cinema, producing meanings through physical means (the body, the articulatory and hearing organs, the brain), cinematic enunciation is more expensive than speech.[34] True enough. That observation is necessary to the understanding of cinema as a social apparatus (of questions of access, monopoly, and power) and underscores its specificity with respect to other signifying practices; but the single economic parameter is not sufficient to define its mode of semiotic production. The problem is not, or not just, that cinema operates with many different matters of expression and more "expensive," less available "machinery" than natural language. The problem is, rather, that meanings are not produced *in* a particular film but "circulate between social formation, spectator and film."[35] The production of meanings, I rephrase, always involves not simply a specific apparatus of representation but several. While each can be described analytically in its matters of expression or its social-economic conditions of production (e.g., the technological or economic modalities of, say, sound cinema), what is at issue is the possibility of accounting for their joint hold on the spectator and, *thus,* the production of meanings for a subject and/or of a subject in meaning across a plurality of discourses.

If—to put it bluntly and circuitously—the subject is where meanings are formed and if, at the same time, meanings constitute the subject, then the notion of semiotic productivity must include that of modes of production. So "the question of how semantic values are constructed, read and located in history" becomes a most pertinent question.[36]

I have argued that a theory of cinema as a social technology, a relation of the technical and the social, can be developed only with a constant, critical attention to its discursive operations and from the awareness of their present inadequacy. I now want to suggest that cinematic theory must displace the questions of representation and subject construction from the procrustean bed of phallic signification and an exclusive emphasis on the signifier; that we must seek, that is, other ways of mapping the terrain in which meanings are produced. To this end, it may be useful to reconsider the notion of code, somewhat emarginated by current film theory after its heyday in semiology, and importantly redefined in Eco's *Theory of Semiotics*.

In the structural formulation of classical semiology, a code was construed to be a system of oppositional values (Saussure's *langue*, or Metz's code of cinematic punctuation) located upstream of the meanings produced contextually in enunciation and reception. "Meanings" (Saussure's signifieds) were supposed to be subsumed in, and in a stable relationship to, the respective signs (Saussure's signifiers). So defined, a code could be envisaged and described, like a structure, independently of any communicative purpose and apart from an actual situation of signification. For Eco this is not a code but, in fact, a structure, a system; whereas a code is a significant *and* communicational framework linking differential elements on the expression plane with semantic elements on the content plane or with behavioral responses. In the same manner, a sign is not a fixed semiotic entity (the relatively stable union of a signifier and a signified) but a "sign-function," the mutual and transitory correlation of two functives which he calls "sign-vehicle" (the physical component of the sign, on the expression plane) and "cultural unit" (a semantic unit on the content plane). In the historical process, "the same functive can also enter into another correlation, thus becoming a different functive and so giving rise to a new sign-function."[37] As socially established, operational rules that *generate* signs (whereas in classical semiology codes *organize* signs), the codes are historically related to the modes of sign production; it follows that the codes change whenever new or different contents are culturally assigned to the same sign-vehicle or whenever new sign-vehicles are produced. In this manner a new text, a different interpretation of a text—any new practice of discourse— sets up a different configuration of content, introduces other cultural meanings that in turn transform the codes and rearrange the semantic universe of the society that produces it. What is important to note here is that, in this notion of code, the content of the sign-vehicle is also a unit in a semantic system (but not necessarily a binary system) of oppositional values. Each culture, for example, segments the continuum of experience by "making certain units pertinent and understanding others merely as variants, 'allophones'."[38]

> When it is said that the expression /Evening star/ denotes a certain large physical "object" of a spherical form, which travels through space some scores of millions of miles from the Earth, one should in fact say that: the expression in question denotes "a certain" corresponding *cultural unit* to which the speaker refers, and which she has accepted in the way described by the culture in which she lives, without having ever experienced the real referent. So much is this so that only the logician knows that the expression in question has the same denotatum as has the expression /Morning star/. Whoever emitted or received this latter sign-vehicle thought that there were *two different things*. And she was right in the sense that the cultural codes to which she referred provided for two different cultural units. Her social life did not develop on the basis of things but on the basis of cultural units. Or rather, for her as for us, things were only known through cultural units which the universe of communication put into circulation *in place of things*.[39]

Even within a single culture, most semantic fields disintegrate very quickly (unlike the field of colors or kinship terms which have been studied systematically precisely because, in addition to being made up of highly structured cultural units, they have been, like syntax or phonemic structure, durable systems). Most semantic fields are constantly restructured by movements of acculturation and critical revision; that is, they are subject to a process of change due to contradictions within each system and/or to the appearance of new material events outside the system. Now, if cultural units can be recognized by virtue of their opposition to one another in various semantic systems, and can be identified or isolated by the (indefinite) series of their interpretants, then they can be considered to some extent independently of the systemic or structural organizations of the sign-vehicles.

The existence, or rather the theoretical hypothesis, of semantic fields makes it possible to envisage a non-linear semantic space constructed not by one system—language—but by the multilevel interaction of many heterogeneous sign-vehicles and cultural units, the codes being the networks of their correlations *across* the planes of content and expression. In other words, signification involves several systems or discourses intersecting, superimposed, or juxtaposed to one another, with the codes mapping out paths and positions in a virtual (vertical) semantic space which is discursively, textually and contextually, constituted in each signifying act. What distinguishes this notion of code is that both planes, expression and content, are assumed at once in the relationship of meaning. Thus it appears to be very close to the notion of cinematic apparatus as a social technology: not a technical device or *dispositif* (the camera, or the film "industry") but a *relation* of the technical *and* the social which involves the subject as (inter)locutor, poses the subject as the place of that relation. Only in this sense, according to Eco, can one speak of transformation of the codes, of the modes of production, of the semantic fields, or of the social.

Eco's emphasis is a productivist one: his view of sign production, and especially of the mode he calls invention, associating it with art and creativity, is from the perspective of the maker, the speaker, the artist, the *producer* of signs. But what about the woman? She has no access to the codes of the invisible city which represents her and absents her; she is not in the place of Eco's "subject of semiosis"—*homo faber*, the city builder, the producer of signs. Nor is she in the representation which inscribes her as absent. The woman cannot transform the codes; she can only transgress them, make trouble, provoke, pervert, turn the representation into a trap ("this ugly city, this trap"). For semiotics too, finally, the founding tale remains the same. Though now the place of the female subject in language, in discourse, and in the social may be understood another way, it is an equally impossible position. She now finds herself in the empty space between the signs, in a void of meaning, where no demand is possible and no code available; or, going back to the cinema, she finds herself in the place of the female spectator, between the look of the camera (the masculine representation) and the image on the screen (the specular fixity of the feminine representation), not one or the other but both and neither.

I have no picture of the city where the female subject lives. For me, historical woman, discourse does not cohere; there is no specific term of reference, no certain point of enunciation. Like the female reader of Calvino's text, who reading, desiring, building the city, both excludes and imprisons herself, our questioning of the representation of woman in cinema and language is itself a re-presentation of an irreducible contradiction for women in discourse. (What does speaking "as a woman" mean?) But a critical feminist reading of the text, of all the texts of culture, instates the awareness of that contradiction and the knowledge of its terms; it thus changes the representation into a performance which exceeds the text. For women to enact the contradiction is to demonstrate the non-coincidence of woman and women. To perform the terms of the production of woman as text, as image, is to resist identification with that image. It is to have stepped through the looking-glass.

As the reader by now has discovered, the title of this essay has little or nothing to do with Lewis Carroll's book or its heroine. It has, however, something to do with a text not cited directly, but whose presence here, as in much feminist writing, is due to our historical memory: Sheila Rowbotham's *Woman's Consciousness, Man's World.*[40] In Part I, also entitled "Through the Looking-Glass," Rowbotham describes her own struggle as a woman with and against revolutionary marxism, which was dominated by what she calls the "male non-experience" of the specific material situation of women. She could be speaking for many others indeed when she says: "When women's liberation burst about my ears I suddenly saw ideas which had been roaming hopelessly round my head coming out in the shape of other people—women-people. Once again I started to find my bearings all over again. But this time we were going through the looking-glass together" (p. 25). Of many keen and moving passages I could cite, the following is particularly relevant to the conclusion of my essay:

> Consciousness within the revolutionary movement can only become coherent and self-critical when its version of the world becomes clear not simply within itself but when it knows itself in relation to what it has created apart from itself. When we can look back at ourselves through our own cultural creations, our actions, our ideas, our pamphlets, our organization, our history, our theory, we begin to integrate a new reality. As we begin to know ourselves in a new relation to one another we can start to understand our movement in relation to the world outside. We can begin to use our self-consciousness strategically. [Pp. 27–28]

Imaging

CINEMA HAS BEEN STUDIED AS AN APPARATUS OF representation, an image machine developed to construct images or visions of social reality and the spectators' place in it. But, insofar as cinema is directly implicated in the production and reproduction of meanings, values, and ideology in *both* sociality and subjectivity, it should be better understood as a signifying practice, a work of semiosis: a work that produces effects of meaning and perception, self-images and subject positions for all those involved, makers and viewers; and thus a semiotic process in which the subject is continually engaged, represented, and inscribed in ideology.[1] The latter emphasis is quite consonant with the present concerns of theoretical feminism in its effort to articulate the relations of the female subject to ideology, representation, practice, and its need to reconceptualize women's position in the symbolic. But the current theories of the subject—Kristeva's as well as Lacan's—pose very serious difficulties for feminist theory. Part of the problem, as I have suggested, lies in their derivation from, and overwhelming dependence on, linguistics. It may well be, then, that part of the solution is to start elsewhere, which is not to say that we should ignore or discard a useful concept like signifying practice, but rather to propose that we rejoin it from another critical path.

If feminists have been so insistently engaged in practices of cinema, as film makers, critics, and theorists, it is because there the stakes are especially high. The representation of woman as image (spectacle, object to be looked at, vision of beauty—and the concurrent representation of the female body as the *locus* of sexuality, site of visual pleasure, or lure of the gaze) is so pervasive in our culture, well before and beyond the institution of cinema, that it necessarily constitutes a starting point for any understanding of sexual difference and its ideological effects in the construction of social subjects, its presence in all forms of subjectivity. Moreover, in our "civilization of the image," as Barthes has called it, cinema works most effectively as an *imaging* machine, which by producing images (of women or not of women) also tends to reproduce woman as image. The stakes for women in cinema, therefore, are very high, and our intervention most important at the theoretical level, if we are to obtain a conceptually rigorous and politically useful grasp of the processes of imaging. In the context of the discussion of iconic signification, the feminist critique of representation has raised many questions that require critical attention and further elaboration. In very general terms, what are the conditions of presence of the image in cinema and film? And vice versa, what are the conditions of presence of cinema and film in imaging, in the production of a social imaginary?

More specifically, what is at stake, for film theory and for feminism, in the notion of "images of women," "negative" images (literally, *clichés*), or the alternative, "positive" images? The notion circulates widely and has acquired currency in private conversations as well as institutional discourses from film criticism to media shop talk, from academic courses in women's studies to scholarly conferences and special journal issues.[2] Such discussions of images of women rely on an often crude opposition of positive and negative, which is not only uncomfortably close to popular stereotypes such as the good guys versus the bad guys, or the nice girl versus the bad woman, but also contains a less obvious and more risky implication. For it assumes that images are directly absorbed by the viewers, that each image is immediately readable and meaningful in and of itself, regardless of its context or of the circumstances of its production, circulation, and reception. Viewers, in turn, are presumed to be at once historically innocent and purely receptive, as if they too existed in the world immune from other social practices and discourses, yet immediately susceptible to images, to a certain power of iconism, its truth or reality effect. But this is not the case. And it is precisely the feminist critique of representation that has conclusively demonstrated how any image in our culture—let alone any image of woman—is placed within, and read from, the encompassing context of patriarchal ideologies, whose values and effects are social and subjective, aesthetic and affective, and obviously permeate the entire social fabric and hence all social subjects, women as well as men. Thus, since the historical innocence of women is no longer a tenable critical category for feminism, we should rather think of images as (potentially) productive of contradictions in both subjective and social processes. This proposition leads to a second set of questions: by what processes do images on the screen produce imaging on and off screen, articulate meaning and desire, for the spectators? How are images perceived? How do we *see*? How do we attribute meaning to what we see? And do those meanings remain linked to images? What about language? Or sound? What relations do language and sound bear to images? Do we image as well as imagine, or are they the same thing? And then again we must ask: what historical factors intervene in imaging? (Historical factors might include social discourses, genre codification, audience expectations, but also unconscious production, memory, and fantasy.) Finally, what are the "productive relations" of imaging in filmmaking and film-viewing, or spectatorship—productive of what? productive how?

These questions are by no means exhaustive of the intricate problematic of imaging. Moreover, they demand consideration of several areas of theoretical discourse that are indispensable in the study of cinematic signification and representation: semiotics, psychoanalysis, ideology, reception and perception theories.[3] In the following pages I will discuss some points at issue in the theoretical accounts of the image given by semiotics and by recent studies of perception; and in so doing I will attempt to outline the notion of imaging more precisely as the process of the articulation of meaning to images, the engagement of subjectivity in that process, and thus the mapping of a social vision into subjectivity.

PROEMIUM

It is customary to begin such epic tales with a classical verse as propitiatory invocation. Therefore: In the beginning was the word. In its earlier stages semiology was developed in the wake of Saussurian linguistics as a conceptual, analytical framework to study sign systems—or better, to study a certain functioning of certain elements, called signs, in the social production of meaning. In the Saussurian account, the system of language is defined by a double articulation of its elementary units, its signs, the smallest meaningful units of language (morphemes, roughly corresponding to words). The first articulation is the combination, linking, or sequential ordering of morphemes into sentences according to the rules of morphology and syntax; the second articulation is the combination of certain distinctive units, sounds in themselves meaningless (the phonemes), into significant units, into signs, according to the rules established by phonology. Each sign, said Saussure, is constituted by an arbitrary or conventional (socially established) bond between a *sound-image* and a *concept,* a signifier and a signified. Note that from the very beginning in semiology the idea of image, of representation, is associated with the signifier, not with the signified, which is defined as "concept."[4] This may be partly responsible for the disregard in which the signified (hence meaning) was held. If we were to call the signified "a mental image," thereby associating meaning with representation rather than with the purely conceptual, we would have, I think, a better sense of the complexity of the sign. For representation (verbal, visual, aural) is in both components of the sign; better still, representation *is* the sign-function, the social work of the sign.[5]

The Saussurian account prompted the assumption that analogous operations were at work in nonverbal sign systems—systems composed of images, gestures, sounds, objects—and the representational apparati utilizing them, such as painting, advertising, the cinema, the theatre, dance, music, architecture. If the first thorough semiological investigations of cinema yielded the result that no exact parallelism, no homology with verbal language could be drawn, nonetheless semiotics has continued to be concerned with the modes and conditions of iconic coding, the rules of visual communication. So it may be useful to retrace something of the history of semiotics from the debate around cinematic articulation, which took place during the mid-sixties around the *Mostra del nuovo cinema* in Pesaro, Italy (also known as the Pesaro Film Festival), and practically set off the semiological analysis of cinema.[6]

CINEMATIC ARTICULATION AND ICONICITY

The debate on articulation in the early years of semiology seemed to crystallize around an opposition between linguistic signs and iconic signs, between verbal language and visual images. Their difference was thought to be inherent in two irreducible modes of perception, signification, and communication: verbal language appeared to be mediated, coded, symbolic, whereas iconism was assumed to be immediate, natural, directly linked to reality. Cinema was at the very center of this theoretical storm, for its status as a semiotic system (a language, as it was then assumed any semiotic system would be) depended on the possibility of determining an articulation, preferably a double articulation, for the cinematic signs. Although a narrow linguistic notion of articulation has proved to be something of a theoretical liability and is no longer adequate to the concerns of film theory, the questions "what is cinematic articulation, how is cinema articulated, what does it articulate?" are still very much at issue. Hence it is important to review the terms of the argument and to follow its development over the years.

According to Metz's first paper on the topic, "Le cinéma: langue ou language?" (1964), taking a position which he later revised, cinema can only be described as a language without a code or language-system ("un langage sans langue"), for it lacks altogether the second articulation (at the phonemic level). Though meaningful, cinematic images cannot be defined as signs in the Saussurian sense, because they are motivated and analogical rather than arbitrary or conventional, and because each image is not generated by a code with a series of fixed rules and (largely unconscious) operations, as a word or a sentence is. The cinematic image is instead a unique, a one-time-only, combination of elements that cannot be catalogued, as words can be, in lexicons or dictionaries. Saussure had said that language is a storehouse of signs, from which all speakers equally draw. But no such thing could be claimed for cinema; for the images it puts together, there is no paradigm, no storehouse. In the cinematic image, concluded Metz, meaning is released naturally from the total signifier without recourse to a code.[7]

Pasolini, on the other hand, maintained that cinema was a language with a double articulation, though different from verbal language and in fact more like written language, whose minimal units were the various objects in the frame or shot *(inquadratura)*; these he called *cinémi*, "cinemes," by analogy with *fonemi*, phonemes. The cinemes combine into larger units, the shots, which are the basic significant units of cinema, corresponding to the morphemes of verbal language. In this way, for Pasolini, cinema articulates reality precisely by means of its second articulation: the selection and combination of real, profilmic objects or events (faces, landscapes, gestures, etc.) in each shot. It is these profilmic and pre-filmic events or objects in reality ("oggetti, forme o atti della realtà"—and hence already *cultural* objects) that constitute the paradigm of cinema, its storehouse of significant images, of image-signs *(im-segni)*.

> Cinemes have this very character of compulsoriness: we cannot but choose from among the cinemes that are there, that is to say, the objects, forms and events of reality which we can grasp with our senses. Unlike phonemes, which are few in number, cinemes are infinite, or at least countless.[8]

Yet, contended Eco, another participant in the debate, the objects in the frame do not have the same status as the phonemes of verbal language.[9] Even leaving aside the problem of the qualitative difference between objects and their photographic image (a difference central to semiotics, for the real object, the referent, is neither the signified nor the signifier but "the material precondition of any coding process"),[10] the objects in a frame are already meaningful units, thus more like morphemes. In fact, within the idea of cinema as a system of signs, the cinematic code could be better described as having not two (as for Pasolini), nor one (as for Metz), but three articulations, which Eco designates as follows. He calls *seme* (semantic nucleus, meaningful unit) each recognizable shape (Pasolini's "object"); each seme is made up of smaller *iconic signs* such as /nose/ or /eye/; each iconic sign can be further analyzed in *figurae* (e.g., angles, curves, light-dark effects, etc.) whose value is not semantic but positional and oppositional, like the phonemes'. The iconic signs (nose, eye, street) would thus be formed from a paradigm of possible iconic *figurae* (angles, curves, light); and this would be the third articulation. In turn the iconic signs would combine into a seme (human figure, landscape), the second articulation. Finally, the combination of semes into a frame would constitute the first articulation. But the process does not stop there. Not only do semes combine to form a frame, but, given that cinema is pictures in motion, a further combination takes place in the projected film, in the passage from frame (or photogram) to shot. Here each iconic sign and each iconic seme generates what kinesics calls *cinemorphs*, i.e., significant units of movement, gestural units. If, continues Eco, kinesics finds difficulty in identifying the non-meaningful units, the *figurae*, of a gesture (the equivalent of phonemes), cinema does not: it is the specific property of the camera that allows cinema to break down the unity of perceived movement, the gestural continuum, into discrete units which in themselves are not significant. It is precisely the motion picture camera that provides a way to analyze kinesic signs in their non-meaningful, differential units, something of which human natural perception is incapable.

Eco's line of reasoning is correct enough, but then a further distinction must be made. The breakdown of movement into photograms is still mechanically imposed, no less than it was in, say, futurist paintings. The "units of movement" are established by the speed of the camera, they are not discrete units in the gesture itself, whereas phonemes are distinguishable and in finite number in language. Then, since cinema depends on the objects whose imprint the light rays inscribe on the film stock, one would also need to distinguish between the articulation of *real* movement (the movement of the objects, studied by kinesics), cinematic movement (the movement of the frames effected by the pull-down mechanism in the camera or the blades of the projector shutter), and apparent movement or motion (perceived by the viewer). And here semiotics must rejoin the study of visual and motion perception.[11]

But let us assume with Eco that cinema, considered as a sign system (independently, that is, of a viewing situation and actually considered merely as image-track), does have a triple articulation. This assumption would explain, for instance, the greater perceptual richness we experience—the so-called impression of reality—and our conviction that cinema is better equipped than verbal language to transmit, capture, or express that reality; it would also account for, as he notes, the various metaphysics of cinema. The question then is: even assuming that we may correctly speak of a triple articulation of the cinematic signs, is it worthwhile to do so? The notion of articulation is an analytical notion, whose usefulness rests on its ability to account for the phenomenon (language, cinema) economically, to account for a maximum of events with a minimum of combinable units. Now the "phenomenon," the events of cinema are not the photogram, the still image, but at the very least the shot (cf. Pasolini's emphasis on *inquadratura*), images in motion which construct not only linear movement but also a depth, an accumulation of time and space that is essential to the meaning, the reading of the image(s).[12] At the conclusion of this phase of the debate Eco admitted that, if cinema as a language can be said to possess a triple articulation, film as discourse is constructed on, and puts into play, many other codes—verbal, iconographic, stylistic, perceptual, narrative. Therefore, he himself remarked, "honesty requires that we ask ourselves whether the notion of triple articulation itself is not possibly complicit with a *semiotic* metaphysics."[13]

With the shift from the notion of language to the notion of discourse began to appear the limitations, theoretical and ideological, of the early semiological analyses. First, the determination of an articulated code (be it a single, double, or triple articulation), even if possible, would offer neither an ontological nor an epistemological guarantee of the event, of what cinema is—to cite the title of Bazin's famous book. For indeed, as Stephen Heath observes, one never encounters "cinema" or "language," but only practices of language, or practices of cinema.[14] And this, I will suggest, is what Pasolini was attempting, unsuccessfully, to formulate: the idea of cinema as a signifying practice, not cinema as system. Second, that notion of articulation, concerned as it was with minimal units and the homogeneity of the theoretical object, and "vitiated [in Pasolini's phrase] by the linguistic mould," was predicated on an imaginary, if not metaphysical, unity of cinema as system, independent, that is, of a viewing situation. Thus it tended to hide or make non-pertinent the other components of the signifying process; for example, to hide the fact that cinematic signification and signification in general are not systemic but rather discursive processes, that they not only engage and overlay multiple codes, but also involve distinct communicative situations, particular conditions of reception, enunciation, and address, and thus, crucially, the notion of spectatorship—the positioning of spectators in and by the film, in and by cinema. In this sense, for example, Claire Johnston writes,

> feminist film practice can no longer be seen simply in terms of the effectivity of a system of representation, but rather as a production of and by subjects already in social practices which always involve heterogeneous and often contradictory positions in ideologies. . . . Real readers are subjects in history rather than mere subjects of a single text.[15]

In short, spectators are not, as it were, either in the film text *or* simply outside the film text; rather, we might say, they intersect the film as they are intersected by cinema. Therefore, it is the usefulness of that notion of iconic and cinematic articulation, and its pretension to provide the proper semiotic definition of the phenomenon cinema, that must be challenged.

This said, however, iconicity—the articulation of meanings to images—does remain an issue for semiotics and for film theory. It should not be too quickly cast aside as irrelevant, false, or superseded, for at least two reasons. On one front, it is important to pursue the question of iconic representation and its productive terms in the relations of meaning as a sort of theoretical resistance: one should not meekly yield to the current trend in semiotics toward an increasing grammatization of discursive and textual operations, toward, that is, logico-mathematical formalization. On another front, it continues to be necessary to reclaim iconicity, the visual component of meaning (including above all visual pleasure and the attendant questions of identification and subjectivity), not so much *from* the domain of the natural or *from* an immediacy of referential reality, as *for* the ideological; to wrench the visual from its vision, as it were, or, as Metz might say, to reclaim the imaginary of the image for the symbolic of cinema.

This is no simple task. For even as most forms of visual communication have become accepted as conventional (coded), our idea of what constitutes "reality" has changed. The paradox of live TV, our "window to the world," is that reality is only accessible as televised, as what is captured by an action camera. The paradox of current Hollywood cinema is that reality must surpass in visual fascination the horrors of, say, Carpenter's *Halloween* or Romero's *Dawn of the Dead,* must be fantasm-agoria, revel-ation, apocalypse here and now. The problem is, the very terms of the reality-illusion dichotomy have been displaced. Thus it is not by chance that all the nature-culture thresholds are being thematized and transgressed in recent movies: incest, life/death (vampires, zombies, and other living dead), human/non-human (aliens, clones, demon seeds, pods, fogs, etc.), and sexual difference (androgyns, transsexuals, transvestites, or transylvanians). Boundaries are very much in question, and the old rites of passage no longer avail. Cinema itself can no longer be the mirror of a reality unmediated, pristine, originary, since industrial technology has forfeited our claim in the earth, now lost to us through ecological disaster. Yet technology alone can simulate the Edenic plenitude of nature and remember it for us. Think of the pastoral landscape unfolding in full color, bathed in the stereophonic sound of Beethoven's Sixth, on the wide screen of the death chamber in *Soylent Green,* the ambiguous title barely hiding a most gruesome irony. The film commemorates at once that loss of Eden and its own loss of innocence, the earlier innocent belief in cinema's perfect capacity to reproduce Eden's perfection, to render reality in its fullness and beauty. But elegy itself is simulated in today's cinema, where reality is hyperreality, not only coded but *absolutely* coded, not merely artificial, artful, made-up, masqueraded, tranvested or perverted, but permanently so, like the vision of its viewers, irreversibly transformed. The eyes of Tommy/David Bowie in *The Man Who Fell to Earth* are an apt metacinematic metaphor for both this elegy of cinema and the glorification of its artfulness, its immense power of vision.

Cinema's hyperreality, its total simulation—as Baudrillard would say—is precisely, conspicuously *imaged,* visually and aurally constructed, and represented as such (think of Truffaut playing the xylophone in *Close Encounters of the Third Kind,* or the canned Muzak and soft pastels of *American Gigolo*). And language becomes more and more incidental, as music used to be in silent cinema, often simply redundant or vaguely evocative, allusive, mythical. The hollow men of Eliot hyper-recited by Kurz/Brando in *Apocalypse Now,* the operatic arias in Bertolucci's *Luna,* serve solely to allude, refer to—not engage—a symbolic order, an abstract code; not to engage the code of opera in all its cultural, historical weight as Visconti does in *Senso,* or in its narrative, thematic, and rhythmic closure as Potter does in *Thriller,* as Rainer does in *Film About a Woman Who.* . . . The opera in *Luna* and myth in Coppola's *Golden Bough* are codes no longer intelligible. But it doesn't matter. What matters is once again the spectacle, as in the earliest days of cinema. Contradiction, paradox, ambiguity in the image as well as in the textualized overlay of sound, language, and image no longer produce distancing effects by baring the device of cinema and thus inducing rationality and consciousness. *They are the spectacle,* the no longer simple but excessive, "perverse" pleasure of current cinema.

In short, cinema's imaging, its complex iconicity, its textual overlay of visual, aural, linguistic, and other coding processes continues to be a crucial problem. And since the old polarity natural-conventional has been displaced, not only in film or semiotic theory, but in the social imaginary through the reality effect produced by the social technology that is cinema, I propose that the question of imaging—the articulation of meaning to image, language, and sound, and the viewer's subjective engagement in that process—must be reformulated in terms that are themselves to be elaborated, recast, or posed anew. Where shall we look for clues or ideas? My present inclination is to go back and read again, think through some of the notions we have taken for granted or perhaps disposed of prematurely. Indeed semiotics, too, has moved along these lines, to some extent, toward the analysis of reading processes and text pragmatics. Eco's own critique of iconism, by displacing the notion of articulation as well as the classical notion of sign to a much less central position in his theory of semiotics, provides a starting point.

Eco's critique of the so-called iconic signs, which he only outlined at the time of the Pesaro debate, has been more fully developed in *A Theory of Semiotics*. There he argues that iconism in fact covers many semiotic procedures, "is a collection of phenomena bundled together under an all-purpose label (just as in the Dark Ages the word 'plague' probably covered a lot of different diseases)" (p. 216). Thus the difference between the image of a dog and the word /dog/ is not the "trivial" difference between iconic (motivated by similarity) and arbitrary (or "symbolic") signs. "It is rather a matter of a complex and continuously gradated array of different modes of producing signs and texts, every sign-function (sign-unit or text) being in turn the result of many of these modes of production" (p. 190), every sign-function being in fact a text. Even if in a given iconic continuum, an image, one can isolate pertinent discrete units or *figurae,* as soon as they are detected, they seem to dissolve again. In other words, these "pseudo-features" cannot be organized into a system of rigid differences, and their positional as well as semantic values vary according to the coding rules instituted each time by the context. In studying iconic signification one sees "the classical notion of sign dissolve into a highly complex network of changing relationships" (p. 49). The very notion of sign, he emphasizes, becomes "untenable" when equated with the notions of significant elementary *units* and *fixed* correlations. Finally, Eco concludes, there is no such thing as an iconic sign; there are only visual texts, whose pertinent units are established, *if at all,* by the context. And it is the code, a purposefully established correlation between expressive and semantic units, that "decides on what level of complexity it will single out its own pertinent features" (p. 235).

The key concepts here are context, pertinence, and purposefulness (of the codes). The context establishes the pertinence of the units, of what counts or functions as a sign in an iconic text for a certain communicational act, a particular "reading." And the purposefulness of the codes, which is embedded in any practice of signification as a condition of communication, determines the level of complexity of the particular communicational act, that is to say, of what and how much one sees or "reads" in an image.[16] Obviously, the definition of context is crucial. While the purpose of the code is not intended by Eco as idiosyncratic motive or individual intentionality (codes are socially and culturally established and usually work, not unlike linguistic structures, below the conscious awareness of the viewers), nevertheless it is possible to link purposefulness to subjectivity. Eco himself speaks of particular communicational acts which establish new codes, and calls them inventions or aesthetic texts, thus admitting the possibility of a subjective purposefulness, such as an artist's creativity, for at least some instances of code-making. The notion of context, however, is more restrictively defined as co-text, as everything that is included within the frame of the picture, so to speak. And although he does take into account the work of intertextuality in the reading of the image, intertextuality too is understood literally, as the relay to other images or other texts; it does not stretch to encompass nontextualized discourses, discursive formations, or other heterogeneous social practices, which however must be assumed to inform the viewer's subjective processes.[17]

The importance, but also the insufficiency of this notion of context for my present concern, imaging, is apparent. Insofar as the notion is applicable to film spectators, it does not admit the possibility of a different reading of the filmic images by, say, women and men; it does not account, that is, for gender or other social factors that overdetermine the engagement of subjectivity in the semiotic process of spectatorship. In light of the developments within semiotics and especially of Eco's critique of iconism, it is interesting to reread Pasolini's essays on cinema, written in the mid-sixties and at the time quickly dismissed as un-semiotic, theoretically unsophisticated, or even reactionary.[18] Ironically, from where we now stand, his views on the relation of cinema to reality appear to have addressed perhaps the central issues of cinematic theory. In particular, his observation that cinematic images inscribe reality as representation and his insistence on the "audio-visuality" of cinema (what I call the articulation of meaning to images, language, and sound) bear directly on the role that cinema's imaging has in the production of social reality.

Pasolini's often quoted slogan, "cinema is the language of reality," was in part provocatively outrageous, in part very earnestly asserted. To be exact, the words he used (it is the title of his best known essay on cinema) were "cinema is the *written language of reality*." This he explained as follows: the invention of the alphabet and the technology of writing revolutionized society by "revealing" language to men (men, this is also the word he used), making them conscious of spoken language as representation; previously, thought and speech must have appeared as natural, whereas written language *instituted a cultural consciousness of thought as representation*. In the same way cinema is a kind of "writing" *(scrittura, écriture)* of reality, in that it permits the conscious representation of human action; hence cinema is "the written language of action," or "the written language of reality" (pp. 238–39). For Pasolini, human action, human intervention in the real, is the first and foremost expression of men, their primary "language"; primary not (or not just) in the sense of originary or prehistoric, but primary to the extent that it encompasses all other "languages"— verbal, gestural, iconic, musical, etc. In this sense he says, what Lenin has left us—the transformation of social structures and their cultural consequences—is "a great poem of action."

> From Lenin's great action poem to the short pages of action prose of a Fiat worker or a petty government official, life is undoubtedly moving away from classical humanistic ideals and is becoming lost in pragma. *Cinema* (with the other audio-visual techniques) *seems to be the written language of this pragma.* But this may be its salvation, precisely *because it expresses it* from within: being produced out of this pragma, [cinema] reproduces it. [P. 211]

Another statement: cinema, like poetry (poetic writing, as a practice of language), is "translinguistic." It encodes human action in a grammar, a set of conventions, a vehicle; but as soon as it is perceived, heard, received by a reader/spectator, the convention is discarded and action (reality) is "recreated as a dynamics of feelings, affects, passions, ideas" in that reader/spectator. Thus in living, in practical existence, in our actions, "we represent ourselves, we perform ourselves. Human reality is this double representation in which we are at once actors and spectators: a gigantic happening, if you will." Cinema, then, is the recorded, stored, "written" moment of a "natural and total language, which is our action in the real."[19]

It is easy to see why Pasolini's arguments could have been so easily dismissed. He himself, only half-jokingly, asked: "What horrible sins are crouching in my philosophy?" and named the "monstrous" juxtaposition of irrationalism and pragmatism, religion and action, and other "fascist" aspects of our civilization (p. 240). Let me suggest, however, that an unconventional, less literal or narrow reading of Pasolini's pronouncements (for such they undoubtedly were), one that would accept his provocations and work on the contradictions of his "heretical empiricism," could be very helpful in resisting, if not countering, the more subtle seduction of a logico-semiotic humanism.

This is not the place for an extensive reading of essays, articles, screenplay notations, interventions and interviews spanning nearly a decade; or for a reassessment of the originality of his insights with regard to, for example, the function of montage as "negative duration" in the construction of a "physio-psychological" continuity for the spectator or the qualities of "physicality" (fisicalità) and oniricità, the dreamlike state film induces in the spectator—insights which he tried to couch in the terms of the theoretical discourse of semiology (and they did not fit) but which, several years later, recast in psychoanalytic terms, were to become central to film theory's concern with visual pleasure, spectatorship, and the complex nexus of imaging and meaning that Metz was to locate in the "imaginary signifier." That relation of image and language in cinema, wrote Pasolini in 1965, is *in* the film and *before* the film; it is to be sought in "a complex nexus of *significant images* [imaginary signifiers?] which *pre-figures* cinematic communication and acts *as its instrumental foundation*."[20] What Pasolini touches upon here is possibly one of the most important and most difficult problems confronting cinematic theory and iconic, as well as verbal, signification: the question of inner speech—of forms of "imagist, sensual, pre-logical thinking" already suggested by Eikhenbaum and Eisenstein in the twenties about the relation of language to sensory perception, of what Freud called word-presentation and thing-presentation in the interplay of primary and secondary processes. A question that, clearly, could not be answered by semiology—but through no fault, no limitation, of Pasolini's—and has been more recently and fruitfully addressed by Paul Willemen.[21]

I will take up just a few other points with regard to Pasolini. First, he imagines cinema as the conscious representation of social practice (he calls it action, reality—reality as human practice). This is exactly, and explicitly, what many independent filmmakers are in fact doing or trying to do today. Pasolini, of course, speaks as a filmmaker—*en poète*, as he said. He is concerned with film as expression, with the practice of cinema as the occasion of a direct encounter with reality, not merely personal, and yet subjective. He is not specifically taking on, as others are, cinema as institution, as a social technology which produces or reproduces meanings, values, and images *for* the spectators. But he is keenly aware, nevertheless, in the passages I quoted and elsewhere, that cinema's writing, its representation of human action, institutes "a cultural consciousness" of that encounter with reality. That is why he says—and this is my second point—that cinema, like poetry, is *trans*linguistic: it exceeds the moment of the inscription, the technical apparatus, to become "a dynamics of feelings, affects, passions, ideas" in the moment of reception. Cinema and poetry, that is, are not languages (grammars, articulatory mechanisms), but discourses and practices of language, modes of representing—signifying practices, we would say; he said "the written language of pragma." The emphasis on the subjective in three of the four terms, "feelings, affects, passions, ideas," cannot be construed as an emphasis on the merely "personal," that is to say, an individual's existential or idiosyncratic response to the film. On the contrary, it points to the current notion of spectatorship as a site of productive relations, of the engagement of subjectivity in meaning, values, and imaging. It therefore suggests that the subjective processes which cinema instigates are "culturally conscious," that cinema's binding of fantasy to images institutes, *for* the spectator, forms of subjectivity which are themselves, unequivocally, social.[22]

One could go on recontextualizing, intertextualizing, overtextualizing Pasolini's "extravagant" statements. But I must go back to semiotics, where it all started—not only my reading of Pasolini's text but also the theoretical discourse on cinema through which I have been reading it. Pasolini's use of semiology, aberrant as it might have seemed, was in fact prophetic. The notion of *im-segno* proposed in the 1965 essays "Il cinema di poesia" and "La sceneggiatura come 'struttura che vuol essere altra struttura'" is much closer to Eco's notion of sign-function than anyone would have suspected, way back then. And so is

Pasolini's attempt to define the "reader's collaboration" in the *sceno-testo*, the screenplay as text-in-movement, as diachronic structure or structure-in-process—another of his scandalous contradictions, yet no longer so if we compare it with Eco's recent reformulation of the notion of open text.[23] As for the question of cinematic articulation and iconism, the *context* of cinema, as Pasolini outlines it, the context which makes certain "features" pertinent and thus produces meaning and subjectivity, is not only a discursive context or a textual co-text (linguistic or iconic), as Eco defines it; it is the context of social practice, that human action which cinematic representation articulates and inscribes from both sides of the screen, so to speak, for both filmmakers and spectators as subjects in history.[24]

In that essay of 1966 Pasolini insisted, "bisogna ideologizzare." Ideologize, he said. Nowhere do those words seem so appropriate still as in a discussion of imaging. An example of what can literally be called the cinematic articulation of human action may serve to demonstrate their appropriateness. We know that the camera can be used, and has been used, to study the relation of movement to time and space. We also know that such studies, whether scientific or aesthetic, are always embedded in concrete historical practices, often indeed are aimed toward very specific economic or ideological objectives. A particular device, a motion camera connected to a clock, was developed by Frank Gilbreth, a management expert, to determine time-motion ratios for industrial workers and thus impose on the workers a higher rate of productivity. The "Gilbreth Chronometer" is described in *The Book of Progress* (1915):

> Every film [frame] reveals the successive positions of a workman in performing each minute operation of the task entrusted to him. The position of the chronometer pointer in successive films indicates the length of time between successive operations. These films are studied under a microscope, and a careful analysis of each operation is made to develop the standard time for each. . . . Any workman may, for a time, deceive an inexperienced efficiency engineer . . . but the camera cannot be deceived. . . . The film records faithfully every movement made, and subsequent analysis and study reveals exactly how many of these movements were necessary and how many were purposely slow or useless.[25]

This apparatus that "cannot be deceived" is used to set a "standard time" of industrial production that eliminates "useless" movements, thus maximizing output. The imposition of such standard time seriously restricts the workers' investment of fantasy (to borrow a term and a concept from Oskar Negt) in the work, fantasy that will then be invested in "leisure-time" activities. Thus the industrial limitation of fantasy, the quantitative and qualitative restrictions on work-related imaging are but the underside of cinema's binding of fantasy to certain images, cinema's articulation of meaning and desire, for the spectators, in particular representations. What we call genres—the narrative filmic organization of content according to specific cinematic codifications in the western, the horror film, melodrama, film noir, the musical, etc.—are also ways in which cinema articulates human action, establishes meanings in relation to images, and binds fantasy at once to images and meanings. This binding of fantasy to certain representations, certain significant images, affects the spectator as a subjective production. The spectator, stitched in the film's spatiotemporal movement, is constructed as the point of intelligibility and origin of those representations, as the subject of, the "figure-for," those images and meanings. In these ways cinema effectively, powerfully participates in the social production of subjectivity: both the disinvestment of fantasy in work-related imaging (the effect of the Gilbreth chronometer) and the investment of fantasy in film's imaging (the movies as the great escape) are modes of subjective production effected by cinema through the articulation of human action, cinema's imaging.

MAPPING

According to physiologist Colin Blakemore, our apparently unified view of the outside world is in fact produced by the interconnected operations of diverse neural processes. Not only are there different kinds of neuron or nerve cells in the brain and in the retina (the retina, the photosensitive layer at the back of the eye, is actually part of the cortex, composed of the same tissue and nerve cells); and not only do those nerve cells have different functions (for example, "the main function of the nucleus is not to process visual information by transforming the messages from the eyes, but to filter the signals, depending on the activity of the other sense organs");[26] but each neuron responds to a specific responsive field, and its action is inhibited or excited by the action of other, adjacent cortical cells. Different parts of the retina project through the optic nerves to different parts of the visual cortex and of the brain stem (the superior colliculus, in the lower part of the brain), producing two maps of the visual world or rather a discontinuous map in which are represented certain features of objects (edges and shapes, position, orientation). In other words, these interacting processes do not merely *record* a unified or preconstituted visual space, but actually constitute a discontinuous *map* of the external world. "Map" is the term used by Blakemore: the activity of the optical and cortical cells constitutes, he says, "a mapping of visual space on to the substance of the brain" (p. 14).

The perceptual apparatus, then, does not copy reality but symbolizes it. This is supported by the fact that "unnatural" stimulations of the retina or cortex (surgical, electrical, or manual) produce visual sensations; hence the familiar comic book truth that a blow on the head makes one see stars. This happens because "the brain always assumes that a message from a particular sense organ is the result of the *expected* form of stimulation" (p. 17). The term "expected" here implies that perception works by a set of learned responses, a cognitive pattern, a code; and further, that the principle of organization or combination of sensory input is a kind of inference (it has been called "unconscious inference").[27] The perceptual apparatus, moreover, is subject to adaptation or calibration, for expectations are readjusted on the basis of new stimuli or occurrences. Finally, perception is not merely patterned response but active anticipation. In the words of R. L. Gregory, perception is "predictive": "the study of perception shows that nothing is seen as 'directly' as supposed in common sense."[28] To perceive is to make a continuous series of educated guesses, on the basis of prior knowledges and expectations, however unconscious.

The term "mapping," interestingly enough, is also used by Eco to define the process of semiosis, sign-making, the production of signs and meanings (without, to the best of my knowledge, any intended reference to Blakemore or psychophysiology). Mapping, for Eco, is the transformation of percepts into semantic units into expressions, a transformation that occurs by transferring—mapping—certain pertinent elements (features that have been recognized as pertinent) from one material continuum to another. The particular rules of articulation, the conditions of reproducibility or of invention, and the physical labor involved are the other parameters to be taken into account in

Eco's classification of what he calls the modes of sign production. Eco's view of sign production, especially of the mode he calls invention, associating it with art and creativity, is from the perspective of the *maker*—the speaker, the artist, the producer of signs; it stems from his background in classical aesthetics as well as marxism. In *A Theory of Semiotics* he defines inventions as code-making, thus:

> We may define as invention a mode of production whereby the producer of the sign-function chooses a new material continuum not yet segmented for that purpose and proposes a new way of organizing (of giving form to) it in order *to map* within it the formal pertinent elements of a content-type. Thus in invention we have a case of *ratio difficilis* realized within a heteromaterial expression; but since no previous convention exists to correlate the elements of the expression with the selected content, the sign producer must in some way *posit* this correlation so as to make it acceptable. In this sense inventions are radically different from recognition, choice, and replica. [P. 245]

Inventions are radically different because, by establishing new codes, they are capable of transforming both the representation and the perception of reality, and thus eventually can change social reality. The perceptual model, on the contrary, is focused on the spectator, so to speak, rather than the filmmaker. While Eco's model requires that, in order to change the world, one must produce new signs, which in turn will produce new codes and different meanings or social values, the other model says nothing about purposeful activity and rather stresses adaptation to external events. But that adaptation is nonetheless a kind of production—of sensation, cognition, memory, an ordering and distribution of energy, a constant activity for survival, pleasure, self-maintenance.

The notion of mapping common to these two models implies that perception and signification are neither direct or simple reproduction (copy, mimesis, reflection) nor inevitably predetermined by biology, anatomy, or destiny; though they are socially determined and over-determined. Put another way, what is called reproduction—as women well know—is never simply natural or simply technical, never spontaneous, automatic, without labor, without pain, without desire, without the engagement of subjectivity. This is the case even for those signs that Eco calls replicas, strictly coded signs for which the code is ready-made and neither requires nor allows invention.[29] Since replicas, like all other signs, are always produced in a communicational context, their (re)production is still embedded in a speech act; it always occurs within a process of enunciation and address that requires the mapping of other elements or the making pertinent of other features, and that also involves memory, expectations, decisions, pain, desire—in short, the whole discontinuous history of the subject. If, then, subjectivity is engaged in semiosis at all levels, not just in visual pleasure but in all cognitive processes, in turn semiosis (coded expectations, patterns of response, assumptions, inferences, predictions, and, I would add, fantasy) is at work in sensory perception, inscribed in the body—the human body and the film body. Finally, the notion of mapping suggests an ongoing but discontinuous process of perceiving-representing-meaning (I like to call it "imaging") that is neither linguistic (discrete, linear, syntagmatic, or arbitrary) nor iconic (analogical, paradigmatic, or motivated), but both, or perhaps neither. And in this imaging process are involved different codes and modalities of semiotic production, as well as the semiotic production of difference.

Difference. Inevitably that question comes back, we come back to the question of imaging difference, the question of feminism. Which is not, can no longer be, a matter of simple oppositions between negative and positive images, iconic and verbal signification, imaginary and symbolic processes, intuitive perception and intellectual cognition, and so forth. Nor can it be simply a matter of reversing the hierarchy of value which underlies each set, assigning dominance to one term over the other (as in the feminine-masculine or female-male dichotomies). The fundamental proposition of feminism, that the personal is political, urges the displacement of all such oppositional terms, the crossing and recharting of the space between them. No other course seems open if we are to reconceptualize the relations that bind the social to the subjective. If we take up the notion of mapping, for instance, and allow it to act as a footbridge across the two distinct theoretical fields of psychophysiology and semiotics, we can envision a connection, a pathway between spheres of material existence, perception, and semiosis, which are usually thought of as self-contained and incommensurable.

Much the same way as classical semiology opposed iconic and verbal signs, perception and signification are usually considered distinct processes, often indeed opposed to one another as pertaining respectively to the sphere of subjectivity (feeling, affectivity, fantasy, pre-logical, pre-discursive, or primary processes) and to the sphere of sociality (rationality, communication, symbolization, or secondary processes). Very few manifestations of culture, notably Art, are thought to partake of both. And even when a cultural form, such as cinema, clearly traverses both spheres, their presumed incommensurability dictates that questions of perception, identification, pleasure, or displeasure be accounted for in terms of individual idiosyncratic response or personal taste, and hence not publicly discussed; while a film's social import, its ultimate meaning, or its aesthetic qualities may be grasped, shared, taught, or debated "objectively" in a generalized discourse. Thus, for example, even as the feminist critique of representation began with, and was developed from, the sheer displeasure of female spectators in the great majority of films, no other public discourse existed prior to it in which the question of displeasure in the "image" of woman (and the attendant difficulties of identification) could be addressed. Thus, whenever displeasure was expressed, it would be inevitably dismissed as an exaggerated, oversensitive, or hysterical reaction on the part of the individual woman. Such reactions appeared to violate the classic rule of aesthetic distance, and with it the artistic-social character of cinema, by an impingement of the subjective, the personal, the irrational. That the focus on "positive" images of woman is now another formula in both film criticism and filmmaking is a measure of the social legitimation of a certain feminist discourse, and the consequent viability of its commercial and ideological exploitation (witness the recent crop of films like *The French Lieutenant's Woman, Tess, Gloria, Nine to Five, Rich and Famous, Personal Best, Tootsie,* etc.).

Feminist film theory, meanwhile, has gone well beyond the simple opposition of positive and negative images, and has indeed displaced the very terms of that opposition through a sustained critical attention to the hidden work of the apparatus.[30] It has shown, for instance, how narrativity works to anchor images to non-contradictory points of identification, so that the "sexual difference" is ultimately reconfirmed and any ambiguity reconciled by narrative closure. The symptomatic reading of films as filmic texts has worked against such closure, seeking out the invisible subtext made of the gaps and excess in the narrative or visual texture of a film, and finding there, concurrent with the repression of the female's look, the signs of her elision from the text. Thus, it has been argued, it is the elision of woman that is represented in the film, rather than a positive or a negative image; and what the representation of woman *as* image, positive *or* negative, achieves is to deny women the status of subjects both on the screen and in the cinema. But even so an opposition is produced: the image and what the image hides (the elided woman), one visible and the other invisible, sound very much like a binary set. In short, we continue to face the difficulty of elaborating a new conceptual framework not founded on the dialectic logic of opposition, as all hegemonic discourses seem to be in Western culture. The notion of mapping and the theoretical bridge it sets up between perception and signification suggest a complex interaction and mutual implication, rather than opposition, between the spheres of subjectivity and sociality. It may be useful as a model, or at least a guiding concept in understanding the relations of imaging, the articulation of images to meanings in the cinema, as well as cinema's own role in mediating, binding, or indeed mapping the social into the subjective.

In what is now considered one of the most important texts of feminist film criticism, Laura Mulvey stated that an alternative, politically and aesthetically avant-garde cinema could only exist in counterpoint to mainstream film as analysis, subversion, and total negation of Hollywood's pleasurable obsessions and its ideological manipulation of visual pleasure. "Unchallenged, mainstream film coded the erotic into the language of the dominant patriarchal order"; woman, inscribed in films as representation/image, is at once the support of male desire and of the filmic code, the look, that defines cinema itself ("she holds the look, plays to and signifies male desire").

> Going far beyond highlighting a woman's to-be-looked-at-ness, cinema builds the way she is to be looked at into the spectacle itself. Playing on the tension between film as controlling the dimension of time (editing, narrative) and film as controlling the dimension of space (changes in distance, editing), cinematic codes create a gaze, a world, and an object, thereby producing an illusion cut to the measure of desire. It is these cinematic codes and their relationship to formative external structures that must be broken down before mainstream film and the pleasure it provides can be challenged. . . . Women, whose image has continually been stolen and used for this end, cannot view the decline of the traditional film form with anything much more than sentimental regret.[31]

The challenge to classical narrative cinema, the effort to invent "a new language of desire" for an "alternative" cinema, entails nothing short of the destruction of visual pleasure as we now know it. But if "intellectual unpleasure" is not the answer, as Mulvey well knows (and her films strive against that problem, too), it nevertheless seems the unavoidable consequent in a binary set whose first term is visual pleasure, when that set is part of a series of oppositional terms subsumed under categories of the type A and non-A: "mainstream" (Hollywood and derivatives) and "non-mainstream" (political-aesthetic avant-garde). The importance of Mulvey's essay, marking and summing up an intensely productive phase of feminist work with film, is not to be diminished by the limitations of its theoretical scope. Indeed the fact that it has not yet been superseded is a major argument for our continued engagement with its problematic and the questions it raises—for one, the impasse reached by a certain notion of political avant-garde, a notion which, like Godard's cinema, today retains its critical force only to the extent that we are willing to historicize it and to give it up as the paragon or absolute model of any radical cinema.

The purpose of the following discussion, therefore, is to displace yet another couple of oppositional terms, mainstream and avant-garde, by traversing the space between them and mapping it otherwise. I shall start from a marvellous sentence, in the passage just quoted, which sets out practically all the specifications—the terms, components, and operations—of the cinematic apparatus: "*cinematic codes* create *a gaze, a world,* and *an object,* thereby *producing* an *illusion* cut to the measure of *desire.*" It is an amazingly concise and precise description of cinema, not only as a social technology, a working of the codes (a machine, institution, apparatus producing images and meanings for, and together with, a subject's vision); but also as a signifying practice, a work of semiosis, which engages desire and positions the subject in the very processes of vision, looking and seeing. It is, or could be, a perfectly good description of cinema *tout court.* But in the context of Mulvey's essay the description only refers to dominant or Hollywood cinema. Within the discursive framework that opposes mainstream to avant-garde cinema, "illusion" is associated with the former and charged with negative connotations: naive reflection-theory realism, bourgeois idealism, sexism, and other ideological mystifications are part and parcel of illusionist cinema, as of all narrative and representational forms in general. Hence, in this Brechtian-Godardian program, "the first blow against the monolithic accumulation of traditional film conventions (already undertaken by radical filmmakers) is to free the look of the camera into its materiality in time and space and the look of the audience into dialectics, passionate detachment" (p. 18). Therefore, within the context of the argument, a radical film practice can only constitute itself against the specifications of that cinema, in counterpoint to it, and must set out to destroy the "satisfaction, pleasure and privilege" it affords. The alternative is brutal, especially for women to whom pleasure and satisfaction, in the cinema and elsewhere, are not easily available. And indeed the program has not been rigorously followed by feminist filmmakers. Which is not meant, again, as a *post-factum* criticism of an ideological analysis that has promoted and sustained the politicization of film practice, and feminist film practice in particular; on the contrary, the point is to assess its historical significance and to locate the usefulness of its lesson in the very limits it has posed and allowed to be tested.

Suppose, however, that the word illusion were to be dislodged from the particular discursive framework of Mulvey's argument and allowed to carry with it the semantic associations it has in the work of E. H. Gombrich. Might it then be possible to reassess the pertinence of her description to all cinema, and to readjust accordingly the specifications of the apparatus? Illusion, according to Gombrich, has been addressed by all aesthetic theories and philosophies since Plato as one of the characteristic functions or qualities of art, though by no means its exclusive property. Because of its capacity to confuse intelligence and critical reason ("the best part of the soul," writes Plato, is "that which puts its trust in measurement and reckoning"), and to appeal instead to "the lower reaches of the soul" and the errors of the senses, Plato banishes "scene-painting" or mimetic art together with poetry from the ideal State in the *Republic*.[32] Thereafter, in the history of Western philosophies and epistemologies, where "Platonism has been victorious all along the line," illusion is typically equated with delusion and deception, so that even an interest in the problem of illusion in painting still "carries the taint of vulgarity . . . like discussing ventriloquism in the study of dramatic art" (p. 194). Yet it is by an illusion not unlike ventriloquism that, for example, we take the sounds and words issuing from our television sets or from the movie theatre's loudspeakers as if they were made or spoken by the images on the screen, i.e., as diegetic sounds and speech (dialogue).

Briefly, Gombrich sees illusion as a process operating not only in representation, visual and otherwise, but in all sensory perception, and a process in fact crucial to any organism's chances of survival.[33] Perception and illusion are inseparably twined in the constant "scanning for meaning" which describes each individual's relation to the environment. As in Gregory's account, perception entails a making of judgments based on inference and prediction, a testing for consistency, the proving or disproving of expectations elicited by contextual and situational clues. In the course of his analysis of diverse forms and mechanisms of illusion, Gombrich makes several observations that are useful to the present discussion. In the first place, he argues, the Platonic dichotomy between opinion *(doxa)* and knowledge *(episteme)* is untenable, as is the equation of illusion with mistaken belief.

> There is no antithesis between reflex and reflection, but a continuous spectrum extending from the one to the other, or rather a hierarchy of systems which interact on many levels. The lower system of impulse and anticipation offers material for the higher centres in a chain of processes that extends from unconscious reaction to conscious scrutiny and beyond to the refined methods of testing developed by science. [P. 219]

No antithesis, no opposition, but a complex interplay links reflex and reflection, perceptual anticipations (which he also calls "pre-images" or "phantom percepts"), and the actuality that confirms or refutes the expectations derived from contextual knowledge—the latter, then, including instinctual responses and "conditioned" reflexes. For example, both self-movement and eye movements, any shift in focus, effect changes in the environment which demand predictive assessment; "the stimulus that reaches us from the margin of the field of vision may lead to an anticipation of what we shall find on inspection." If confirmation or refutation rarely enters our awareness, it is because we usually have no need to stop and reflect on the correctness of our hypotheses, and thus "prediction and actuality merge in our awareness, just as the two retinal images fuse in binocular vision." However, the existence of prognostic perception may become apparent in situations where "the predictive phantom does become available to introspection . . . when the erasure mechanism fails in the absence of contradictory percepts or when the phantom becomes too strong to yield to the pressures of refutation" (p. 212). The most dramatic instance of this is hallucination, but Gombrich suggests that the process may similarly account for the phenomenon of "closure" studied in *Gestalt* psychology, the viewer's tendency to fill in or ignore the gap in a circle that is exposed to view for a moment. Here again the "filling-in," the phantom percept, would be determined by contextual expectations, "the interpretation of what is represented" (p. 228).

The hypothesis of phantom percepts and their occurrence in complex situations involving other, often contradictory, percepts, is of particular interest for iconic signification and visual representation, especially in cinema. When Gombrich reports an experiment (looking at a seascape through a tube) that masks the contradictory percepts of the frame and the wall, thus mobilizing our response and projection, he could be speaking of the standard film viewing situation: the tube "cuts out binocular disparity which normally enables us to perceive the orientation and location of the canvas"; it both eliminates many of the contradictory percepts and makes it difficult to estimate the viewer's distance from and relation to the painting; and therefore it contributes to the working of illusion, since "where our perception is unsettled . . . illusion more easily takes over" (p. 232). (One has cause to be reminded here of the conditions in which, while censorship is relaxed during sleep, unconscious formations surface in the dreamwork. Similarly, the "willing suspension of disbelief" which marks our complicity in illusion, our love of fiction, even the willingness to act or hold beliefs at variance with the cognitive systems of our culture, would be but the general form of the specific operations of fetishism as described by Freud, and cinema as proposed by Metz.)[34] However, Gombrich adds, what distinguishes the world of "make believe" in games and fantasies from the dream is the inner logic of play—in Huizinga's definition, the social contract by which external consistency is given up or traded against the internal coherence of the illusion. (And here no one will fail to recognize the very process on which narrative cinema is founded.)

Significantly, when Gombrich eventually addresses cinematic illusion *per se*, it is in the terms of narrative cinema (and television). Paintings, he says, afford a double perception—one requiring concentration within the frame, the other taking in the wall and the surround; but with moving pictures it is "almost impossible" to read the pictures and also attend to the screen, their surface, as an object like any other in the room. This is so because the "sequence imposed upon us within the frame . . . carries the confirmation and refutations we employ in real-life situations" (p. 240). In other words, the picture "coheres" in the manner in which a real "scene" coheres in our daily perception. From Gombrich's account one has to conclude that the impression of reality imputed to cinema by general consensus is not the physical imprint of objects and shapes onto the film, the capturing of actual reality in the image, but rather the result of cinema's ability to reproduce in film our own perception, to reconfirm our expectations, hypotheses, and knowledge of reality.

What about phantom percepts then? Though Gombrich does not seem to observe the presence of any other contradictory percepts in cinematic representation (possibly due to an insufficiently or otherwise "keyed" attention), the notion is still very interesting and could be further pursued. For instance, with regard to avant-garde practices which foreground frame, surface, montage, and other cinematic codes or materials, including sound, flicker, and special effects; could contradictory or phantom percepts be produced not to negate illusion and destroy visual pleasure, but to problematize their terms in cinema? Not to deny all coherence to representation, or to prevent all possibility of identification and subject reflection, or again to void perception of all meaning formation; but to displace its orientation, to redirect "purposeful attending" toward another object of vision, and to construct other ways of seeing? Clearly the question is relevant to both the theory and the practice of cinema, and I shall come back to it. For the moment, however, further consideration must be given to the relationship between vision and the object of vision.

For Gombrich, vision and perception are homologous and equally bound up with meaning, equally dependent on illusion. The object of vision, be it represented or perceptual, image or real world, is constructed by a purposeful attending and selective gathering of clues which may cohere into meaningful percepts.

What may make a painting like a distant view through a window is not the fact that the two can be as indistinguishable as is a facsimile from the original; it is the similarity between the mental activities both can arouse, the search for meaning, the testing for consistency, expressed in the movements of the eye and, more important, in the movements of the mind. [P. 240]

In short, the similarity of represented (images) to real objects—which is the burden of iconicity and the problem of any theory of pictorial or cinematic realism—is transferred from the representation to the viewer's judgment. But the problem is not resolved because that judgment is itself anchored in reality, in the viewer's experience of "real life" and "natural objects." The argument is circular, and only achieves its closure in the corollary that the systematic relations between picture and object of depiction are to be sought in culturally defined "standards of truth."[35] This, as Joel Snyder points out, "only underscores the futility of seeking a standard of correctness that resides outside of the reciprocal relationship between skills of representation and skills of perception."[36] Our belief in a natural or privileged relation of images to the real world, of picture to referent (object of depiction), is not to be easily dispelled and continues perniciously to mock us even as refutations are advanced. Finally, Snyder suggests, the obduracy of the illusion inherent in iconic representation can only be convincingly explained by posing vision itself as pictorial.

In "Picturing Vision," Snyder traces the problem of photographic realism back to the development of the camera. Designed and built as a tool to help in the production of realistic pictures, the camera incorporates the particular standards of pictorial representation established in the early Renaissance and actually based in a medieval notion of vision. Since a critical history of the camera has been provided within film theory, I shall not dwell on this section of his essay, however valuable, and proceed instead to what I think is its main project and most interesting contribution, a rereading of Alberti's *Della pittura*.[37] This earliest, fundamental text on linear perspective, Snyder argues, is first an account of vision and perception, and then a method or set of rules for making pictures. "Throughout *De Pictura*, Alberti insists that the aim of the painter is to depict 'visible things'.... The primary problem in the interpretation of Alberti's text is to provide an account of what Alberti takes a visible thing to be, for, as I will show, the definition of visible thing carries with it the manner and means of depiction" (p. 238). Alberti's standard of pictorial correctness, which enables the artist "to construct a pictorial equivalent to vision," (p. 234) as well as his definition of visible things, derive from the scientific account of vision and the formal principles of *perspectiva*, a medieval theory of perception based in part on Aristotle's *De Anima*.[38] A misunderstanding of the central role played by medieval optics in the Renaissance theory of linear perspective has caused art historians to overlay it with more recent theories of vision (Panofsky's notion of a "visual image" produced by rays, for instance, was totally alien to classical or medieval optics) and thus miss the full import of Alberti's *conceptual* achievement. According to *perspectiva*,

> images are completed perceptual judgments about the objects of sense. They are made in the mind where one would expect to find them—in the imagination. What Alberti did was to conceive of this mental construct, the image, as a picture. . . . This picture metaphor controls the text. But the genius of Alberti was not simply in conceiving of a visual image as a picture; he also provided a method by means of which that image could be projected and copied by art. [P. 240]

Snyder's reading shows how Alberti, having listed the "things that are seen," the elements of the visible which alone concerns the painter (i.e., point, line, surface, light and color), goes on to describe how those elements are measured and placed in relation to one another and to the viewer's eye by rays, the "ministers" of vision; and finally gives a step-by-step outline of how the painter, in order to make the picture, follows a sequence of looking and seeing identical to that which constitutes the systematic process of vision. In sum, because for Alberti "the structure of depiction is the structure of perception," his system permits the painter "to depict the rational structure of perceptual judgments." And because "Alberti's window is literally a frame of reference with the standard units of measurement incorporated into its periphery . . . the viewer is given a warrant to make his own certified judgments about visible things depicted on the surface of the window" (p. 245).

In this account, the system of linear perspective appears to be much more than a technique for painting, whether we take it to accord itself to the physiological structure of the eye or to an inherent structure of reality, and whether we assume it to reflect "the movements of the mind" or the natural organization of the physical world. In the terms that have been specified above for cinema, it is not only a technical and conceptual-discursive apparatus which produces the object of vision, but also a signifying practice, for both painter and viewer, which instates vision itself as representation and, more important, as subject vision. A veritable social technology, linear perspective produces and confirms a vision of things, a *Weltanschauung,* inscribing the correct judgment of the world in the act of seeing; the congruence of sociality and individual, the unity of the social subject, are borne out in the very form and content of the representation. Not surprisingly, then, Alberti's demonstrations affected his contemporaries like "miracles"; to early Renaissance audiences, "the sight of those pictures must have been extraordinary—something akin to looking into the soul" (p. 246), as Snyder comments. What does seem surprising, is that we can still subscribe to that medieval notion of vision and to the quattrocento concept of depiction. Or do we? Even without invoking obvious examples to the contrary (video games, x-ray photography, or other scientific and military uses of film and video), we are daily exposed to forms of representation and image production, all kinds of trick photography, cinematic special effects, telecasts of news or live events, that simply cannot be construed according to linear perspective. The postulated relationship between skills of representation and skills of perception would suggest that something else, or something more, is involved for us in the relations of vision and meaning—of imaging.

Alberti's name stands for the confluence, in a particular historical moment, of artistic practices and epistemological discourses that coalesced to define a certain vision as knowledge and standard of meaning: the knowledge and the meaning of the object of vision (the sensible world) are given, represented, in the subject's vision.[39] I wish to suggest that, in our century, cinema has been the instance of another such confluence. It has performed a function similar in all respects to that of perspective in the previous centuries and, what is more, continues to inform the social imaginary, working through other media and apparati of representation, other "machines of the visible," as well as through social practices.

It is now time to return to Mulvey's description: "cinematic codes create a gaze, a world, and an object, thereby producing an illusion cut to the measure of desire." Only one term, desire, has not appeared in the above discussions of vision and illusion. And indeed if there is a term paradigmatic of the sensibility of the twentieth century, directly linked to the Romantic and post-Romantic notion of memory, to the linguistic and expressive experimentation of modernism, and surreptitiously scattered through the libidinal economies of postmodernism, that is desire. The twin birth of cinema and psychoanalysis around the year 1900 has been often noted, as well as their inheritance of the novel, or better, the novelistic, with its built-in standard of truth, its "vérité romanesque." Cinema's privileged relation to desire is built on that: the operations of narrativity construct a full and unified visual space in which events take place as a drama of vision and a memory spectacle. The film re-members (fragments and makes whole again) the object of vision for the spectator; the spectator is continually moved along in the film's progress (*cinematography* is the inscription of movement) and constantly held in place, in the place of the subject of vision.[40] If narrativity brings to cinema the capacity for organizing meaning, which is its primary function since the time of the classical myths, the inheritance of Renaissance perspective, that comes to cinema with the camera, could perhaps be understood as *Schaulust* (scopophilia), Freud's word for visual pleasure. The scopic drive that maps desire into representation, and is so essential to the work of the film and the productive relations of imaging in general, could be itself a function of social memory, recalling a time when the unity of the subject with the world was achieved and represented as vision. Together, narrativity and scopophilia perform the "miracles" of cinema, the modern equivalent of linear perspective for early Renaissance audiences. If psychoanalysis was dubbed by its inventor "the royal road" to the unconscious, surely cinema must be our way of "looking into the soul."

In a sense, then, narrative and visual pleasure constitute the frame of reference of cinema, one which provides the measure of desire. I believe this statement must apply to women as it does to men. The difference is, quite literally, that it is men who have defined the "visible things" of cinema, who have defined the object and the modalities of vision, pleasure, and meaning on the basis of perceptual and conceptual schemata provided by patriarchal ideological and social formations. In the frame of reference of men's cinema, narrative, and visual theories, the male is the measure of desire, quite as the phallus is its signifier and the standard of visibility in psychoanalysis. The project of feminist cinema, therefore, is not so much "to make visible the invisible," as the saying goes, or to destroy vision altogether, as to construct another (object of) vision and the conditions of visibility for a different social subject. To this end, the fundamental insights gained by the feminist critique of representation must be extended and refined in a continuing and self-critical analysis of the positions available to women in cinema and to the female subject in the social. The present task of theoretical feminism and of feminist film practice alike is to articulate the relations of the female subject to representation, meaning, and vision, and in so doing to construct the terms of another frame of reference, another measure of desire. This cannot be done by destroying all representational coherence, by denying "the hold" of the image in order to prevent identification and subject reflection, by voiding perception of any given or preconstructed meanings. The minimalist strategies of materialist avant-garde cinema—its blanket condemnation of narrative and illusionism, its reductive economy of repetition, its production of the spectator as the locus of a certain "randomness of energy" to counter the unity of subject vision—are predicated on, even as they work against, the (transcendental) male subject.[41] Valuable as that work has been and still is, as a radical analysis of what Mulvey calls "the monolithic accumulation of traditional film conventions," its value for feminism is severely curtailed by its discursive context, its "purposefulness," and the terms of its address. (This point will be further developed in chapter 3, through a reading of Michael Snow's *Presents*.)

The ideas and concepts explored in the attempt to outline a more flexible and articulated notion of imaging may be usefully considered in this respect: the concept of mapping as a complex, mutual intersecting of perceptual and semiotic processes; the suggestion that contradictory or phantom percepts, elided by the purposefulness of dominant codes, are nevertheless an indelible if muted aspect of perception (and thus could be played against the dominant codes to question and displace them); the idea that illusion works toward survival (whose or what manner of survival is clearly a political question, one that requires the constant examination of our relation to the instance of power); finally, the complicity of image production with visual theories and hegemonic social discourses, but equally the latter's coexistence with heterogeneous and even contradictory practices and knowledges. All of this suggests that narrative and visual pleasure need and should not be thought of as the exclusive property of dominant codes, serving solely the purposes of "oppression." If it is granted that the relations between meanings and images exceed the work of the film and the institution of cinema, then it must be possible to imagine how perceptual and semantic contradictions may be engaged, worked through, or redirected toward unsettling and subverting the dominant formations. The achieved hegemony of both the cinematic and the psychoanalytic institutions proves that, far from destroying visual and sexual pleasure, the discourse on desire produces and multiplies its instances. The question then is how to reconstruct or organize vision from the "impossible" place of female desire, the historical place of the female spectator between the look of the camera and the image on the screen, and how to represent the terms of her double identification in the process of looking at her looking. Pasolini's observation that cinematic representation is both the inscription and the performance of social reality points to one interesting direction: by foregrounding the work of its codes, cinema could be made to re-present the play of contradictory percepts and meanings usually elided in representation, and so to enact the contradictions of women as social subjects, to perform the terms of the specific division of the female subject in language, in imaging, in the social. That such a project specifically demands an attention to strategies of narrative and imagistic figuration is explicitly suggested, for example, in Yvonne Rainer's *Film About a Woman Who.* . . . Some of those strategies will be discussed in subsequent chapters in relation to films like Potter's *Thriller* and Roeg's *Bad Timing,* which also attempt an articulation of the female subject and thus address women spectators in a contradictory, but not impossible space of female desire.

Snow on the Oedipal Stage

3

MICHAEL SNOW'S FILM, *PRESENTS* (1981), OPENS with a shot of what appears to be a white vertical line quivering in the middle of the black screen. Slowly the line begins to stretch out horizontally to form a column, then a rectangle, and to reveal its image content, to "present" an image. As it widens, the vertical "slit" on the screen unfolds its vision: a naked woman reclining on a bed. The image continues to stretch, forming a more and more horizontally elongated rectangle, still defined as "an image" by the margins of darkened screen that frame it above and below; when it reaches the two small sides of the screen, it has become a horizontal line. Then it begins to stretch out vertically, until it reaches the aspect ratio of a movie screen, though smaller than the real screen whose proportions it maintains. Then it stops. The image is now fully revealed as a nude, its size that of a painting—but the actress's body has been moving intermittently all along, as if in sleep: it is clearly a filmed nude, not a painted one, a motion picture, a filmic image, not a still photograph or a painting.

The next shot, marking a transition to the second scene or segment of the film, shows the same woman, bed, and room, but now the image is in pastel colors—pink, blue, ivory—and takes up the full screen. The pulsating sound that has provided a continuous surface until this moment, ceases. There is a knock at a door. The woman jumps out of bed, puts on a blue robe and pink shoes, and starts walking screen-right toward the off-screen door. The camera seems to follow her into a living room, a locale contiguous with the bedroom in what is very obviously a stage set. And the stage, not the camera, has been moving, rotating in the opposite direction, in front of a fixed camera.

The second scene of the film presents the woman and her visitor, a fully clothed man who brings her flowers. They search for something (a paper, some form of writing, a script?) misplaced somewhere in the living room. Truck noises are heard, as the set tilts, shakes and vibrates. Again the camera seems to follow the movements of the two people, "trucking" back and forth from one end of the room to the other—or is it the stage that moves? Then the camera begins to conduct a search of its own, investigating objects and furniture, which wobble and fall. With increasing aggression, it attacks tables, a couch, the TV set, until they crack, break up, and shatter. The objects also appear reflected on a transparent, windowlike surface moving with the camera. On the sound track, in addition to the truck noises, is recorded an angry squeaky sound very much reminiscent of that made by the alien in Ridley Scott's *Alien*. (As Michael Snow explained, the reflection was obtained by a slab of plexiglass mounted in front of the lens; the shaking and shattering of the set was effected by two fork lifts [hence the truck noises], which literally picked up and moved the stage during the filming of the scene.)

The film's third section is composed of a sequence of quite unrelated shots of landscapes and skylines, vehicles, birds in flight, women walking, etc., some of which are distinctly marked culturally and geographically (East Coast maples, the Roman Colosseum, Dutch canals, Goya's *Maja desnuda* at the Prado, photos of women on magazine covers, beaches, Eskimo sleds and igloos, tropical vegetation) as if to suggest a "travelogue." An irregular drum beat underscores each cut, re-marking the end/the beginning of every shot.

Even from this brief description, one can infer some of the film's concerns—with cinematic representation and voyeuristic pleasure, the activity of the camera as inscription of the scopic drive and sexualization of the female body as object of the look; with *mise en scène* and montage, referentiality and signification; and with several expressive modalities and modes of sign production from painting to photography to video, from classical (studio, staged) cinema to avant-garde or "structural" film.

At first, *Presents* seems very much unlike Snow's other works, primarily because for well over two-thirds of its ninety minutes the dominant element is montage. (It would not be difficult, however, to point to references to or at least traces of *Back and Forth* (↔) in the set and camera movement of section II; of *One Second in Montreal* in the images of snowy trees and parks in winter; of *Wavelength* in the shots of waves, framed and unframed, and in the continuous "surface" sound and slow transformation of the image in section I, as well as in the fragments of narrative—minimal characters, shreds of dialogue, the "search"—in section II; of *La région centrale* in the shots of clouds, sky, and ground in section III, where the omnidirectionality of movement is now constructed in the editing room rather than by a special camera mount, thus discontinuous instead of continuous; and so forth.) Moreover, unlike the structurally overdetermined coherence we have come to associate with Snow's films since *Wavelength* (1967) and *La région centrale* (1971), there is here a formal discrepancy, an unrelatedness between the first two sections, dependent on a specifically constructed material apparatus (video used for film, the stage, the fork lifts, the "prepared" camera), and the third, whose constructive principle, montage, is one of the basic and intrinsic codes of cinematic discourse. That the latter may be new in Snow's filmmaking is beside the point, for it is this seeming discrepancy, rather than the new element of montage, that constitutes both the novelty of the film and its textual coherence, providing the terms in which is articulated its aesthetic unity.

In discussing the film after its first screening at the Chicago Art Institute (April 1981), Snow himself posed a series of relationships between the second and third sections: indoor/outdoor; staged *mise en scène*/shots of the real world (taken during a year of travel in Canada, Europe, and the United States); single long take with prepared camera and stage apparatus/three-month work at the editing table. The transition between these sections, he indicated, is marked by the theme of the Fall (downward traveling shots of buildings, of red and gold maples in the fall, and of Niagara Falls echo, at the beginning of the montage, the glass falling in the prior scene, as does a painting of Adam and Eve later on); while the overriding concern of all three sections is with the camera: with the process of looking through it and with its inscription of distance and desire. These are, of course, central to the first section as well, which appropriately carries one of the film's main "themes" (again, in Snow's words), "women."

The set of conceptual oppositions so precisely identified by Snow and the mythical (narrative) theme of the Fall he eloquently described are perfectly consistent with one another, the latter being the condition of the former. It is the fallen state of man, exiled from Eden or imprisoned in the dark cave of Plato's myth, barred from the plenitude of body, vision, and meaning, that imposes the separation of man from nature, of self from world. After the Fall, and in the effort to recapture the lost totality of being, unity, and bliss, have come the dialectical oppositions that characterize our culture and Snow's film: inside/outside, camera/event, active gaze/passive image, male/female. "Oppositions are drama," he once said.[1]

It would be possible, following his lead, to read the three sections of the film as a Lacanian passage: from the infant's gaze on the breast—a continuous, contiguous unfolding of vision on the woman's body (the wholeness of the video image unfolding on the screen, re-marked by the sound surface); to the mirror stage (the woman's body as a "painterly" representation, as a nude, framed, in long shot), and the concomitant acquisition of language (on the collapsing set of section II, the man and the woman do exchange a few words); on to the aggressivity of the camera on the Oedipal stage and, beyond that, to the fully achieved entry into the symbolic (montage as the articulatory code of cinematic language, underscored and strengthened by the formal, musical "punctuation" of the rhythmic drumbeat). Except that this entry into the symbolic, though it allows one to leave the closed, constricted space of the stage for the open, unlimited world of reality, is really, Snow suggests, a "fall" into language. For that reality can never be wholly seen or grasped as a totality: the more variety in the sights and objects offered to vision, the more obvious and constraining is montage as the principle of articulation; and the length of this section contributes to the spectator's awareness of that constraint. Nor can reality ever be totalized as meaning, since the project of Snow's montage, unlike Eisenstein's, is to prevent any associations between contiguous or alternate shots. Thus their succession would suggest, almost literally, a chain of signifiers on which meaning slides, with the movement of the camera, in every direction, the drumbeat signaling moments of suture, the appearing and disappearing of the subject, the constant turn of imaginary and symbolic, and so on.

Not inconsistently with this reading, made possible by a theoretical-aesthetic framework whose foundation is woman as both object and support of representation and desire, one could also see the film as a history: a presentation and an exploration of the history of cinematic representation and its modes of production (painting, photography, music, language, theatre, film, video), of the narrative strategies which anchor image to meaning, of the discourses and institutions which guarantee image circulation—museums, magazines, travelogues, documentaries, home movies, cinema from classical studio films to contemporary "electronic" and SFX (special effects) movies.

What is far less easy, for me, is to reconcile the film's critical, even self-critical, position with regard to forms of visual representation and artistic practices (cf. the irony of the title, Michael Snow presents . . .) with its assumption of the traditional modernist view that the "origin" of art is (in) the artist, *whose* desire is inscribed in the representation, *whose* distance from, and longing for, the object desired is both mediated and effected by the lens, the camera, the apparatus; and *to whom*, finally, the film returns as to its only possible reference, its source of aesthetic unity and meaning. For if reality cannot be grasped and totalized by the symbolic of cinema, which fragments, diffuses, limits, and multiplies the object of vision, it is precisely that vision, at once constrained and constructed by the cinematic apparatus, that *Presents* in the last instance re-presents.

Classical narrative cinema poses the spectator as subject of vision, the "figure for," and term of reference of, its constructed "narrative space."[2] It does so through the operations of narrativization, that hidden work of narrative, which Snow's films in particular have exposed by excess, stretching its rules to the very limits, almost beyond recognition (e.g., the 45-minute zoom of *Wavelength*). With *Presents* the pendulum swings back to the filmmaker as subject of vision; is it perhaps to test, expose, exceed *that* limit? In view of the decade or more of critical work in and on cinema, bearing directly on the nexus of representation and sexual difference, and on the ideological fallacy of the subject-object dichotomy, one has to wonder. It would be tempting, in a way, to see Snow's film as the deployment of that epistemological-aesthetic-ideological paradigm to its farthest limits, the critical working out of its expressive and productive possibilities from the painterly, artistic nude to commercial pornography on the magazine stand, from the individual's private fantasy in the bedroom to the mass-media fantasy of the world—both constituted, like the artist's/subject's vision, by the clichés of patriarchal culture. Tempting, perhaps generous. But even so the film presents, and presents itself as, a statement, an assertion, a taking of position, a last stand. It is not, as were Snow's earlier ones, a film working on a problem; at least not a problem for the spectator.

For some time now the cinematic apparatus has been under scrutiny by filmmakers as well as theorists. Much of the work around both classical and avant-garde, mainstream and independent, cinema has aimed at analyzing or engaging what Heath has called "the problematic of the apparatus." Of Oshima's work, for instance, he writes:

> *Empire of the Senses* produces and breaks the apparatus of look and identification; it does so by describing—in the geometrical acceptation of the word: by *marking out*—the problematic of that apparatus; hence its drama is not merely 'of vision' but . . . of the relations of cinema's vision and of the demonstration of the terms—including, above all, the woman—of those relations.[3]

But there are problems and there are problems. What concerns me here is the problem of identification, the relation of subjectivity to the representation of sexual difference, and the positions available to female spectators in film; in other words, the conditions of meaning-production and the modalities of spectatorship for women. Heath's claim for Oshima's film, that it "produces and breaks the apparatus of look and identification," is an important one, suggesting as it does that both are necessary, and simultaneously so; both rupture and production of the terms sustaining the relations of "vision" (image and narrative, then, pleasure and meaning) must occur at once. However, for a film to describe or to set out the limits of the apparatus is not sufficient to ensure the rupture; nor is Heath's notion sufficient, theoretically, to explain the relation of women spectators to the film's process.

Presents, for example, in setting up (literally) some of the problems and limitations of the apparatus, does demonstrate the relations and the terms of its vision—including, above all, the woman as object, ground, and support of the representation. Yet in this film, the nexus of look and identification is produced and broken in relation to "cinema" ("It's all pretty self-referential—referential both to itself and to film in general," says Snow), hence to its spectator as traditionally construed, as sexually undifferentiated; and women spectators are placed, as they are by classical cinema, in a zero position, a space of non-meaning. Because the epistemological paradigm which guarantees the subject-object, man-woman dichotomy is still operative here, as it is in classical cinema, *Presents* addresses its disruption of look and identification to a masculine spectator-subject, whose division, like that of the Lacanian subject, takes place in the enunciation, in the sliding of the signifier, in the impossible effort to satisfy the demand, to "touch" the image (woman), to hold the object of desire and to secure meaning. Spectator identification, here, is with *this* subject, with *this* division, with the masculine subject of enunciation, of the look; finally, with the filmmaker.

Asked about his "use of pinups and women's bodies as objects . . . like the page from a girly magazine," in an interview with Jonathan Rosenbaum, Snow responds:

> There *is* that one shot. It seems to stand out in your memory, it's nice, isn't it? *(Laughs.)*
> J.R. There are a lot of walking women. But men aren't photographed in the same way that women are.
> M.S. No. Should they be? . . . There are so many shots of women, it's really funny when that stands out, because there are some rather elderly ladies, and lots of shots of women doing work of various kinds. It *is* a panorama, you know, and that aspect of looking at women is important, because *I* look at women, and so do other men, and so do women.[4]

The doubt that these three entities—"I," "other men," and "women"—may "look at women" in different ways does not cross Snow's film. Nor does that fact that the eye looking through the lens is not the eye looking at the screen. If the eye that has looked through the camera is a divided, a fallen "I," it is nevertheless the only source and point of reference of its own vision, and the site of any possible spectator identification. In relation to this film, then, women spectators find themselves placed once again in a negative semantic space, between the "active" look of the camera and the "passive" image on the screen, a space where, though invested by the cone of light from the projector, they cast no shadow. They are not there.

This is not the least "present" of the film for feminist theorists: it allows us to understand and to locate with some precision the modalities of inscription of sexual difference in non-feminist avant-garde filmmaking, and therefore to begin to specify for ourselves how a feminist film practice is in itself a practice of difference, testing, as Kristeva has suggested, "the two boundaries of language and socialisation": how to be "that which is unspoken" and at the same time to speak "that which is repressed in discourse"; how at once to be *and* to speak, to be *and* to represent difference, otherness, the elsewhere of language.[5] Hence the magnitude of the stakes women have in cinematic representation and the constant urgency to engage and intervene in man-made cinema—but not in order to demonstrate the functioning of woman as the support of masculine vision, or "the production of woman as fetish in a particular conjuncture of capitalism and patriarchy."[6] This is no longer the task of feminist critical practice, though it may be crucial to men's work as they attempt to confront the structures of their sexuality, the blind spots of their desire and of their theories.[7] For even in the most overt gesture of opposition, in the political re-marking of its irreducible difference, the feminist critique is not pure, absolute negativity but rather historically conscious negation; the negation of existing cultural values, of current definitions, and of the terms in which theoretical questions are couched. At a time when increasing numbers of individuals and institutions are staking their claims and asserting their "rights" to address "the woman question," it is especially necessary to negotiate the contradiction that threatens feminism from within, pushing it to choose between negativity and positivity, between either unqualified opposition, pure negativity, on the one hand, or purely affirmative action in all quarters, on the other. To negotiate that contradiction, to keep it going, is to resist the pressure of the binary epistemological model towards coherence, unity, and the production of a fixed self/image, a subject-vision, and to insist instead on the production of contradictory points of identification, an elsewhere of vision.

In this sense, the notion of a film working on a problem, "a problem of 'seeing' for the spectator," is a good starting point. But how does a film produce *and* break the apparatus of look and identification? Speaking of Oshima's *In the Realm of the Senses*, a narrative film which deliberately seeks to articulate the sexual, the political, and the cinematic in its questioning of vision, Heath indicates that three main issues are involved: narrative, identification, and the shifting of the film's question on to the spectators. I believe that these issues are also involved in avant-garde cinema, for they are central to cinema as a mode of semiotic production.

> This order of the look in the work of the film is neither the thematics of voyeurism (note already the displacement of the look's subject from men to women) nor the binding structure of a classic narrative disposition. . . . Its register is . . . that of the edging of every frame, of every

shot, towards a problem of 'seeing' for the spectator. . . .
In the Realm of the Senses is acutely the film of the impossibility of 'the seen', haunted not by a space 'off' that must and can be unceasingly caught up into a unity, the position of a view for a viewer, but by a 'nothing seen' that drains the images of any full presence, of any adequate view. [P. 150]

That possibility of a "nothing seen," that uncertainty of vision which Oshima's film poses from within the system of representation it works with, narrative cinema, is not only the question of the film, but the very mechanism which allows that question to be shifted and put to the spectator. Although Snow's film, unlike Oshima's, is not narrative in the usual sense of the word, the question of spectatorship—of the ways in which the spectator's view is included, of the spectator's place as it is produced by the film's enunciation and address—is not an impertinent one.

As my reading of *Presents* suggests, the production of meaning and, thus, the engagement of subjectivity in the processes of seeing and hearing a film are never wholly outside of narrative. They are never exempt from the tendency to narrativize, the culturally ever present complicity of narrative with meaning. If in classical cinema it is the logic of narrative that "orders our memory of the film, *our* vision," as Heath states, yet according to Barthes meanings are also produced through a rhetoric of the images, with language serving as their anchorage and relay. I will propose that narrativity, perhaps even more than language, is at work in our "ways of seeing," that its logic, its patterns of repetition and difference, affect our ordering of sensory "data" at least as much as the primary rhythms of rhetorical tropes.

Discussing several formulations of cinematic identification and their implications for female spectatorship, Mary Ann Doane points out that Metz's influential definition of primary cinematic identification, based on the analogy with the mirror stage, in effect excludes women spectators much in the same way classical cinema (or Snow's *Presents*) does; that is to say, it provides the two familiar polarities of identification: with the masculine, active gaze and narrative point of view or with the feminine, specular, masochistic position.[8] Is it accidental, she then asks, "that Freud's description of identification with respect to the woman frequently hinges on . . . pain, suffering, aggression turned round against the self?" And that "while in the case of the boy, the super-ego is the relay of identification, in the girl's situation, it is the symptom"? Doane goes on to say that Mulvey, unlike Metz, suggests that primary and secondary identification operate in a common space where they are articulated together: primary, narcissistic identification, which is involved in the constitution of the ego and thus considered to be a precondition for the subject-object relations constituting secondary identification, is in fact "from the beginning inflected by, overlaid by secondary identification," for the latter depends upon "the existence of an object 'outside' the subject." Thus, Doane concludes, the mirror-effect is not a precondition of understanding images, but "the after-effect of a particular mode of discourse."[9]

In stating that secondary identification is "articulated with the father, the super-ego, and the Oedipal complex," Doane does not make an explicit connection between secondarization and narrative, or narrativity. But I should like to do so, and continuing her argument, propose that any imagistic identification and any reading of the image, including its rhetoric, are inflected or overlaid by the Oedipal logic of narrativity; they are implicated with it through the inscription of desire in the very *movement* of narrative, the unfolding of the Oedipal scenario as *drama* (action). Can it be accidental, I ask, that the semantic structure of all narrative is the movement of an actant-subject toward an actant-object (Greimas), that in fairy tales the object of the hero's quest (action) is "a *princess* (a sought-for person) and *her father*" (Propp), that the central Bororo myth in Lévi-Strauss's study of over eight hundred North and South American myths is a variant of the Greek myth of Oedipus? And that even the circus act of the lion and lion tamer is semiotically constructed along a narrative, Oedipal trajectory?[10] In short, I am proposing that narrativity, because of its inscription of the movement and positionalities of desire, is what mediates the relation of image and language. For both filmmakers and spectators, insofar as they are always historical subjects of signifying practices, images are already, "from the beginning," overdetermined by narrative through its symbolic inscription of desire. Images are implicated with narrative, we might say, as dreams are with secondarization in analytic practice, and as Lacan's imaginary or Kristeva's semiotic is with the symbolic in actual practices of language. Positions of identification, visual pleasure itself, then, are reached only *après coup,* as after-effects of an engagement of subjectivity in the relations of meaning; relations which involve and mutually bind image and narrative.

If this is the case, narrative or narrativity is more than just a code among others employed either cinematically or metacinematically by a film. It is a condition of signification and identification processes, and the very possibility or impossibility of "seeing" is dependent on it. That Snow's recent work comes back to a referential and representational ("thematic") content, while still concerned with the exploration of specific cinematic codes and their effects on perception (camera movement and speed, image transformation, sound, language, and now also montage), may evidence an awareness of this insistence of narrativity in imagistic meaning and of the tendency to narrativize at work in perception itself. In *Presents,* however, that tendency is explored as a mode of production of the film, as a code of cinema, inherent in the material apparatus; and consequently an expressive problem for the filmmaker vis-à-vis the form and the matter of expression—a struggle of the artist with the angel of his material, so to speak.

Writing on the textual relations between semiotic systems that have spatial structure and semiotic systems that have temporal structure, between the iconic and the verbal registers in a text, J.M. Lotman argues that film narrative is "a fuller form of the iconic narrative text as it combines the semantic essence of painting with the transformational syntagmatic quality of music. However, [he adds] the question would be simple, or even primitive, if this or that art were automatically to realize the constructive possibilities of its material. . . . It is a question of freedom vis-à-vis the material, of those acts of conscious artistic choice that can either preserve the structure of the material or violate it."[11]

The specific code of narrative (*fabula* and characters) is taken up self-reflexively, metacinematically, in the staged "Oedipal drama" of *Presents,* where the camera itself is an actor, in fact the protagonist; while the musical (abstract) rhythm of montage in section III struggles precisely against the tendency of (representational) images to make a story by association and contiguity. Yet the narrative "meanings" set up by the prior two sections are not to be dispelled. Would they be, without those sections? Probably not. As J. Hoberman notes, "close-ups of heart surgery or a woman's pubic area are bound to

have more impact than shots of cars or trees, no matter how franti-
cally the camera is jiggling. *Presents* doesn't dehierarchize its images, it
trivializes them."[12] What the film, finally, demonstrates is the grand
illusion of a non-illusionist cinema so dear to some sectors of the
avant-garde, and the ideological weight of a purely "materialist"
cinema.

While the importance of Snow's work on perception and cinematic
codes is not to be diminished by what that work does not do, other
recent films have taken on cinematic representation as a production
of meaning for the spectators, posing the problem of seeing, not as
one of expressive modalities, a problem of "art," but as a questioning
of identification and subject identity. It is not by chance that such
films, whether commercially or independently distributed, mainstream or avant-garde, work with and against narrative, and that for
them, as for Oshima's film, "the question lies in the articulation of the
sexual, the political and the cinematic, and in the impossibilities discovered in the process of such an articulation" (p. 48).

One of those "impossibilities," perhaps the most serious for feminism, is that while no "positive images" of woman can be produced by
simple role reversal or any thematics of liberation, while no direct
representation of desire can be given except in the terms of the
Oedipal, masculine-feminine polarity, it is only through narrative that
the questions of identification, of the place and time of women spectators in the film, can be addressed. I do not mean "narrative" in the
narrow sense of story (*fabula* and characters) or logical structure (actions and actants), but in the broader sense of discourse conveying the
temporal movement and positionalities of desire, be they written,
oral, or filmic narrative forms: the case history, the postcard in *Sigmund Freud's Dora;* pornographic literature and sentimental novels
read aloud in *Salò* and *Song of the Shirt,* respectively; strictly coded
narrative genres such as opera and film noir in *Thriller;* the "news
story" in *Realm of the Senses;* myth in *Riddles of the Sphinx;* porno films
and TV commercials in *Dora;* science fiction in *The Man Who Fell to
Earth* (or less so: philosophical writing in *Salò,* the political mythology
of Nazi-Fascism in *The Night Porter,* historical and journalistic writing
in *Song of the Shirt,* medical-juridical discourse in *Bad Timing*); as well
as filmic narration in its voice-over, synch-sound, and other varieties.
Each of these films engages a number of narrative discourses dis-
persed across the text, showing their congruence and cooperation in

the general "deployment of sexuality," as Foucault calls it, of which cinema is one institutionalized technology.

The privileged position of cinema (and television or, to a lesser extent, photography) in that deployment, and therefore in the constitution of social subjects, has to do with what used to be called the referentiality of the image, its direct or analogical "impression of reality," which today, in a poststructuralist or, better, postsemiological climate, is more accurately understood as an imagistic representation. The fascination with the human body, documented by film historians and guaranteed by sponsors and producers, is explained by Foucault's hypothesis of sexuality as an "implantation" of pleasures in the body, which sustains the social network of power relations.[13] As a direct result of the historical formation of sexuality, then, the imagistic representation of the body, cinema's gift of visual pleasure, is a focal point of any process of identification, exerting a pull on the spectator comparable only to the tension of narrativity. The scandalous pleasures afforded by Marlene Dietrich in top hat and tails performing Maurice Chevalier to Cary Grant's audience in *Blonde Venus*, Tim Curry's drag in *The Rocky Horror Picture Show*, Richard Gere's *American Gigolo* or, more subtly, David Bowie's alien body in *The Man Who Fell to Earth*, and the more overtly ideological insistence of Pasolini's camera on Terence Stamp's trousers in *Teorema* are perhaps no more than minor violations of the standard code of spectatorship; but they have disrupted it to such a degree that, on seeing again *Ben Hur* (1959), for example, we notice with surprise the insistence of Wyler's camera on Charlton Heston's bare midriff and legs.

It has often been objected that "feminizing" the male body does not alter the polarity by which *the* body is desired, can be *seen*, only as female. The objection comes from the terms in which phallic desire is constructed, its requirements of disavowal, hence, for cinema, voyeurism and fetishism. But I do not think it holds outside of that construction. A more interesting objection would be that those representations of the body, like the "nude" of Snow's film, are not pure images, pure imaginary, but are already implicated in narrativity, thus overdetermined by certain positionalities of desire, a certain placing of identification. That is why it is not androgyny that we read in Tommy/David Bowie's body, but the signified of a sexual difference not reducible to the terms of a phallic or Oedipal polarity. It is not homosexuality that we read in Dietrich's body, look, and gesture, but the simultaneous presence of two positionalities of desire, the masculine (in her drag performance) and the feminine (in her other acts as dancer, mother, and "lost woman"), perversely and hilariously brought together in her ape-suit act. For the same reason, simple role reversals do not work as well. The body of John Travolta in *Moment by Moment* is not disturbing or exciting, but merely another pretty body on the Malibu scene; it even lacks the imaginary possibility, explicitly contained in the narrative of *American Gigolo,* that the function of a man's body may be nothing more (and nothing less!) than to give pleasure to women.

It is in the play of these two tensions, image and narrative, not just one or the other, that the spectator's subjectivity is engaged, in the twofold pull of a film's imaging, body and meaning. If the masculine-feminine polarity can be disrupted to open other spaces for identification, other positionalities of desire, the work of the film should be on these problems: how to address the spectator from an elsewhere of vision, how to construct a different narrative temporality, how to position the spectator and the filmmaker not at the center but at the borders of the Oedipal stage.

Now and Nowhere:
Roeg's Bad Timing

4

—You said you loved me!
—I said I'd arrest you.
—You know it means the same thing.

> Angie Dickinson as "Feathers" to John Wayne
> as Sheriff John T. Chance in *Rio Bravo*, Hawks,
> 1959; screenplay by Leigh Brackett

THE NOW AGING DEBATE WITHIN AVANT-GARDE and independent cinema on the ideological effects and political effectivity of representational, "illusionist," or "anthropomorphic" film versus abstract or structural-materialist film may have found new life in the writings of Michel Foucault, particularly in his notion of the social as a "practical field" in which technologies and discourses are deployed.

Whether cinema is taken to be an art or a mass industry, experiment or entertainment, a language-system or a subjective, fantasmatic production, cinema depends on technology, or better, is implicated with it. The particular advantage of Foucault's historical methodology is that it opposes the bourgeois tradition of an autonomous history of ideas in favor of the analytical transcription of "empirical knowledges"; it thus bypasses the base-superstructure model in which technology, like language, is usually associated with the base, as the ensemble of purely technical or instrumental means, while "ideas" are considered to be superstructural. Redefined as a set of regulated procedures, mechanisms and techniques of reality-control, deployed by power, the notion of technology is expanded to include the production of social subjects, practices, and knowledges; consequently, ideas themselves assume a practical, pragmatic character in their articulation with power relations.

Were one to adopt, and to adapt, Foucault's method of historical analysis to cinema, one would have to shift the terms of the question "cinema" away from the ideas of cinema as art, documentation, or mass communication, and from the idea of cinema history as the history of those ideas; away from *auteur* theory as well as from the project of an economic history of cinema *per se;* from the presumption that a film expresses the filmmaker's individual creativity, the artist's "visionary" draw on the bank of some collective unconscious; and from the assumption that historical research is done by collecting and assembling "data." It would also mean abandoning—theoretically, that is—the concept of an autonomous or internal development of cinema's "technological means," whether mechanical, chemical, or electronic, the techniques supposed to derive from them, even the expressive styles elaborated against or in spite of them; abandoning, too, the idea of cinema as a device to capture phenomena and guarantee their reality and historical occurrence, their taking or having taken place. In short, one would have to abandon the idea of cinema as a self-contained system, semiotic or economic, imaginary or visionary.

Some of this shifting has already taken place in film theory and practice. That is why there is a growing interest in Foucault's work and, perhaps ironically, on the part not of film historians but of those concerned with current film practice and with the practical field in which cinematic discourse is deployed. Foucault's views appear most relevant to cinema, to its elaboration of genres and techniques, to the development of audiences through tactical distribution and exhibition, to the ideological effects it produces (or seeks to produce) in spectatorship.[1] In this context, and not as an "application" of Foucault's proposals but in the attempt to engage them from a feminist critical position, is offered the following reading of Nicolas Roeg's *Bad Timing.*

But first we must ask: what is the practical field in which technologies, cinema for example, are deployed? It is the social in general, understood as a crisscrossing of specific practices, involving relations of power and pleasure, with individuals and groups assuming variable positions or positionalities. Power is exercised "from below," says Foucault, "from innumerable points, in the interplay of nonegalitarian and mobile relations"; and so are resistances. In fact, the existence

of power relations "depends on a multiplicity of points of resistance
. . . present everywhere in the power network." Resistances are not "in
a position of exteriority in relation to power, [but] by definition, they
can only exist in the strategic field of power relations." Moreover,
both power relations and points of resistance pass through "apparatuses and institutions, without being exactly localized in them," but
rather traversing or spreading across "social stratifications and individual unities."[2] This map of the social as a field of forces (discourses,
and the institutions which anchor and guarantee them, are for
Foucault—much like signs are for Eco—social forces), where individuals, groups, or classes move about assuming variable positions,
exercising at once power and resistance from innumerable points
defined by constantly shifting relations, is a very appealing, almost
optimistic vision of an unlimited political semiosis. Groups form and
dissolve, relations of power are not fixed and egalitarian, but multiple
and mobile. If the political is a continuous production of meanings,
positionalities, and struggles in an open range of practices and discourses, everyone really has a chance to resist. Pleasures are practically guaranteed.

This, incidentally, may not be the least reason why Foucault's writings, eminently quotable in themselves, seem to be more and more
often quoted in relation to cinema. Technology, power and pleasure,
sexuality and the body, the family and other forms of confinement,
prisons and hospitals, psychoanalysis—what other historian or
philosopher has put together and spoken of things that so directly
concern cinema? Who can resist, for example, applying his notion of
sexuality as a "technology of sex" to cinema: a set of regulated procedures which produce sex and the desire for sex as their end result, sex
as not just the object of desire but at the same time its very support? In
its "sixty years of seduction" (as ABC has recently reminded us),
cinema both exemplifies and employs, even perfects, that technology
of sex. It exemplifies the deployment of sexuality by its endless investigations and confessions, its revealing and concealing, its search for
vision and truth; and it perfects its technology by "implanting" images
and patterns of meaning in the spectator's body, in perception and
cognition, implanting the very terms of its imaging, its mechanisms of
capture and seduction, confrontation and mutual reinforcement. Few
can resist it. Yet I think we should.

There may be some danger in simply accepting Foucault's representation as a description of the social (which one may be led to do by virtue of the fact that it presents itself as historical writing instead of, say, philosophical or literary writing). While it is not divergent, epistemologically, from several neomarxist conceptions of the public sphere, from Negt and Kluge to Eco's view of sign production, unlike them it tends to account for everything, leaving no phenomenon or event outside the reach of its discursive order; nothing exceeds the totalizing power of discourse, nothing escapes from the discourse of power.[3] Thus if one asks, what can cinema do? what films shall we make or exhibit? should women filmmakers bother to go to Hollywood? should black students study filmmaking? and so forth, Foucault assures us that power comes from below, and that the points of resistance are present everywhere in the power network. According to him, then, the question of political effectivity should be posed in these terms: how do we seek out "the most immediate, the most local power relations at work," how do we analyze them, how do we weigh "the effect of resistance and counterinvestments?"[4] The critical tools for this kind of history, this "microanalytics" of cinema, are yet to be developed. And herein lies, I think, the usefulness of Foucault's work for current film theory and practice. But caution should be exercised lest the very congruence between Foucault's view of the social and the ideological operations of cinema blind us to the complexity of the task. My reading of *Bad Timing* seeks to suggest something of that complexity and, in particular, the difficulty in weighing the effects of resistance and counterinvestments, as evidenced by the film's reception.

Nicolas Roeg's *Bad Timing: A Sensual Obsession* seems to have caused more displeasure than pleasure to virtually everyone: general audiences (it was not a box office success) and official media critics, on the one hand, and women's groups involved in the antipornography campaign, on the other. It has been found boring and confusing, over-reaching and pretentious, "technically good" and offensive to women. The X-rating and pattern of exhibition (art cinemas in first run, then, immediately, the revival circuit), plus the director's cult reputation (*Performance, Don't Look Now, Walkabout, The Man Who Fell to Earth*), place *Bad Timing* in a special category of commercially distributed, non-mainstream films such as Oshima's *In the Realm of the Senses*, Cavani's *The Night Porter*, Pasolini's *Salò*, or, to a lesser degree,

Godard's *Every Man for Himself,* and, lesser still, Bertolucci's *Last Tango in Paris.*

All these films deliberately seek to articulate the sexual, the political, and the cinematic through a sustained questioning of vision and power; and though not "independently" produced (thus undeserving of the moral commendations extended to low-budget movies, the ethical rewards of poor cinema), they urge us to reconsider the current definitions of cinema no less forcefully than do other, more explicitly and programmatically "alternative" practices: avant-garde filmmaking and political film, or what Solanas and Getino called "third cinema" in 1970, to distinguish it from European art cinema on one side and Hollywood on the other.[5] Today we do not speak of only three kinds of cinema; categories have multiplied, discourses and practices intersect and overlap (*The Love Boat* remakes Busby Berkeley; Michael Snow makes a travelogue [*Presents,* 1981]; Bruce Beresford's *Breaker Morant* finally shows that socialist realism can be effectively beautiful, and more effective than Marlon Brando as antiwar protest).

Still there are films that do not seem to fit anywhere, and *Bad Timing* is one such film. That it does not belong in the "great artist's film" slot with the latest Fellini-Mastroianni hoopla (*City of Women*) and Truffaut's *Last Metro,* or in a package of "new foreign cinema"— German, French, Australian, whatever—or with "independent," social-issue oriented films like John Sayles's *The Return of the Secaucus Seven* or Connie Fields's *Rosie the Riveter,* is one more reason for its production of displeasure. Then there is the question of genre: neither a thriller nor a love story, though the opening and closing songs pay homage to both; no appeal to the political mythology of Nazi-Fascism; not a remake of a James Cain novel, nor a meta-cinematic remake of *Psycho* or *8½, Bad Timing* has a well chosen title indeed. Yet—Harvey Keitel is everyone's favorite actor, Theresa Russell is very beautiful, the sound wonderful, the cinematography impressive as always in Roeg's films, and the editing is almost as stunning as Thelma Schoonmaker's in *Raging Bull.*

Its problem, I think, is not displeasure but *unpleasure. Bad Timing* undercuts the spectators' pleasure by preventing both visual and narrative identification, by making it literally as difficult to see as to understand events and their succession, their timing; and our sense of time becomes uncertain in the film, as its vision for us is blurry. The nexus of look and identification, which has been discussed in chapter 3 with regard to films by Snow and Oshima, is central to Roeg's film as well, with its thematics of voyeurism twice relayed through the generic pattern of the police investigation, which in turn encases the "confessional" investigation of sexuality. The work of this film, however, is less with vision than narrative, or better, less on the problem of seeing as such than on the problem of *seeing as understanding* events, behaviors, and motivations. A common viewer-response to *Bad Timing*'s "love story" is: why does Milena stay with him, why is she attracted to him, what does she *see* in him (that I don't)? He—Art Garfunkel as Dr. Alex Linden, an American research psychoanalyst who teaches at the University of Vienna, photos of Freud looming large behind his office desk and couch (actual shot location, the Freud Museum), on which couch Milena twice lies down (and once Alex joins her)—he, for most viewers, is not a particularly attractive character, with his tweed suits, humorless conversation, low-key voice, and overall dull, uncommanding personality. Nor is he a star, glamorous by association with previous roles or gossip columns. He's an ex-sixties songwriter, whose image simply hasn't kept up with the times, hasn't gone punk or whatever the new fashions are, and never had the bisexual versatility of a Mick Jagger or a David Bowie (who is primarily responsible for the box-office success of Roeg's prior film, *The Man Who Fell to Earth*); or, for that matter, the beauty of Oshima's actor, Fuji Tatsuya. If beauty is by no means considered essential to the sexiness of male characters and stars (or even important, as witness the appeal to both men and women of Harvey Keitel as Inspector Netusil), Garfunkel/Alex Linden seems to have none of the qualities that allow viewers to like him or to identify with him.

Thus the point of entry into the film's narrative, the path of access to its inscription of desire, is through the character of Milena/Theresa Russell and what she sees in him (that we don't). That for many this path is not accessible, we know from recent role-reversal films like Jane Wagner's *Moment by Moment* and, of course, from the history of unpleasure that has kept Dorothy Arzner's movies confined to the morgue of film archives. Much in the same way, in *Bad Timing*, access to narrative pleasure is blocked rather than enhanced by the film's generic contiguity with familiar patterns of expectations. The love story *cum* investigation spreads across a generic spectrum that goes from the psychological thriller (*Marnie, Vertigo*) and film noir (*The Big*

Sleep, Double Indemnity) up to the "woman's film" *(Rebecca, Letter from an Unknown Woman),* only the latter genre allowing some measure of identification with the female protagonist and thus access, through her, to the narrative trajectory of (Oedipal) desire. In *Bad Timing,* however, the remembering of the events of the relationship, presented in flashback, cannot be attributed to Milena, who, in terms of the diegetic present, is unconscious for all but the very last scene.

Literally, Milena is the "object" of Alex's desire; she is most desirable when unconscious, body without speech, look, or will, in the infamous "ravishment" scene, which we see but which Alex never confesses to Inspector Netusil. That he does not "confess" is very important: it establishes ravishment not as an individual aberration, a deviation from "normal" sexuality, a perversion to be punished or cured (Netusil has no interest in the law as such; Alex is not a practicing but a "research" analyst), avowed, and most of all confessed ("Confess. Please, Dr. Linden, as a personal favor," begs Netusil; "what is detection, if not confession? . . . between us, it might help . . . I can help you, Dr. Linden. Confess, between us, tell me what you dare not"); and once confessed, then to be attributed to, and serve to characterize, a certain type of deviant personality.[6] On the contrary, if not admitted and disavowed, ravishment remains a sadofetishistic fantasy inherent in the masculine structure of desire and perfectly congruent with the power relations sustained by other social discourses and practices which the film engages—juridical, politico-diplomatic, psychoanalytic, legal, medical, surgical. The security check (a psychological "profile") that Alex runs for Nato on Milena's file, stored in a locked vault like a body in the morgue, conveys the chilled passion of necrophilia; Netusil's investigation is conducted, much like Quinlan's in *Touch of Evil,* from the "hunch" that the real crime is not suicide or murder but rape or ravishment; the vaginal examination performed on Milena's unconscious body, ordered by Netusil, is intercut with shots of her sexual intercourse with Alex; even the emergency room efforts to revive her, to make her expel the ingested amphetamines, show doctors inserting several objects into her throat—matched to a soundtrack of thumping, gulping, and bedroom sounds—before finally cutting her trachea. Nor is psychoanalysis exempted from this imagery as Milena, stretched out on the couch in Alex's office, asks: "Well, Doctor, is there hope for us?"

In the terms of Foucault's argument, Alex's refusal to confess, thus to collaborate with the mechanisms of the "technology of sex," could be read as a resistance to the power/knowledge paradigm; but that refusal is precisely what places him in a position of power in relation to Netusil ("My need is a confession. Would you like to confess, Dr. Linden?" pleads the inspector). For Alex knows that "through the gratification of curiosity, one acquires knowledge," as he tells his students, backed by screen-size projections of "some famous spies," which include "the first spy" (a male child) and the "the first to be spied on" (a couple making love, the child's "primal scene"), as well as Freud, J. Edgar Hoover, and Stalin ("two of whom might be called political voyeurs")—and the equation, knowledge is power, couldn't be clearer. "I prefer to label myself an observer," lectures Dr. Linden; "the guilt-ridden voyeur is usually a political conservative." Nevertheless, that he and Netusil play by the same rules and duplicate or implicate one another as do phychoanalysis and the law, knowledge and power, is visually and aurally established throughout the film, beginning immediately after the lecture scene, with a continuous soundtrack of classical music (not accidentally, Beethoven's *Fidelio* overture) over crosscut shots of the two men in their respective homes, Harvard diplomas hanging in full view in Netusil's study. The inspector is a family man, and so indeed is Alex, who wants to marry Milena and go back to America. It is her refusal to marry him, her "resistance" in Foucault's terms, that places them both in jeopardy with the law ("Husband? relation? boyfriend?" the police keep asking Alex, who replies reluctantly, "You can say a friend") and makes Netusil suspect Alex of some kind of crime. But a distinction must be made with respect to the man's and the woman's relation to the law.

Milena's offense is against propriety, an offense not juridical but moral: her excess, the sexual, physical, and domestic "disorder" that, at least in the movies, marks women who choose to be outside the family ("What a mess! Just like my sister's," says an officer of the law searching her apartment); it is an offense contemplated by the law, not even a violation. Ravishment and rape, on the other hand, are crimes against property, against the legal institution of marriage as sexual ownership of the spouse's body ("you don't own me, I don't own you," protests Milena at first, declining cohabitation). By refusing to confess, and thus to acknowledge guilt, Alex resists the "politically conservative" discourse on sexuality upheld by the police inspector ("creatures who live in this sort of disorder . . . a sort of moral and physical sewer . . . they spread it around them like an infectious disease. . . . They envy our strength, our capacity to fight, our will to master reality").[7] But his resistance comes from and is made possible by the same power/knowledge apparatus; and Alex's politically liberal discourse wins out, with our sympathies going out to Netusil/Keitel, who, though perfectly correct in his "assessment of the truth" and in the logic of his detection—operating as he is from the very same emotional and conceptual paradigm—has been outsmarted and outdone.

This kind of resistance, located within the terms of diverse but congruent practices and discourses, may either succeed and become power (as it does for Alex) or fail and end up in confinement, the morgue or the archive (as for Milena and for Arzner's films). The fact that in matters sexual and cinematic, those who line up with power are men and those who end up in confinement women, is not particularly new or surprising. But it should be kept in mind when reading Foucault's conclusion, which fairly well sums up Alex's tactical position in the film:

> We must not think that by saying yes to sex, one says no to power. . . . It is the agency of sex that we must break away from, if we aim—through a tactical reversal of the various mechanisms of sexuality—to counter the grips of power with the claims of bodies, pleasures, and knowledges, in their multiplicity and their possibility of resistance. The rallying point for the counterattack against the deployment of sexuality ought not to be sex-desire, but bodies and pleasures.[8]

Foucault's rallying point, bodies and pleasures, which in a way is represented in the character of Milena, turns out to be useful and good for Alex, and very clearly bad, in fact impossible, for Milena.

Bad Timing, however, poses the possibility of another kind of resistance, and does so thematically as well as formally, working through the problematic of temporality, narrative, and montage. It suggests a resistance, in the film and within the practice of cinema, to be understood as radical difference, an absolute negativity which resists integration into the discourses of power/knowledge/vision. Actually, this other kind of resistance is also sketched out by Foucault (and thus must now be discussed), but its relation to power is much more ambiguous; in fact he does not distinguish between the two, and in *The*

History of Sexuality leaves the notion of resistance underdeveloped so that, if anything, it seems to be a subsidiary of power. He writes: "Resistances do not derive from a few heterogeneous principles; but neither are they a lure or a promise that is of necessity betrayed. They are the odd term in relations of power; they are inscribed in the latter as an irreducible opposite."[9] For me, irreducible and opposite don't go together; an "opposite" is already "reduced," led back into a logic of unity, a dialectic or a dialogue. Elsewhere, however, it should be noted, he speaks of a pure negativity, an indeterminate force capable of escaping or dodging all controls and constrictions, all processes of normalization and determination. This negativity appears to be less a resistance, a force that can be set against power, than a non-force, an absolute difference with respect to power. For the latter, far from being a negative element of repression, is the positive condition of knowledge, the only productive force; in other words, it is power, not negativity or resistance, which spreads across the social body as a productive network of discourses, forms of knowledge and subjectivity. Foucault's examples of this pure negativity—Pierre Rivière, popular justice as a form of judiciary guerrilla, the quasimystical idea of a "non-proletarianised common people"—remain, themselves, indeterminate in his discourse.[10]

Here one is drawn to a comparison with the notion of a proletarian or plebeian public sphere, elaborated by Negt and Kluge's *Oeffentlichkeit und Erfahrung* in opposition to and as a development of Habermas's analysis of the bourgeious public sphere.[11] However, despite the similarities, Foucault's plebeian resistance is precisely *not* proletarianized, not mediating toward political praxis. Hence the impression of "paradoxical conservatism" it has generated, "a sort of mysticism of indetermination."[12] Foucault's non-proletarianized masses appear somehow free of ideology: when they perceive someone to be their enemy and decide to punish or to reeducate this enemy, he argues, the masses "do not rely on an abstract universal idea of justice" but rather "on their own experience, that of the injuries they have suffered, that of the way in which they have been wronged, in which they have been oppressed"; thus their justice is not an "authoritative" one, "backed up by a state apparatus which has the power to enforce their decisions; they *purely and simply* carry them out."[13] Purely and simply? He speaks as if these plebeian masses were sexually or otherwise undifferentiated, as if these "common people" were untouched by "abstract" ideas, unencumbered by symbolic processes, mythical production, patriarchal structures—in short, as if they were immune to ideology, which is to say, outside of culture. Later on in the discussion, pressed on by the "Maoists" (who object that popular justice during the French Resistance missed its real enemy-target by going after the women who had slept with Germans and shaving their heads [cf. Emmanuelle Riva/Nevers in *Hiroshima, Mon Amour*], instead of punishing the real collaborators), Foucault elegantly contradicts himself: "This does not mean that the non-proletarianised plebs has remained unsullied. . . . [The bourgeois] ideological effects on the plebs have been uncontestable and profound."[14] Nevertheless, the pure and simple masses must be kept unsullied for the sake of his argument: "if people went rushing after women to shave their heads it was because the collaborators . . . against whom they should have exercised popular justice, were presented to the masses as being too difficult to deal with in that way: it was said, 'Oh, those people's crimes are too great, we'll bring them before a court.'. . . In this case the courts were just used as an excuse for dealing with things other than by acts of popular justice."[15]

"Paradoxical conservatism" is a very appropriate phrase for a major theoretician of social history who writes of power and resistance, bodies and pleasures and sexuality as if the ideological structures and effects of patriarchy and sexual differentiation had nothing to do with history, indeed as if they had no discursive status or political implications. The rape and sexual extortion performed on little girls by young and adult males is a "bit of theatre," a petty "everyday occurrence in the life of village sexuality," purely "inconsequential bucolic pleasures."[16] What really matters to the historian is the power of institutions, the mechanisms by which these bits of theatre become, presumably, pleasurable for the individuals involved, the men *and* the women—former little girls, proletarianized or not—who then become complicit with those institutional apparati. Here is where, despite Foucault's elegant rhetoric and radical politics (his interventions in issues of capital punishment, prison revolts, psychiatric clinics, judiciary scandals, etc.), his efforts to define political resistance and theoretical negativity sink like a paper boat in a street puddle.

A more convincing definition of negativity, and one which is directly pertinent to my reading of *Bad Timing*, is Julia Kristeva's, also given in an interview:

Believing oneself 'a woman' is almost as absurd and obscurantist as believing oneself 'a man'. I say almost because there are still things to be got for women: freedom of abortion and contraception, childcare facilities, recognition of work, etc. Therefore, 'we are women' should still be kept as a slogan, for demands and publicity. But more fundamentally, women cannot *be*: the category woman is even that which does not fit into *being*. From there, women's practice can ony be negative, in opposition to that which exists, to say that 'this is not it' and 'it is not yet'. What I mean by 'woman' is that which is not represented, that which is unspoken, that which is left out of namings and ideologies.[17]

This "unspoken" of femininity, this "not represented" or not representable, this negativity as the underside of discourse is the sense in which, I will attempt to show, Roeg's film inscribes the figure of a radical and irreducible difference.

In the last scene of the film, the only one in which Milena is shown not in flashback but in a diegetic time subsequent to her hospitalization—thus possibly the only "real" time for her as a character independent of the investigative frame—Alex catches a glimpse of her getting out of a cab in New York City. He, and we, are not sure it is Milena until we see the scar on her chest. Then he calls out her name; she looks at him and remains silent; the film cuts back to Alex looking out of the cab, then to her as she turns and walks away, then back to Alex and follows his cab disappearing into the city traffic. The effect of this scene, Milena's survival having been previously reported, is something of an epilogue, or a moral in the Brechtian manner. Her stern, silent look and changed demeanor suggest an actor who, stepping out of the play (Alex's memory drama), confronts the audience with the play's question. The scar that identifies her for Alex and for us, like the snake-bite scars on the bodies of the Moroccan snake charmers, like the surgical modifications performed on the sensory apparatus of Tommy/David Bowie in *The Man Who Fell to Earth*, is a mark at once of subjection and of resistance. This scar is a sign of a radical difference inscribed and displayed in the body, a resistance not congruent, not commensurable with the dialectic of the system, as Alex's is, thus not its political negation but an absolute negativity.

This resistance, the film suggests, is not located within the terms of the productive apparati of power/knowledge, for no "truth" is produced there about Milena's character; but neither is it located outside of those practices and discourses which constitute the given social world. It is, quite simply, difference. The "man" who fell to earth cannot go back out there whence "he" came. "He" will remain on earth indefinitely as an alien, marked by a radical, though barely perceptible, difference. Milena, too, is neither bound by the rules and institutions of power/knowledge nor "free" of them, and *this* contradiction is what the scar signifies: her passion and her silence, her experience of difference, her history—past, present—inscribed and displayed in her sexed body, which now, as throughout the film's alternating images, is both there and not there, conscious and unconscious, in contradiction, in excess of those dialectical oppositions.

In *The Man Who Fell to Earth*, difference—physical and cultural—is represented primarily in spatial terms; however, it is the fact that Tommy's body does not age like the others around him which in the end, despite the surgical intervention that makes it *absolutely* impossible for him to go back to his distant planet, conclusively re-marks his radical otherness. Possibly because Tommy's expanded temporal dimension and his superior (tele)vision are elements of content accounted for by the generic code of science fiction, the film's montage plays mainly on spatial displacement and discontinuities. In *Bad Timing*, as the title insists, temporality is directly in question, and its different orders must be established symbolically, i.e., cinematically. For both Tommy and Milena, the surgical operation is but the symbolic representation of a lengthy and multiple process of cultural determination, conditioning, and adaptation that has preceded it. While the destruction of Tommy's vision occurs toward the end of the film, for Milena the surgical intervention is there from the beginning, so that the only way to imagine her "before"—the only representation of woman possible in discourse—is through Alex's re-membering; when we see her in "real" time, "her" time, outside of Alex's and Netusil's fantasmatic construction, which coincides with narrative time, she is *already* scarred. And although the linear temporal dimension of the investigation seeks to reduce her contradiction and to establish it as an opposition (to the law, to patriarchy, to phallic desire), the montage resists that time, makes it bad, prevents it from producing the truth. The question of time, the "bad timing" of conflicting orders of temporality and the filmic representation of non-congruent temporal registers, is the problem of the film, its work with and against narrative: how to articulate the sexual, the political, and the cinematic, and "the impossibilities discovered in the process of such an articulation."[18]

There is the linear time of the investigation, with its logical succession of cause and effect, crime and punishment, guilt and reparation, its movement toward resolution and backward toward the original scene, the traumatic moment of an Oedipal drama which narrativity endlessly reconstructs. All narrative cinema, in a sense, is the making good of Oedipus, the restoration of his vision by the film's re-presentation (reenactment) of the drama. Linear time, with its logic of identity and non-contradiction, its predication of a definite identification of characters and events, before or after a "now" which is not "not now," a here where "I" am, or an elsewhere where "I" am not, is a necessary condition of all investigation and of all narrative. It regulates the detection of an already certain "crime" and the making good of the film's vision for the spectators. In Roeg's film this time is "bad," for the sequence of events between Milena's phone call to Alex and his call for the ambulance, and the lapse of time between them, cannot be reconstructed (except in his "confession"); the "evidence" is insufficient. As Netusil's detection hangs on Alex's confession, we depend on the film's structuring of visual and aural clues, but find ourselves adrift between narrative and shot, amidst mismatching images and sounds. For example, the tape of her voice on the phone is played back at several different points in the film, suggesting the non-logical, symptomatic processes of compulsive repetition; even the ravishment scene, placed as it is concurrently with the direct confrontation between Alex and Netusil—the moment when they come together in the scenario of voyeurism and fetishism that sustains their common "sensual obsession"—cannot furnish conclusive proof, factual or logical.

By not producing the truth, by preventing a certain identification of events and behaviors, the film denies the legality of this temporal order and of the investigative, narrative vision. Our sympathy for Netusil is a measure of our identification with his loss. Indeed, the temporal order of loss, the second register of "bad" time in the film, is that of symptomatic repetition and primary processes, the relentless, unruly return of an image-fetish—the female body, bound, strapped down, violated, powerless, voiceless or nearly inarticulate, lifeless—signaling the dimension of obsession, its compulsive timing, an illegality of vision.[19] Together, in a systemic opposition which by definition "projects" one onto the other (as Jakobson would say, but does not Foucault as well?), the sequential, metonymic order of the investigation and the metaphoric register of obsessive repetition define the legal and illegal times of masculine, phallic desire.[20] But a third possibility is posed in the film, questioning the first two: the possibility of a different temporality, another time of desire.

"What about my time," shouts Milena in a context where time stands for desire (and significantly not in a Vienna apartment but on a sunbathed Moroccan terrace from which she watches the snake charmers in the market square below); "what about now? . . ." she asks in response to Alex's marriage proposal, which is accompanied not by a diamond ring but by a one-way ticket from Casablanca to New York.[21] Alex does not reply, though in our mind's ears echoes the answer given for him by all the movies we remember, "We'll always have Paris." That question, indeed, could not be answered in the film in any other way: the apparatus of cinema—both classical narrative and avant-garde cinema—has been developed in a culture founded exactly on the exclusion of all discourse in which that question could be posed.[22] Milena's "now," her "time," the time of her desire is in another register altogether, not congruent or commensurate with Alex's time, which leads forward to possession as marriage and/or backward to fetishistic possession. "If I told you I was married, you'd think it meant in your way, and it wasn't like that, so better I . . . I don't think it was a lie. . . . Words . . . [it's] not important," explains Milena. "Not important to whom? To whom? To whom? To whom?" pounds and cajoles Alex's voice over her body, which the montage locates simultaneously on their bed and on the operating table.

Along the linear dimension of his time, in the unified trajectory of phallic desire, marriage and love can only "mean" in his way, and Milena's "now" has no place. As he tells her, again apropos of her marital status, "either you're married or divorced, you can't be in between. To be in between is to be no place at all." A not atypical exchange between them, and one which exemplifies their mismatched, nonsynchronous registers of time and desire, occurs on the bridge over the Danube that serves as border and "neutral ground" between Vienna, where the story of Alex and Milena takes place, and Bratislava, where Milena's Czech husband, Stefan, lives.[23] This scene parallels the one, early on in the film, when Milena and Stefan part on the same border bridge (and "it does not mean I'm going away," she says). Now, again she's returning to Vienna:

Milena: How're you doin'?

Alex: What happened?

Milena: You don't like it . . . the way I look . . . I bought it for you [a new dress] . . .

Alex: You're a day late.

Milena: I wired you, didn't I?

Alex (as she walks back on the bridge toward Bratislava): Where are you going?

Milena: Nowhere.

And it is Pinter's *No Man's Land* that Yale Udoff, the author of *Bad Timing*'s screenplay and himself a playwright, has Milena read in the German translation, *Niemandsland*.

If "nowhere" and "now" are the place and time of feminine desire, they can only be stated as negativity, as borders; this is what the film finally says, and it is the most it can "say." Borders are not gaps—in a story, in a chain of signifiers, in a presumed continuity of the drive from excitation to discharge to excitation—that can be filled, overtaken, and thus negated. Borders stand for the potentially conflictual copresence of different cultures, desires, contradictions, which they articulate or simply delineate. Like the river between two cities, two countries, two histories, in the surprising last shot of the film, borders mark difference itself; a difference that is not just in one or in the other, but between them and in both. Radical difference cannot perhaps be represented except as an experiencing of borders. In the thematic image of the river, in the incongruous, inconclusive, or impossible "conversations" on the bridge in Vienna, Casablanca, New York, the film inscribes the cinematic figures of non-coherence: non sequiturs in the dialogue, visual and aural split ends, a running over of the sound beyond "its" image, a bleeding of one image into another, the cuts which articulate narrative and shot, and mismatch them.

For me, spectator, *Bad Timing* does more than demonstrate the terms of cinema's vision, the functioning of woman as the support of masculine desire and "the odd term in the relations of power." It effectively breaks the narrative complicity of look and identification with the wedge of a question: what about now? what about my time and place in the apparatus, in the nexus of image, sound, and narrative temporality? To say that Roeg's film poses that question for me, however, is not to say that it is "a feminist film"—a label that at best serves industrial profits—but to suggest that it be considered next to more explicitly political and avant-garde practices of cinema, next to films like Sally Potter's *Thriller* or *Sigmund Freud's Dora: A Case of Mistaken Identity* (not made by Sigmund Freud, against the rules of grammatical identification and authorial ownership, but by A. McCall, C. Pajaczkowska, A. Tyndall, and J. Weinstock). Like those films, *Bad Timing* plays on two concurrent tellings of the story, several temporal registers, and a voice somewhere, nowhere, that asks a question without answer. What is retold, in all three cases, is "the same old story," as Billie Holiday sings over the rolling end-credits,

> The same old story
> Of a boy and a girl in love,
> The scene, same old moonlight,
> The time, same old June night,
> Romance's the theme . . .
> . . . .
> The same old story.
> It's been told much too much before.
> The same old story.
> But it's worth telling just once more . . .

In *Sigmund Freud's Dora*, the other telling of the story is, of course, Freud's own case history, a narrative genre *par excellence*, dependent as it is on the Oedipal drama and the "family romance." *Thriller* engages opera, specifically Puccini's *Bohème*, whose narrative appeal is closer to the sentimental novel and the "weepie" film genre than are the grand historical spectacles of Verdi or the mythical-mystical total theatre of Wagner. And in *Bad Timing*, it is the story of narrative cinema, from *Broken Blossoms* to *Chinatown*, or vice versa.[24] It starts out as film noir and ends by reclaiming the love story, but both are off-key, embarrassed by the difficulty of vision and understanding: the ambiguity of Klimt's mosaic figures, of Schiele's disturbing bodies, of Blake's lovers; the incoherence or unintelligibility of language (Waits's slurred words, Milena's barely articulate voice on tape, the doctors' German, the Czech embassy intercom messages, the broken French of Alex and Milena hitchhiking in Morocco, the snake charmers' chant); and the disphasure of image and word, pleasure and meaning in Alex's slide lecture. In the latter, the image, supposed to appear on the screen in front of the students to match the lecturer's words, suddenly appears on a screen behind them, but by the time the students/viewers turn their heads, the words refer to another image, which is now in front of them. And, as they turn around again, that too is gone. This short sequence, on the very theme of voyeurism, is a condensed and perfect metaphor of the entire film's work with and against narrative cinema: it frustrates the expected correspondence of look and identification, power and knowledge, while it emphasizes their historical, social, and cinematic complicity.

But, as I suggested, something else takes place in *Bad Timing*, as in *Thriller* and *Sigmund Freud's Dora:* the disruption of look and identification is concurrent with a dispersal of narrative, temporal, visual, and aural registers. Specifically, these films construct a double temporality of events, where the linear dimension of the narrative, backward and forward (they all have something of an investigation going on), is constantly punctuated, interrupted, and rendered ineffectual by a "now" that mocks, screams, and disturbs (the TV commercials and porno clips in *Dora*, ambulance siren and the *Tel Quel* recitation in *Thriller*). In *Bad Timing* that "now" is the constant presence of Milena's sexed body, which the montage succeeds in making present as at once conscious and unconscious, alive and dead, there and not there: never totally unconscious, for it moves and gasps, shivers and groans—registering sensations, unknown perceptions, feelings perhaps—even in the deep coma of the emergency room and of the ravishment scene (especially then); nor ever fully conscious in the sense of having full "presence of mind" as Alex does, full self-control or self-possession; but drunk, drugged, high, caught up in hysterical elation or depression, screaming or nearly inarticulate. And then, because of this memory of montage, that joins together in the "now" distinct and contradictory temporal registers, the scar on her chest in the last scene assumes its particular significance. It is still, to be sure, the "wound" which psychoanalysis correctly identifies as the mark of woman, the inscription of (sexual) difference in the female body; just as Milena still functions narratively in the film as "the woman," image to be looked at, body of desire. But the scar *also* assumes the value of a difference much more radical than the lack of something, be it the phallus, being, language, or power. What the filmic image of the scar inscribes is the figure of an irreducible difference, of that which is elided, left out, not represented or representable.

It is such a figure, constructed by the montage as a memory of borders, contradiction, here and there, now and nowhere, that addresses me, spectator, as historical woman. And it is just in the split, in that non-coherence between registers of time and desire, that figural and narrative identification are possible for me, that I can pose the question of my time and place in the terms of the film's imaging.

Desire in Narrative

5

"SADISM DEMANDS A STORY," WRITES LAURA MULVEY in the essay already cited on several occasions. The proposition, with its insidious suggestion of reversibility, is vaguely threatening. (Is a story, are all stories, to be claimed by sadism?) The full statement reads: "Sadism demands a story, depends on making something happen, forcing a change in another person, a battle of will and strength, victory/defeat, all occurring in a linear time with a beginning and an end."[1] This sounds like a common definition of narrative, yet is offered as a description of sadism. Are we to infer that sadism is the causal agent, the deep structure, the generative force of narrative? Or at least coextensive with it? We would prefer to think the proposition is biased or at best particular, pertinent to some narrative genres like the thriller (after all, she is speaking of Hitchcock's films), but surely not applicable to all narratives, not universally valid. For, as Roland Barthes once stated, narrative is universal, is present in every society, age, and culture:

> Carried by articulated language, spoken or written, fixed or moving images, gestures, and the ordered mixture of all these substances; narrative is present in myth, legend, fable, tale, novella, epic, history, tragedy, drama, comedy, mime, painting (think of Carpaccio's *Saint Ursula*), stained glass windows, cinema, comics, news item, conversation. . . . Caring nothing for the division between good and bad literature, narrative is international, transhistorical, transcultural: it is simply there, like life itself.[2]

Barthes's famous essay served as introduction to the 1966 issue of

Communications, devoted to the structural analysis of narrative, a seminal work in what has become known as narratology and undoubtedly a cornerstone in narrative theory. The volume and the work of its contributors owed much to a variety of sources, from structural linguistics to Russian Formalism and Prague School poetics, as did all semiological research in its early stages; but its coming to existence at that particular time must be traced directly to the publication, in 1958, of Lévi-Strauss's *Anthropologie structurale* and the English translation of Propp's *Morphology of the Folktale.*[3] The early structural studies were concerned with the logic of narrative possibilities, of actions and their patterned arrangement, be it the logic of a diachronic unfolding of the actions performed by the characters (Propp's "functions" and *"dramatis personae"*); or the logic of a paradigmatic distribution of semantic macrounits (Lévi-Strauss's "mythemes") and the relations among them; or, in Barthes's own, more finely articulated model, the logic of a vertical ("hierarchical") integration of narrative instances and levels of description.

Not surprisingly, none of these models would support or even admit of a connection between sadism and narrative that may presuppose the agency of desire. Or more exactly, none would admit of a *structural* connection between sadism and narrative; that is to say, one by which the agency of desire might be seen somehow at work in that logic, that "higher order of relation," that "passion of meaning" which narrative, Barthes says, excites in us. The structural models would consider sadism or desire as types of thematic investment, to be located on the level of content, and thus preempt the possibility of an integral relationship, a mutual structural implication of narrative with desire and *a fortiori* sadism. Curiously, however, Barthes ends his essay with this statement: "It may be significant that it is at the same moment (around the age of three) the the little human 'invents' at once sentence, narrative, and the Oedipus" (p. 124). He will of course pursue the relation between narrative and Oedipal structuration, as it is mediated by language, in later works from *S/Z* to *The Pleasure of the Text.* But in so doing—this too may be significant—Barthes drifts further and further away from his own semiological model, and, far from seeking to establish an analytic structural framework, his writing will become increasingly fragmented and fragmentary, personal, a subject's discourse. Nevertheless, once suggested, the connection between narrative and the Oedipus, desire and narrative, not only appears to be incontestable but, divesting itself from Barthes's singular critical *iter,* urges a reconsideration of narrative structure—or better, narrativity.

Since the early structural analyses, semiotics has developed a dynamic, processual view of signification as a work(ing) of the codes, a production of meaning which involves a subject in a social field. The object of narrative theory, redefined accordingly, is not therefore narrative but narrativity; not so much the structure of narrative (its component units and their relations) as its work and effects. Today narrative theory is no longer or not primarily intent on establishing a logic, a grammar, or a formal rhetoric of narrative; what it seeks to understand is the nature of the structuring and destructuring, even destructive, processes at work in textual and semiotic production. It was again Barthes who, in his notion of the text, sketched out a new direction and a useful critical approach to the question of narrativity: "The work can be held in the hand, the text is held in language, only exists in the movement of a discourse . . . or again, *the Text is experienced only in an activity of production*" (p. 157).

To ask in what ways and by what means desire works along with narrativity, within the movement of its discourse, requires attention to two distinct but interrelated lines of inquiry. First, the reexamination of the relations of narrative to genres, on the one hand, and to epistemological frameworks on the other; thus, the understanding of the various conditions of presence of narrative in forms of representation that go from myth and folktale to drama, fiction, cinema, and further, historical narration, the case history, up to what Turner calls "social dramas." Narrative has been the focus of much recent critical debate. A comparison of the 1980 special issue of *Critical Inquiry* on narrative, for example, with the 1966 *Communications* mentioned earlier indicates a shift in emphasis. The "transhistorical," narratological view of narrative structures seems to have given way to an attempt to historicize the notion of narrative by relating it to the subject and to its implication in, or dependence on the social order, the law of meaning; or to the transformative effects produced in processes of reading and practices of writing. More often than not, however, those efforts all but reaffirm an integrative and ultimately traditional view of narrativity. Paradoxically, in spite of the methodological shift away from the notion of structure and toward a notion of process, they end up dehistoricizing the subject and thus universalizing the narrative process as such. The problem, I believe, is that many of the current formulations of narrative process fail to see that subjectivity is engaged in the cogs of narrative and indeed constituted in the relation of narrative, meaning, and desire; so that the very work of narrativity is the engagement of the subject in certain positionalities of meaning and desire. Or else they fail to locate the relation of narrative and desire where it takes place, where that relation is materially inscribed—in a field of textual practices. Thus, finally, they fail to envisage a materially, historically, and experientially constituted subject, a subject engendered, we might say, precisely by the process of its engagement in the narrative genres.

Second, then, the relation of narrative and desire must be sought within the specificity of a textual practice, where it is materially inscribed. This is especially obvious when one considers narrativity in cinema, where the issue of material specificity (not simply of "techniques") is unavoidable and in fact has long been a central question of film theory—whence the value, the relevance of cinema for any general theory of narrative. But within film theory, too, a certain shifting of emphasis has occurred with regard to narrative. While narrative film has always been the primary area of reference for critical and theoretical discourses on cinema, narrative structuration has received on the whole much less attention than have the technical, economic, ideological, or aesthetic aspects of filmmaking and film viewing.[4] Moreover, as I discuss in previous chapters, the issue of narrative has served as a bone of contention, as well as a rigid criterion of discrimination, between dominant, mainstream cinema and avant-garde or independent practices. The distinction is not unlike that often made between mainstream fiction and metafiction or antinarrative; except that in cinema that distinction is articulated and defined in political terms.

Because of the material specificity of cinema—its near-total and unmediated dependence on the socioeconomic and the technological—film theory and film practice stand in a close-knit relationship, bound by strict ties of historical proximity. Thus it is not by pure coincidence that the return to narrative on the part of theory, its increasing concern with narrativity, corresponds to a return of narrative in alternative and avant-garde film practices. That does not mean that the emergence of narrative would mark an apolitical or reactionary turn. On the contrary, as Claire Johnston first noted back in 1974, narrative is a major issue in women's cinema; a feminist strategy should combine, rather than oppose, the notions of film as a political tool and film as entertainment. The political, analytical work of women's cinema is to bring home the fact that "cinema involves the production of signs," and "the sign is always a product"; that what the camera grasps is not reality as such but "the 'natural' [naturalized] world of the dominant ideology. . . . The 'truth' of our oppression cannot be 'captured' on celluloid with the 'innocence' of the camera: it has to be constructed, manufactured." Thus, she insisted, the project of feminist film criticism was to build up a systematic body of knowledge about film and to develop the means to interrogate male bourgeois cinema; but that knowledge must then feed back into filmmaking practices, where what is at stake is "the working through," the question, of desire. "In order to counter our objectification in the cinema, our collective fantasies must be released: women's cinema must embody the working through of desire: such an objective demands the use of the entertainment film."[5] Very much out of this same concern, in a recent essay on sexual identity in melodrama, Laura Mulvey addresses the question of pleasure for the female spectator and turns to consider the positionalities of identification available to her in narrative cinema, which are "triggered by the logic of narrative grammar."[6]

For feminist theory in particular, the interest in narrativity amounts to a *theoretical return* to narrative and the posing of questions that have been either preempted or displaced by semiotic studies. That return amounts, as is often the case with any radical critique, to a rereading of the sacred texts against the passionate urging of a different question, a different practice, and a different desire. For if Metz's work on *la grande syntagmatique* left little room for a consideration of the working of desire in narrative structuration, Barthes's discourse on the pleasure of the text, at once erotic and epistemological, also develops from his prior hunch that a connection exists between language, narrative, and the Oedipus. Pleasure and meaning move along the triple track he first outlined, and the tracking is from the point of view of Oedipus, so to speak, its movement is that of a masculine desire.

> The pleasure of the text is . . . an Oedipal pleasure (to denude, to know, to learn the origin and the end), if it is true that every narrative (every unveiling of the truth) is a staging of the (absent, hidden, or

hypostatized) father—which would explain the solidarity of narrative forms, of family structures, and of prohibitions of nudity.[7]

The analogy that Robert Scholes proposes between narrative and sexual intercourse again affirms, in the manner of a *reductio ad absurdum,* what seems to be the inherent maleness of all narrative movement:

> The archetype of all fiction is the sexual act. In saying this I do not mean merely to remind the reader of the connection between all art and the erotic in human nature. Nor do I intend simply to suggest an analogy between fiction and sex. For what connects fiction—and music—with sex is the fundamental orgastic rhythm of tumescence and detumescence, of tension and resolution, of intensification to the point of climax and consummation. In the sophisticated forms of fiction, as in the sophisticated practice of sex, much of the art consists of delaying climax within the framework of desire in order to prolong the pleasurable act itself. When we look at fiction with respect to its form alone, we see a pattern of events designed to move toward climax and resolution, balanced by a counter-pattern of events designed to delay this very climax and resolution.[8]

Lightly gliding over a further parallelism linking the content of the fictional work with the "possible procreative content" and the "necessary emotional content" of the sexual act, Scholes proceeds to look closely at what he calls "the meaning of the fictional act." The analogy still holds. In both cases, fiction and sex, the act "is a reciprocal relationship. It takes two." Unless the writer writes or the reader reads "for his own amusement," pursuing solitary pleasures ("but these are acts of mental masturbation," observes the critic, determined to run his metaphor into the ground), "in the full fictional act [they] share a relationship of mutual dependency. The meaning of the fictional act itself is something like love." And in the end, "when writer and reader make a 'marriage of true minds,' the act of fiction is perfect and complete."

Those of us who know no art of delaying climax or, reading, feel no incipient tumescence, may well be barred from the pleasure of this "full fictional act"; nor may we profit from the rhythm method by which it is attained. But knowing, as one does, how rare a thing a marriage of true minds can be, and then how rarely it lasts beyond the first few chapters; and knowing, furthermore, how the story usually goes, one might be brought to wonder: is Mulvey perhaps not wrong, after all, in seeing a connection between sadism and narrative? And the suggestion that the connection is one of mutual implication already appears much less far-fetched, and all the more outrageous. In the following pages I shall seek to explore further the nature of that connection which, I suspect, is constitutive of narrative and of the very work of narrativity.

Suppose we were to ask the question: what became of the Sphinx after the encounter with Oedipus on his way to Thebes? Or, how did Medusa feel seeing herself in Perseus' mirror just before being slain? To be sure, an answer could be found by perusing a good textbook of classical mythology; but the point is, no one knows offhand and, what is more, it seldom occurs to anyone to ask. Our culture, history, and science do not provide an answer; but neither do the modern mythologies, the fictions of our social imagination, the stories and the images produced by what may be called the psychotechnologies of our everyday life. Medusa and the Sphinx, like the other ancient monsters, have survived inscribed in hero narratives, in someone else's story, not their own; so they are figures or markers of positions—places and topoi—through which the hero and his story move to their destination and to accomplish meaning.

Classical mythology of course was populated with monsters, beings awesome to behold, whose power to capture vision, to lure the gaze, is conveyed in the very etymon of the word "monster." But only a few have survived past the dark ages into Renaissance epos, and beyond the age of reason into the imaginary of modernism; and perhaps not by chance the few that have survived are narratively inscribed within stories of heroes and semantically associated with boundary. What these monsters stand for, to us, is the symbolic transposition of the place where they stand, the literary topos being literally, in this case, a topographical projection; the *limen,* frontier between the desert and the city, threshold to the inner recesses of the cave or maze, metaphorizes the symbolic boundary between nature and culture, the limit and the test imposed on man.

The ancient monsters had a sex, as did the gods, in a mythology whose painstakingly rich articulation of sexual difference was to be boiled down to the stark Platonic opposition man/non-man. And again in the modern mythologies, the gender of monsters, unlike the sex of angels, is a carefully worked out representation. The Minotaur, for example, imprisoned at the center of the labyrinth in Crete, exacts his toll in human lives indiscriminately (seven girls, seven boys) as would a natural plague; more beast than man, he represents the bestial, animal side of man that must be sought out and conquered. The issue of Pasifae's unnatural union with a bull, he is described as "half bull and half man" but referred to as "the Cretan Bull" or even, with unwitting irony, by the patronymic "Minos' bull."[9] In *Fellini's Satyricon* he is represented with a man's body and the head of a bull. Medusa and the Sphinx, on the contrary, are more human than animal, and definitely female: the latter has the body of a winged lion but a woman's head; Medusa is female and beautiful, although she too is connected with bestiality (she was Poseidon's lover and pregnant with his offspring when Perseus killed her, and from her body, as her head was severed, sprang forth the winged horse Pegasus). Medusa's power to cast the spell which in many cultures is actually called "the evil eye," is directly represented in her horribly "staring eyes," which are a constant feature of her figurative and literary representations; while the serpents in their hair or "girdles" are a variable attribute of all three Gorgons, together with other monstrous features such as wings, "a lolling tongue," or "grinning heads."[10]

Medusa's power, her evil look, is more explicit than the Sphinx's but both achieve analogous long-term effects: they not only kill or devour, but blind as well. The legends of Perseus and Oedipus in which they are inscribed, make it clear that their threat is to man's vision, and their power consists in their enigma and "to-be-looked-at-ness" (in Mulvey's word), their luring of man's gaze into the "dark continent," as Freud put it, the enigma of femininity. They are obstacles man encounters on the path of life, on his way to manhood, wisdom, and power; they must be slain or defeated so that he can go forward to fulfill his destiny—and his story. Thus we don't know, his story doesn't tell, what became of the Sphinx after the encounter with Oedipus, though some may claim to have caught a glimpse of her again in the smile of Mona Lisa, and others, like mythologist H. J. Rose, simply state that she "killed herself in disgust," after Oedipus solved her riddle—and married Jocasta.[11] Medusa, of course, was slain, though she too is still laughing, according to Hélène Cixous.[12] The questions we might ask are obvious. Why did the Sphinx kill herself (like Jocasta), and why the disgust? Why did Medusa not wake up to her own slaying, or did she perhaps *have* to be asleep? Let us ask our questions, then—if we can.

In an essay entitled "Rereading Femininity" Shoshana Felman points out how Freud's own interrogation of the "riddle" of femininity, his very asking of the question "woman" ("What does a woman want?"), paradoxically excludes women from the question, bars them from asking it themselves. She quotes Freud's words:

> Throughout history people have knocked their heads against the riddle of the nature of femininity. . . . Nor will *you* have escaped worrying over this problem—those of you who are men; to those of you who are women this will not apply—you are yourselves the problem.

And she comments:

> A question, Freud thus implies, is always a question of desire; it springs out of a desire which is also the desire for a question. Women, however, are considered merely as the *objects* of desire, and as the *objects* of the question. To the extent that women "*are* the question," they cannot *enunciate* the question; they cannot be the speaking *subjects* of the knowledge or the science which the question seeks.[13]

What Freud's question really asks, therefore, is "what is femininity—for men?" In this sense it is a question of desire: it is prompted by men's desire for woman, and by men's desire to know. Let me now elaborate this point a little further. Freud's is a question addressed to men, both in the sense that the question is not asked of women ("to those of you who are women, this will not apply") and that its answer is *for* men, reverts to men. The similarity between this "riddle" and the riddle of the Sphinx is striking, for in the latter, also, the term of address is man. Oedipus is addressed, he solves the riddle, and his answer, the very meaning or content of the riddle, is—man, universal man, Oedipus therefore. However, the apparent syntactical parallelism of the two expressions, "the riddle of the Sphinx" and "the riddle of femininity," disguises one important difference, the source of enunciation: *who* asks the question? While Oedipus is he who answers the riddle posed by the Sphinx, Freud stands in both places at once, for he first formulates—defines—the question and then answers it. And we shall see that his question, what is femininity, acts precisely as the impulse, the desire that will generate a narrative, the story of femininity, or how a (female) child with a bisexual disposition becomes a little girl and then a woman.

What must be stressed in this respect, however obvious it may seem, is that Freud's evocation of the myth of Oedipus is mediated by the text of Sophocles. The Oedipus of psychoanalysis is the *Oedipus Rex*, where the myth is already textually inscribed, cast in dramatic literary form, and thus sharply focused on the hero as mover of the narrative, the center and term of reference of consciousness and desire. And indeed in the drama it is Oedipus who asks the question and presses for an answer that will come back to him with a vengeance, as it were. "Not Creon, you are your own worst enemy," foretells Tiresias. As for the Sphinx, she is long gone and little more than a legend in the world of the tragedy, the plague-ridden city of Thebes. She only served to test Oedipus and qualify him as hero. Having fulfilled her narrative function (the function of the Donor, in Propp's terms), her question is now subsumed in his; her power, his; her fateful gift of knowledge, soon to be his. Oedipus's question then, like Freud's, generates a narrative, turns into a quest. Thus not only is a question, as Felman says, always a question of desire; a story too is always a question of desire.

But whose desire is it that speaks, and whom does that desire address? The received interpretations of the Oedipus story, Freud's among others, leave no doubt. The desire is Oedipus's, and though its object may be woman (or Truth or knowledge or power), its term of reference and address is man: man as social being and mythical subject, founder of the social order, and source of mimetic violence; hence the institution of the incest prohibition, its maintenance in Sophocles' Oedipus as in Hamlet's revenge of his father, its costs and benefits, again, for man. However, we need not limit our understanding of the inscription of desire in narrative to the Oedipus story proper, which is in fact paradigmatic of all narratives. According to Greimas, for instance, the semantic structure of all narrative is the movement of an actant-subject toward an actant-object. In this light, it is not accidental that the central Bororo myth in Lévi-Strauss's study of over eight hundred North and South American myths is an autochthonous variant of the Greek myth of Oedipus; or that the circus act of the lion tamer, analyzed by Paul Bouissac, is semiotically constructed along a narrative and clearly Oedipal trajectory.[14]

THE MYTHICAL SUBJECT

However varied the conditions of presence of the narrative form in fictional genres, rituals, or social discourses, its movement seems to be that of a passage, a transformation predicated on the figure of a hero, a mythical subject. While this is already common knowledge, what has remained largely unanalyzed is how this view of myth and narrative rests on a specific assumption about sexual difference. I shall endeavor to retrace some steps in the development of notions of plot from Propp's still-fundamental work to recent studies of the relation between myth, narrative, and the Oedipus.

In Propp's *Morphology of the Folktale* the hero's quest or action is directed toward "the sphere of action of a *princess* (a sought-for person) and of *her father*."[15] This formulation, rather surprising on the part of a scholar of folklore working outside the psychological tradition of mythical exegesis, is better understood in the context of his later and regrettably little-known studies on the social historical roots of the fairy tale. There he presents convincingly the hypothesis that the intimate connection between the functions of the princess and her father in folk narratives derives from her historical key role in dynastic succession, the transfer of power from one ruler to another and from one form of succession, in a matriarchal system, to another in the patriarchal state.

In a splendidly erudite and fascinating essay, "Oedipus in the Light of Folklore," written in the years between the *Morphology* (1928) and "The Historical Roots of the Fairy Tale" (1946), Propp combines the synchronic or "morphological" study of plot types and motifs with their diachronic or historical transformations, which are due, he argues, to the close relationship between a society's folklore production and its modes of material production. However, he cautions, plots do not directly "reflect" a given social order, but rather emerge out of the conflict, the contradictions, of different social orders as they succeed or replace one another; the difficult coexistence of different orders of historical reality in the long period of transition from one to the other is precisely what is manifested in the tensions of plots and in the transformations or dispersion of motifs and plot types.

A broad study of folklore in its historical development shows that whenever historical change creates new forms of life, new economic conquests, new forms of social relations, and all of these filter down into folklore, what is old does not die out, nor is it always entirely replaced by what is new. The old continues to exist along with the new, either parallel to it or combining with it to bring forth several associations of a hybrid nature [e.g., the winged horse, which emerged in folklore as the cultural function of the bird passed on to the domesticated horse] which are neither possible in nature nor in history. . . . One such hybrid formation is the basis of the story of the character who kills his father and marries his mother.[16]

Oedipus would come into being at the historical crossroads where two forms of succession meet and clash: an earlier one in which power was transferred from the king to his son-in-law through marriage with the king's daughter, thus through the agency of the "princess," and a later form in which the transfer occurred directly from the king to his own son. Because the transfer of power implied the necessary death, usually the killing, of the old king by the new one, the later form of succession gives rise in folklore to the theme of patricide and its corollary, the prophecy. In folklore "prophecy is absolutely unknown to peoples who did not yet know the state. Prophecy appears concurrently with the social system of the patriarchal state" (p. 97). The theme of the prophecy, Propp claims, is absent from the tales reflecting the earlier, matriarchal form of succession, where the function of regicide is performed by a son-in-law who is a stranger, often unknown, and unrelated by blood. But with the advent of patriarchy and the strengthening of paternal power as the very foundation of the state, that function (regicide, now patricide) becomes extremely ambiguous. For in such a system, a son cannot wish, let alone execute, the killing of his father; Oedipus is a criminal, though unwittingly. Hence the role of the prophecy: "the intentional and willful killing [of the king] is replaced by a killing demanded by the gods, for in the meantime the gods too have made their appearance" (p. 97).

Propp's analysis proceeds through all the functions and twists of the Oedipus plot, comparing its four main types (Judas, Andreas of Crete, Gregory, and Alban—the Oedipus story is the paradigm for the medieval accounts of the lives of saints!) disseminated in legends and folktales of Europe, Asia, and Africa. For each phase or theme, Propp shows the mediations effected by several variants between external (historical) developments and internal (formal) motivations. Just as Oedipus, who is at once the king's son and the king's son-in-law (Propp argues for the morphological identity of king's daughter and king's widow), combines in his own conflicted person the clash of the old form of succession with the new one, so do many figures and themes of the myth represent the real contradictions that developed historically in the transition from one social system to the other. The Sphinx, for instance, is an "assimilation of the princess who poses a difficult task or enigma [to the hero], and the serpent who exacts a human tribute" (p. 122). In the earlier tales, in fact, it is "the princess or *her* father" (Propp does not say "the king or his daughter") who assigns the difficult task to *her fiancé* in order to prove the worthiness of his claim to her and to the power (the throne) that she alone can bestow; his success enables him to marry her and so accede to her line, which reflects the matriarchal marriage. (For this reason, Propp remarks, the fairy-tale princess normally has no brother: she is the only one who can transfer the throne; her brother only appears in folklore when he acquires a function in history, when patriarchy makes him the heir to the throne.)

In the Oedipus story, which emerged during the patriarchal system, the role of the princess had to be attenuated, played down; however, it did not disappear altogether. Hence the figure of the Sphinx, a condensation of the princess with the serpent, which latter is a figure from the previous stage of the plot—the hero's initiation in the forest, whence he receives strength, wisdom, and the mark of leadership (this in the folktale is the function of the Donor). But, Propp notes, the Sphinx clearly still "contains the image of the woman, and in some versions Oedipus deprives her of her strength in the same way as the princess-sorceress is usually deprived of her power, that is by sexual union" (p. 122). The forest, place of the hero's education, is a female domain. The animal who nurtures the child hero is female (e.g., the she-wolf in the legend of the foundation of Rome), representing the carnal mother; and the nature of the initiation rite itself, in preparing the adolescent for adult sexuality, is closely linked with the woman-mother, she who rules over the animals (e.g., Circe). Subsequently, a woman replaces the female animal as the child's nurse, but she is usually only a presumed mother (e.g., Merope) or bears traces of the animal in her name.

These hybrid formations continue to appear in tales until the full establishment of patriarchy, when the importance of the paternal function is manifested in the theme of the child-hero who does not know his father and sets out to find him. (One might easily speculate that this is what motivates the insistent thematic of the good and nurturing father in recent movies from *Kramer vs. Kramer* to *Ordinary People*: the need to reaffirm a patriarchal order that has been badly shaken by feminism and the lesbian and gay movements.) According to Propp, then, the complex Oedipus plot appears to be located during the period of transition and merging of two social orders whose difficult, conflictual coexistence is inscribed in the many variants of the widely disseminated myth.[17] If the Oedipus story has been read as a tragedy, Propp concludes, in the light of a fate god-given and inherent in human existence, it is because the two events central to it—the victory over the Sphinx and the unwitting murder of the father—have been taken to be metaphysically rather than historically motivated. If we examine the myth in the context of its multiple links with folklore, the concept of fate must yield its exegetic force to more authentic social historical determinations (p. 124).

We now go on to a recent essay on plot typology by Jurij Lotman, the Soviet semiotician whose work on cultural texts may be said to belong to the same tradition as Propp's. Because the two essays are not only equally erudite but equally concerned with narrative typology, they provide an excellent opportunity to examine the historical transformation of the theoretical discourse itself. We find that an epistemological development has taken place during the time between Propp's work in the thirties and forties and Lotman's in the sixties and seventies, a theoretical move that, in a sense, almost repeats the historical move from matriarchal systems to patriarchal state, a transition studied by Propp through its manifestations in folklore. That time, the fifties and early sixties, is marked for anthropology and any theory of culture by the increasing influence of structural linguistics and, with the publication of the major works of Lévi-Strauss and Lacan, the establishment of structuralism as the epistemological foundation of the "sciences of man."

According to Lotman, the origin of plot must be traced to a text-generating mechanism located "at the the center of the cultural *massif*" and thus coextensive with the origin of culture itself.[18] This central mechanism engenders myths, or texts subject to an exclusively cyclical-temporal movement and synchronized with the cyclical process of the seasons, the hours of the day, the astral calendar. Because linear-temporal categories, such as beginning and end, are not pertinent to the type of text thus generated, human life itself is not seen as enclosed between birth and death, but as a recurrent, self-repeating cycle which can be told starting from any point. Although in the retelling, to our modern consciousness, the mythical texts seem to be plot-texts (i.e., based on the succession of discrete events), Lotman states, in themselves they were not so.

> Even if the narration concerned the death of a god, the dismember-ment of his body, and his subsequent resurrection, what we have be-fore us is not a plot-narration in our sense. These events are thought of an inherent to a certain position in the cycle, and repeating themselves from time immemorial. The regularity of the repetition makes of them not an excess, a chance occurrence, but a law, immanently inherent in the world. [P. 163]

The function of such texts, in the non-discrete world of myth, was to establish distinctions and, from them, to construct a picture of the world in which the most remote phenomena could be seen as inti-mately related to one another. By reducing the diversity and variety of phenomena and occurrences to invariant images, these texts could play the role of science, a "classifying, stratifying and regulating role. They reduced the world of excesses and anomalies which surrounded man to norm and system" (p. 162).

The central, cyclical textual mechanism, however, required as its counterpart another text-generating mechanism capable of fixing not laws, but anomalies. And it is the latter which, organized according to a linear, temporal succession of events, generated oral tales about incidents, calamities, crimes, chance occurrences—in short, anything contravening, or in excess of, the mythically established order of things. "If the one mechanism fixed the principle, the other described the chance occurrence. If historically from the first there developed statutory and normative texts of both a sacral and a scientific charac-ter, the second gave rise to historical texts, chronicles and annals" (p. 163). The latter was also primarily responsible, if etymology can be credited, for the historical development of the novel (from the *novella*, or "piece of news"), thus of fictional narratives in general, which Lotman calls plot-texts, adding however that the modern (literary) plot-text is the result of the reciprocal influence of the two typologi-cally older kinds of texts. In this manner he explains the widespread recurrence in modern comedy, drama, and novels of character-doubles (twins or functional pairs), who in a mythical system would be "precipitated" in one single or cyclical text-image. And the same would be true of multi-heroed texts, where heroes of successive generations (say, father and son) function as diachronic character-doubles of each other (while twins would be synchronic doubles). As for the totality of different characters distributed across the plot-text, this is how Lotman maps their genesis in the cyclical system:

> Characters can be divided into those who are mobile, who enjoy freedom with regard to plot-space, who can change their place in the structure of the artistic world and cross the frontier, the basic topological feature of this space, and those who are immobile, who represent, in fact, a function of this space. Looked at typologically, the initial situation is that a certain plot-space is divided by a *single* boundary into an internal and an external sphere, and a *single* character has the opportunity to cross that boundary; this situation is now replaced by a more complex derivative. The mobile character is split up into a paradigm-cluster of different characters on the same plane, and the obstacle (boundary), also multiplying in quantity, gives out a sub-group of personified obstacles—immobile enemy-characters fixed at particular points in the plot-space ("antagonists" to use Propp's term). [P. 167]

Several considerations are in order. First, in the notion of immobile characters or personified obstacles, fixed at a certain point of the plot-space and representing, standing for (on) a boundary which the hero alone can cross, we easily recognize the Sphinx (and Oedipus) and Medusa (and Perseus); but also, if less immediately, Jocasta and Oedipus, or Andromeda and Perseus. Second, by reducing the number and functions of what Propp would call the *dramatis personae* to the two involved in the primary conflict of hero and antagonist (obstacle), Lotman outlines a pattern of mythical narrative strongly suggestive of the one Mulvey ascribes to sadism. Third, as he further translates in cyclical terms the elementary sequence of narrative functions, which Propp had found to be thirty-one in the folktale plot-text, Lotman finds a simple chain of two functions, open at both ends and thus endlessly repeatable: "entry into a closed space, and emergence from it." He then adds: "Inasmuch as closed space *can be interpreted* as 'a cave', 'the grave', 'a house', 'woman' (and, correspondingly, be allotted the features of darkness, warmth, dampness), entry into it *is interpreted* on various levels as 'death', 'conception', 'return home' and so on; moreover all these acts *are thought of as mutually identical*" (p. 168; my emphasis).

In this mythical-textual mechanics, then, the hero must be male, regardless of the gender of the text-image, because the obstacle, whatever its personification, is morphologically female and indeed, simply, the womb. The implication here is not inconsequential. For if the work of the mythical structuration is to establish distinctions, the primary distinction on which all others depend is not, say, life and death, but rather sexual difference. In other words, the picture of the world produced in mythical thought since the very beginning of culture would rest, first and foremost, on what we call biology. Opposite pairs such as inside/outside, the raw/the cooked, or life/death appear to be merely derivatives of the fundamental opposition between boundary and passage; and if passage may be in either direction, from inside to outside or vice versa, from life to death or vice versa, nonetheless all these terms are predicated on the *single* figure of the hero who crosses the boundary and penetrates the other space. In so doing the hero, the mythical subject, is constructed as human being and as male; he is the active principle of culture, the establisher of distinction, the creator of differences. Female is what is not susceptible to transformation, to life or death; she (it) is an element of plot-space, a topos, a resistance, matrix and matter.

The distance between this view and Propp's is not merely "methodological"; it is ideological. Suffice it to point out that in very similar terms René Girard interprets the Oedipus myth in its double link to tragedy and to sacrificial ritual, and defines the role of Oedipus as that of surrogate victim. Ritual sacrifice, he states, serves to reestablish an order periodically violated by the eruption of violent reciprocity, the cyclical violence inherent in "nondifference," or what Lotman calls "non-discreteness." By his victory over the Sphinx, Oedipus has crossed the boundary and thus established his status as hero. However, in committing regicide, patricide, and incest, he has become "the slayer of distinctions," has abolished differences and thus contravened the mythical order. "Patricide represents the establishment of violent reciprocity between father and son, the reduction of the paternal relationship to 'fraternal' revenge," which is exemplified by the enemy brothers Eteocles and Polyneices or by the brothers-in-law Oedipus and Creon. Regicide is but the equivalent, vis-à-vis the polis, of patricide. And therefore, with Oedipus in Thebes,

> violent reciprocity is left in sole command of the battlefield. Its victory could hardly be more complete, for in pitting father against son *it has chosen as the basis of their rivalry an object solemnly consecrated as belonging to*

the father and formally forbidden the son: that is, the father's wife and son's mother. Incest is also a form of violence, an extreme form, and it plays in consequence an extreme role in the destruction of differences. It destroys that other crucial family distinction, that between the mother and her children. Between patricide and incest, the violent abolition of all family differences is achieved. The process that links violence to the loss of distinctions will naturally perceive incest and patricide as its ultimate goals. No possibility of difference then remains; no aspect of life is immune from the onslaught of violence.[19]

What is important here, for the purposes of our discussion, is the relation of mythical thought to the narrative form, the plot-text. As Girard states that tragedy must be understood in its mythological framework, which in turn retains its basis in sacrificial ritual or sacred violence, so does Lotman insist on the mutual influence of the two textual mechanisms, the mythical text and the plot-text. The Soviet scholar exemplifies their coexistence or interrelatedness in a great variety of texts from Shakespeare's *Comedy of Errors* to works by Dostoevsky, Tolstoy, and Pushkin, from Greek myths and Russian folktales to the *Acts of the Apostles*. He notes how, in spite of the fact that historically-specific ideas are transmitted by means of the linear plot mechanism, the mythical or eschatological schema continues to be imposed on the secular identity of literary characters; the recurrence in modern texts of themes like fall-rebirth, resurrection, conversion or enlightenment, bears witness to its presence. And further, this imposition achieves the effect of fashioning the ordinary man's individual, inner world on the model of the macrocosm, presenting the individual as a "conflictingly organized collective." Thus, he concludes, if "plot represents a powerful means of making sense of life," it is because plot (narrative) mediates, integrates, and ultimately reconciles the mythical and the historical, norm and excess, the spatial and temporal orders, the individual and the collectivity.[20]

It is neither facile nor simply paradoxical, in light of such convincing evidence, to state that if the crime of Oedipus is the destruction of differences, the combined work of myth and narrative is the production of Oedipus.[21] The business of the mythical subject is the construction of differences; but as the cyclical mechanism continues to work through narrative—integrating occurrences and excess, modeling fictional characters (heroes and villains, mothers and fathers, sons and lovers) on the mythical places of subject and obstacle, and projecting those spatial positions into the temporal development of plot—narrative itself takes over the function of the mythical subject. The work of narrative, then, is a mapping of differences, and specifically, first and foremost, of sexual difference into each text; and hence, by a sort of accumulation, into the universe of meaning, fiction, and history, represented by the literary-artistic tradition and all the texts of culture. But we have learned from semiotics that the productivity of the text, its play of structure and excess, engages the reader, viewer, or listener as subject in (and for) its process. Much as social formations and representations appeal to and position the individual as subject in the process to which we give the name of ideology, the movement of narrative discourse shifts and places the reader, viewer, or listener in certain portions of the plot space. Therefore, to say that narrative is the production of Oedipus is to say that each reader—male or female—is constrained and defined within the two positions of a sexual difference thus conceived: male-hero-human, on the side of the subject; and female-obstacle-boundary-space, on the other.

If Lotman is right, if the mythical mechanism produces the human being as man and everything else as, not even "woman", but non-man, an absolute abstraction (and this has been so since the beginning of time, since the origin of plot at the origin of culture), the question arises, how or with which positions do readers, viewers, or listeners identify, given that they are already socially constituted women and men? In particular, what forms of identification are possible, what positions are available to female readers, viewers, and listeners? This is one of the first questions to be asked or rearticulated by feminist criticism; and this is where the work of people like Propp and Freud must be seriously reconsidered—Propp's because of its emphasis on the interdependence of material social relations and cultural production, Freud's because of its emphasis on the inscription of those relations into the sphere of subjectivity. But, for the time being, from the previous discussions we reach a provisional conclusion: in its "making sense" of the world, narrative endlessly reconstructs it as a two-character drama in which the human person creates and recreates *himself* out of an abstract or purely symbolic other—the womb, the earth, the grave, the woman; all of which, Lotman thinks, can be interpreted as mere spaces and thought of as "mutually identical." The drama has the movement of a passage, a crossing, an actively experienced transformation of the human being into—man. This is the sense in which all change, all social and personal—even physical—transformation is finally understood.

Take Lévi-Strauss's reading of the Cuna incantation performed to facilitate difficult childbirth, a reading which prompts him to draw a daring parallel between shamanistic practices and psychoanalysis, and allows him to elaborate his crucial notion of the unconscious as symbolic function. The shaman's cure consists, he states, "in making explicit a situation originally existing on the emotional level and in rendering acceptable to the mind pains which the body refuses to tolerate," by provoking an experience "through symbols, that is, through meaningful equivalents of things meant which belong to another order of reality."[22] Whereas the arbitrary pains are alien and unacceptable to the woman, the supernatural monsters evoked by the shaman in his symbolic narrative are part of a coherent system on which the native conception of the universe is founded. By calling upon the myth, the shaman reintegrates the pains within a conceptual and meaningful whole, and "provides the sick [*sic*] woman with a *language,* by means of which unexpressed, and otherwise inexpressible, psychic states can be immediately expressed" (p. 193). Both the shaman's cure and psychoanalytic therapy, argues Lévi-Strauss, albeit with an inversion of all the elements, are effected by means of a manipulation carried out through symbols which constitute a meaningful code, a language.[23] In that language, however,

> the vocabulary matters less than the structure. Whether the myth is re-created by the individual or borrowed from tradition, it derives from its sources—individual or collective (between which interpenetrations and exchanges constantly occur)—only the stock of representations with which it operates. But the structure remains the same, and through it the symbolic function is fulfilled. [P. 199]

Let us consider now the structure of the myth in question and the performative value of the shaman's narrative. The incantation is a ritual, though based on myth; it has, that is, a practical purpose: it seeks to effect a physical, somatic transformation in its addressee. The main actors are the shaman, performing the incantation, and the woman in labor, whose body is to undergo the transformation, to become actively engaged in expelling the full-grown fetus and producing (bringing forth) the child. In the myth which subtends the incantation, one would think, the hero must be a woman or at least a female spirit, goddess, or totemic ancestor. But it is not so. Not only is the hero a male, personified by the shaman, as are his helpers, also symbolized through decidedly phallic attributes; but the very working of the incantation promotes the childbearing woman's identification with the male hero in his struggle with the villain (a *female* deity who has taken possession of the woman's body and soul). And, more importantly, the incantation aims at detaching the woman's identification or perception of self from her own body; it seeks to sever her identification with a body which she must come to perceive precisely as a space, the territory in which the battle is waged.[24] The hero's victory, then, results in his recapturing the woman's soul, and his descent through the landscape of her body symbolizes the (now) unimpeded descent of the fetus along the birth canal. In short, the effectiveness of symbols—the work of the symbolic function in the unconscious—effects a splitting of the female subject's identification into the two mythical positions of hero (mythical subject) and boundary (spatially fixed object, personified obstacle). Here we can again recognize a parallel with the double or split identification which, film theory has argued, cinema offers the female spectator: identification with the look of the camera, apprehended as temporal, active or in movement, and identification with the image on the screen, perceived as spatially static, fixed, in frame.

The extent to which such mythical positioning of the discursive agents works through the narrative form can hardly be overestimated. In a popular, illustrated medical text, for example, the human reproductive cycle is described as "the long journey," and the epic proportions of the narrativized account make it worth a brief digression, and a long quotation. After a preamble introducing the main actors of the epic, sperm and ovum, the difference between man and woman is briefly set out. It "consists in their way of reacting as the pituitary sends out its stimulating hormones to the blood during early puberty. In him, balance and constant readiness; in her, a continuous swing between preparation and destruction."[25] Then the chapter entitled "The Long Journey" begins:

> Travelling over these two pages [an enlarged color photo of sperm cells under microscope occupies the upper half of the pages] is an army of sperm, swimming eagerly in straight ranks. The tails stream behind and the heads show in the direction of movement as they swim through the glassy, fluid cervical mucus on about the fourteenth day of the

menstrual cycle—the day the ovum enters the oviduct. . . . The pene-
tration of sperm in the cervical mucus is very much like the progress of
a fleet of small boats up a river full of invisible logs. . . . Their swimming power will be useful soon enough when they must search for the
waiting ovum. For the great majority of sperm the way up through the
uterus and the oviduct is the road to destruction. Millions succumb in
the acid secretions of the vagina. Presumably half of those who reach
the uterine cavity enter the wrong oviduct. The rest run the risk of
swimming astray in the labyrinth of folds and recesses in the widest
part of the oviduct, where the ovum awaits their arrival. There has
been much speculation as to how the sperm find their way to the hiding
place of the ovum. When observed in glass tubes, sperm have a tendency to swim upstream; they must swim against the stream of fluid
which runs, due to the action of cilia, from the abdominal cavity toward
the uterus. Apparently the ovum sends out some attracting substances
as well, so that the sperm bear straight toward it. A few hours' sojourn
in the oviductal secretion appears to be essential; if an unfertilized
ovum is placed among sperm that have not been within the uterus or
oviduct, the interest on the part of the sperm is not very impressive.
After ovulation the ovum is capable of being fertilized for only about
24 hours, perhaps even fewer. But sperm are patient suitors. They can
endure for at least a couple of days. . . . Considering all the obstacles
along the way, we may well imagine that the best man wins. [Pp. 28–31]

This amazing passage, by representing biological difference in fully
mythical terms, actually bears out Lévi-Strauss's claim for the symbolic function. It also demonstrates how Lotman's mythical-textual
mechanism, embedded in the narrative (epic) form, works within
(pseudo) scientific discourse to construct biology itself as myth and,
consequently, as *a result* of "sexual difference." The paradox that the
passage and its context bring into focus is that sexual difference is not
the production of spermatozoa and ova in human organisms; quite
the contrary, sexual difference is what allows the "millions of sperm"
and the villainous "ovum" to be anthropomorphized as actors in a
drama which the text, appropriately enough, dubs "The Everyday
Miracle." Ironically, we note, it was none but Freud who questioned
the certainty of anatomical science ("the spermatozoon, and its vehicle
are male; the ovum and the organism that harbours it are female")
and, with the theory of bisexuality, concluded that "what constitutes
masculinity or femininity is an unknown characteristic which anatomy
cannot lay hold of."[26]

ON NARRATIVE AND FREUD

The work of Lévi-Strauss, culturally situated between ethnography and psychoanalysis, sheds light not only on the implication of both with the mythical-narrative order but equally, in turn, on the influence of psychoanalysis on current critical discourses; it allows us to see the presence of the mythical mechanism at work in the very epistemological bases of structuralism and cultural semiotics. Though Lotman is no Freudian, his analysis of narrative and myth, presumably based on materialist assumptions about culture, all but brings out the unique achievement of Freud's theory of psychoanalysis and its potentially radical suggestions. In fact, I would go so far as to say that it is precisely the theories of narrative and myth offered by scholars such as Lotman and Girard and Turner that make it difficult to see in Freud, as they do, a staunch rationalist or, as is too often claimed, the prime promoter of a reactionary, integrative, or reductive theory of human development.[27] On the contrary, we cannot but admire his valiant effort, toward the end of a life-work devoted to recasting, in a major theoretical construct, the cultural knowledge of his time about man's love affair with myth, to make a place for woman in myth—to imagine woman as subject in culture, to understand female subjectivity, to ask the question "what does a woman want?"—in short, to tell *her* story, the story of femininity. And if her story again turned out to be his story, I shall go on to show, it may be less Freud's doing than the work of Lotman's "text-generating mechanism," honed by a centuries-long patriarchal culture and still at work with a vengeance in contemporary epistemologies and social technologies.

It was not an accident of cultural history that Freud, an avid reader of literature, chose the hero of Sophocles' drama as the emblem of Everyman's passage into adult life, his advent to culture and history. All narrative, in its movement forward toward resolution and backward to an initial moment, a paradise lost, is overlaid with what has been called an Oedipal logic—the inner necessity or drive of the drama—its "sense of an ending" inseparable from the memory of loss and the recapturing of time. Proust's title, *A la Recherche du temps perdu*, epitomizes the very movement of narrative: the unfolding of the Oedipal drama as action at once backward and forward, its quest for (self) knowledge through the realization of loss, to the making good of Oedipus' sight and the restoration of vision. Or rather, its sublation into the higher order attained by Oedipus at Colonus, the superior being capable of bridging the visible and the invisible worlds. That Freud envisioned human social development in narrative terms—as did Dante and Plato, Vico and Marx, as most of us do in writing (auto)biographies and diaries or speaking about our personal or public lives—was not an accidental or idiosyncratic choice on Freud's part, but the effect and the demonstration of the "structuring capacity" (as Lévi-Strauss might say) of the narrative form, its coding function in the attribution of meaning, its patterning of experience as epic or dramatic action. In this light, I suggested, must be examined the semiotic postulate that narrative is trans-cultural and trans-historical, that it "is simply there, like life itself," as Barthes so elegantly put it; which also makes necessary, of course, the examination of the critical discourses and their quest for knowledge, their Oedipal or anti-Oedipal logic.

In a recent issue of *Critical Inquiry* devoted to a reconsideration of narrative, Victor Turner sees in "social drama" the universal form of political processes and societal transformation within a culture. Be it in medieval England during the power struggle between Henry II and Thomas Beckett, or in the US of Watergate, or in a struggle for village headmanship among the Ndembu of Zambia in West Central Africa, social drama has a two-way connection to narrative. On the one hand, social dramas are "spontaneous unit[s] of social process and a fact of everyone's experience in every human society";[28] as such they constitute "the social ground" of many types of narrative, from myth, folktale, ballad, and folk epic to chronicle, legend, or even eyewitness report. On the other hand, the latter, as mythical stories,

> feed back into the social process, providing it with a rhetoric, a mode of emplotment, and a meaning. Some genres, particularly the epic, serve as paradigms which inform the action of important political leaders—star groupers of encompassing groups such as church or state—giving them style, direction, and sometimes compelling them subliminally to follow in major public crises a certain course of action, thus emplotting their lives. [P. 153]

The notion of social drama as political process seems to point to a dynamic, dialectical view of narrative, one that would require an analysis of the historical context and material practices in which narrativity is inscribed. But Turner's is still an Aristotelian view, based, he avows, on the fact that "there is an interdependent, perhaps dialectic, relationship between social dramas and genres of cultural performance in perhaps all societies" (p. 153). He is therefore entitled, without risk of Western bias, to see the social process as made up of "spontaneous" units, social dramas, each having four phases (breach, crisis, redress, and reintegration or schism) and corresponding in form to the *Poetics'* description of tragedy. Thus, while breach, crisis, and outcome provide the content of performance genres, their form is derived from redressive ritual and legal procedures, and is a form of catharsis. Despite his quarrel with structuralism on the point of sequence (the stages of social drama are irreversible, the movement of ritual is transformative, he insists), Turner's model is also very much an integrative one. As "action-paradigm" and "redressive ritual," he concludes, narrative is "the supreme instrument for binding the 'values' and the 'goals', in Dilthey's sense of these terms, which motivate human conduct into situational structures of 'meaning'."[29]

The inherent connection between narrative and social history is also articulated by Hayden White as a relation of mutual implication, though in different and much more far-reaching terms. Speaking of the fortunes of narrative in historical writing, he notes that

> historiography is an especially good ground on which to consider the nature of narration and narrativity because it is here that our desire for the imaginary, the possible, must contest with the imperatives of the real, the actual. If we view narration and narrativity as the instruments by which the conflicting claims of the imaginary and the real are mediated, arbitrated, or resolved in a discourse, we begin to comprehend both the appeal of narrative and the grounds for refusing it.[30]

The view currently dominant among historians of historiography, he states, asserts that the modern historical narrative is superior to earlier, imperfect forms of historical representation such as the annals and the chronicle form, consisting respectively of a simply chronological listing of events (the annals) and an account of events that aspires to but fails to achieve narrative closure (the chronicle)—for it "starts out to tell a story but breaks off *in medias res,* in the chronicler's own present" (p. 9). The history proper, in the modern definition, achieves both narrativity and historicality by filling in the gaps left in the annals and by endowing events with a plot structure and an order of meaning. This achievement is possible only when the historian works from an ideological frame of reference, that is to say, when the history is grounded in "the idea of a social system to serve as a fixed reference point by which the flow of ephemeral events can be endowed with specifically moral meaning" (p. 25). That order of moral meaning, according to Hegel's *Lectures on the Philosophy of History,* only exists "in a State cognizant of Laws."[31] Therefore, according to White, "historicality as a distinct mode of human existence is unthinkable without the presupposition of a system of law in relation to which a specifically legal subject could be constituted" (p. 17); and historical self-consciousness itself is conceivable only in relation to that. He then remarks on the "intimate relationship" Hegel has alerted us to between law, historicality, and narrativity: "where there is no rule of law, there can be neither a subject nor the kind of event which lends itself to narrative representation. . . . And this raises the suspicion that narrative in general, from the folktale to the novel, from the annals to the fully realized 'history', has to do with the topics of law, legality, legitimacy, or, more generally, *authority*" (pp. 16–17).

White's argument centers on the *value* of narrativity in historical discourse, which he calls "the discourse of the real," as opposed to pure fiction, or "the discourse of the imaginary" (and admittedly the Lacanian terms are employed but loosely). That value, he suggests, is conferred by the historian's desire for a moral order underlying the aesthetic aspect of historical representation. For the historians themselves, the "value attached to narrativity in the representation of real events arises out of a desire to have real events display the coherence, integrity, fullness, and closure of an image of life that is and can only be imaginary" (p. 27). Aside from the merits of this hypothesis in relation to historical writing as such—which it is not within my competence or my purpose to discuss—two points are of intrinsic interest with regard to narrative theory. First, the retracing of current semiotic and psychoanalytic discourses on narrative to a seldom-acknowledged source, the Hegelian paradigm, could be usefully pursued toward a critical reevaluation of just how much of the despised structuralism is still active, however repressed, in the so-called age of poststructuralism.[32] Secondly, and more to the immediate issue, the intimate relationship binding authority, historicality, and narrative, the Hegelian notion that it is a moral order of meaning, a system of law, which regulates historical narrative, is recast by White, after

Barthes and Lacan, in the terms of a slightly different triad: law, desire, and narrative. The equation of narrative with meaning, in other words, is mediated by the agency of desire. This is how the question is initially formulated:

> What is involved in the discovery of the "true story" within or behind the events that come to us in the chaotic form of "historical records"? What *wish is enacted*, what *desire is gratified*, by the *fantasy* that real events are properly represented when they can be shown to display the formal coherency of a story? In the *enigma of this wish, this desire,* we catch a glimpse of the cultural function of narrativizing discourse. [P. 8; my emphasis]

The very language of the passage, by the author of *Tropics of Discourse,* follows and represents a certain theoretical drift that links Freud to Hegel via the agency of Lacan (*and* Lévi-Strauss).[33] Words like wish, desire, fantasy, enigma belong to that universe of discourse in which Barthes's reading of Balzac's classical narrative text, in *S/Z,* stands at the intersection of semiotics and psychoanalysis, defining a field of critical inquiry. That field and that theoretical intersection were already implicit, as we noted, in the introduction to the 1966 volume of *Communications,* where Barthes saw it significant that at the same moment "the little human 'invents' at once sentence, narrative, and the Oedipus."[34] With regard to narrative theory, this line of critical inquiry may be seen as an attempt to effect a mediation of Hegel and Freud, posing desire as a function of narrative and narrativity as a process engaging that desire. For if the function of desire was already implicit in Hegel's notion of the Other—and its relevance to literary fiction has been argued by Girard's *Deceit, Desire and the Novel*—it is Freud who allows us to see, in the very process of narrativity (the movement of narrative, its dramatic necessity, its driving tension) the inscription of desire, and thus—only thus—of the subject and its representations.[35]

The extent to which psychoanalysis itself is implicated in narrative has often been remarked upon: the theory of evolutionary stages of the human psyche, marked by the interactions of agents such as the id, the ego, and the superego, parallels the metapsychological story of Freud's development of several models of mental functioning from the topographical model of Conscious/Preconscious/Unconscious to the later energetic or thermodynamic conception of the psychic apparatus. These are intimately connected and find their paradigmatic exempla in the psychoanalytic fictional genre *par excellence*, the case history. However, in this age of metafiction, the narrative form of the case history must be subjected to critical scrutiny. Roy Schafer, for one, puts it like this:

> Psychoanalytic theorists of different persuasions have employed different interpretive principles or codes—one might say different narrative structures—to develop their ways of doing analysis and telling about it. These narrative structures present or imply two coordinated accounts: one, of the beginning, the course, and the ending of human development; the other, of the course of the psychoanalytic dialogue. Far from being secondary narratives about data, these structures provide primary narratives that establish what is to count as data. Once installed as leading narrative structures, they are taken as certain in order to develop coherent accounts of lives and technical practices.[36]

The two accounts are not simply coexistent, but coordinated. The analysis being a dialogic process of construction and reconstruction of the patient's personal history—past, present and future—it is important to stress that "the analysand joins in the retelling (redescribing, reinterpreting) as the analysis progresses. The second reality becomes a joint enterprise and a joint experience" (p. 50); and therefore "the sequential life historical narration that is then developed is no more than a second-order retelling of clinical analysis" (p. 52). For Schafer, in short, the individual life history jointly produced in the analytic situation is not, as the positivistic approaches to analysis would have it, a set of factual findings, a recovery of real life events, but rather a "second-order history," a "retelling" of the clinical dialogue. The main narrative problem of the analyst writing up a case, he observes, is "not how to tell a normative chronological life history; rather, it is how to tell the several histories of each analysis" (p. 53). The suggestion is clear: a case history is really a metahistory, a metadiscursive operation in which the "analysand" (this is the emphasis of the neologism, and why it is preferred to "patient") has had equal opportunity to participate. Nevertheless, in spite of and against this important insight, Schafer concludes that the developmental accounts given in case histories are to be seen as "hermeneutically filled-in narrative structures"; and with a sleight of hand turns the sense of the argument all the way around.

> The narrative structures that have been adopted *control* the telling of
> the events of the analysis, including the many tellings and retellings of
> the analysand's life history. . . . The analysand's stories of early child-
> hood, adolescence, and other critical periods of life get to be retold in a
> way that both *summarizes* and *justifies* what the analyst requires in order
> to do the kind of psychoanalytic work that is being done. [P. 53; my
> emphasis.]

"Summarizes" and "justifies" are terms that signal the continuing
dominance of the structural-Hegelian paradigm which "controls,"
through the agency of the analyst (the analyst's discourse and the
analyst's desire), the production of the subject's histories.

It is Freud's contribution to materialist thought, or at least his claim
to a materialist rereading, that the events of his stories, the events of
psychic life, which he presents in narrative form, much as the events
of social life are emplotted by historiography, are not elements of a
moral drama.[37] But they are elements of a drama nonetheless, the
Oedipus drama. Freud states it unequivocally. In *Fragment of an Analysis of a Case of Hysteria,* the famous case of Dora, speaking of the sexual
attraction between parents and children at an early age, which, in his
view, informs all subsequent libidinal investments, he writes: "the
myth of Oedipus is probably to be regarded as a poetical rendering of
what is typical in these relations."[38] There is no small irony in the fact
that this reaffirmation, on Freud's part, of the paradigmatic nature of
the Oedipus occurs in a story that cannot be concluded. By breaking
off analysis, "Dora" refused to join in the telling of her life history.
Unlike "Little Hans" (or rather, his father), "Dora" questioned the
analyst's account and denied it narrative closure, turning what should
have been her case history into a doubtful, unreliable chronicle. Yet, I
would repeat, one feels indebted to Freud more than any other male
theorist for attempting to write the history of femininity, to understand female subjectivity, or simply to imagine woman as mythical and
social subject.

Freud's story of femininity, as we know, is the story of the journey
of the female child across the dangerous terrain of the Oedipus complex. Leaving home, she enters the phallic phase where she comes
face to face with castration, engages in the uneven battle with penis
envy, and remains forever scarred by a narcissistic wound, forever
bleeding. But she goes on, and the worst is still to come. No longer a

"little man," bereft of weapon or magical gift, the female child enters the liminal stage in which her transformation into woman will take place; but only if she successfully negotiates the crossing, haunted by the Scylla and Carybdis of object change and erotogenic zone change, into passivity. If she survives, her reward is motherhood. And here Freud stops. But let's go on, with the help of Lotman, Lévi-Strauss, and the mythologists. Motherhood brings with it the ambiguous, negative power of Demeter—the power to refuse, to withdraw, to plead and struggle anew, and undergo separation and loss with every change of season. Her body, like Demeter's, has become her battlefield and, paradoxically, her only weapon and possession. Yet it is not her own, for she too has come to see it as a territory staked out by heroes and monsters (each with their rights and claims); a landscape mapped by desire, and a wilderness. Nature indeed, Freud laments, has been less kind to women. In the manner of a spiteful stepmother, she has assigned woman "two extra tasks" to be performed in the course of her sexual development, "whereas the more fortunate man has only to continue at the time of his sexual maturity the activity that he has previously carried out."[39]

> Furthermore, it is our impression that more constraint has been applied to the libido when it is pressed into the service of the feminine function, and that—to speak teleologically—Nature takes less careful account of its [that function's] demands than in the case of masculinity. And the reason for this may lie—thinking once again teleologically—in the fact that the accomplishment of the aim of biology has been made to some extent independent of women's consent. ["Femininity," p. 131]

The difficult journey of the female child to womanhood, in other words, leads to the fulfillment of her biological destiny, to reproduction. But the statement, objective though regretful, that reproduction is "to some extent independent of women's consent" makes us pause. We are reminded of the *attack* launched by the army of sperm on the hiding place of the ovum in the epic of *The Everyday Miracle;* of the *battle* waged by the shaman's phallic spirits inside the pregnant woman's body; of the *slaying* of Medusa; of Lotman's hero who *penetrates* into the other space and *overcomes* the obstacle. . . . And all these images add up to Mulvey's phrase, "sadism demands a story," only reversed: "Story demands sadism, depends on making something happen, forcing a change in another person, a battle of will and strength, victory/defeat, all occurring in a linear time with a beginning and an end." All of which is, to some extent, independent of women's consent. But to what extent? Let us read Freud's story again, this time more closely.

The end of the girl's journey, if successful, will bring her to the place where the boy will find her, like Sleeping Beauty, awaiting him, Prince Charming. For the boy has been promised, by the social contract he has entered into at his Oedipal phase, that he will find woman waiting at the end of *his* journey. Thus the itinerary of the female's journey, mapped from the very start on the territory of her own body (the first "task"), is guided by a compass pointing not to reproduction as the fulfillment of *her* biological destiny, but more exactly to the fulfillment of the promise made to "the little man," of his social contract, *his* biological and affective destiny—and to the fulfillment of his desire. This is what predetermines the positions she must occupy in her journey. The myth of which she is presumed to be the subject, generated by the same mechanism that generated the myth of Oedipus, in fact works to construct *her* as a "personified obstacle"; similarly the narrative transforms a human child into a womb,"a cave," "the grave," "a house," "a woman." The story of femininity, Freud's question, and the riddle of the Sphinx all have a single answer, one and the same meaning, one term of reference and address: man, Oedipus, the human male person. And so her story, like any other story, is a question of his desire; as is the teleology that Freud imputes to Nature, that primordial "obstacle" of civilized man.

But all is not well in Thebes. The promised and much hoped for fulfillment of his desire comes to pass but seldom. The social contract has a catch tucked in the fine print; a bug is hidden in the wings of the Oedipal stage. For a mother too, like Nature, is often less kind to female children, and makes it difficult for her daughter to identify with her and so learn how to "fulfill her role in the sexual function and perform her invaluable social tasks."

> It is in this identification too that she acquires her attractiveness to a man, whose Oedipus attachment to his mother it kindles into passion. How often it happens, however, that it is only his son who obtains what he himself aspired to! One gets an impression that a man's love and a woman's are a phase apart psychologically. ["Femininity," p. 134]

Desire itself, then, is in question. If desire is the question which generates both narrative and narrativity as Oedipal drama, that question is an open one, seeking a closure that is only promised, not guaranteed. For Oedipal desire requires in its object—or in its subject when female, as in Freud's little girl—an identification with the feminine position. And while "the aim of biology" may be accomplished independently of women's consent, the aim of desire (heterosexual male desire, that is) may not. In other words, women *must either* consent *or* be seduced into consenting to femininity.

This is the sense in which sadism demands a story or story demands sadism, however one prefers to have it, and hence the continuing significance, for feminism, of a "politics of the unconscious"; for women's consent may not be gotten easily but is finally gotten, and has been for a long time, as much by rape and economic coercion as by the more subtle and lasting effects of ideology, representation, and identification. This is a big issue, and should be broached in relation to specific practices if we are to avoid the usual and universalizing generalizations. The phrase "the politics of the unconscious," which for me recasts the feminist notion that the personal is political in more adequate and useful terms, is from the sound-track of a film by Laura Mulvey and Peter Wollen, *Riddles of the Sphinx*.[40] I would like to use it as a bridge to the last section of the chapter, in which I will take up the problem of identification in narrative cinema.

OEDIPUS INTERRUPTUS

My question at the beginning of this chapter, what did Medusa feel seeing herself reflected in Perseus' shield just before being slain, was intended very much in the context of a politics of the unconscious. It is a rhetorical question, but one that nonetheless needs to be posed within the feminist discourse and urgently demands of it further theoretical attention. It is a rhetorical question in the sense that, I believe, some of us do know how Medusa felt, because we have seen it at the movies, from *Psycho* to *Blow Out*, be the film a *Love Story* or *Not a Love Story*. Yet our knowledge, and the experience of that feeling are discounted by film critics as subjective and idiosyncratic, and by film theorists as naive or untheoretical. Some, for example, would remind us that when we see Medusa being slain (daily) on the screen, as film and television spectators, we have a "purely aesthetic" identification.[41]

Others—and probably you, too, reader—would object that my

question about Medusa is tendentious, for I pretend to ignore that in
the story Medusa was asleep when Perseus entered her "cave"; she did
not see, *she did not look*. Precisely. Doesn't an "aesthetic" identification
mean that, though we "look at her looking" throughout the movie, we
too, women spectators, are asleep when she is being slain? And only
wake up, like Snow White and Sleeping Beauty, if the film ends with
the kiss? Or you may remark that I am indeed naive in equating
Perseus' shield with a movie screen. Yet, not only does that shield
protect Perseus from Medusa's evil look, but later on, after her death
(in his further adventures), it serves as frame and surface on which
her head is pinned to petrify his enemies. It is thus, pinned up on the
shield of Athena, that the slain Medusa continues to perform her
deadly task within the institutions of law and war . . . and cinema (I
would add), for which Cocteau (not I) devised the well-known
definition, "death at work."

In an equally well-known paper of 1922, entitled "Medusa's Head,"
Freud reiterated his theory that "the terror of castration . . . is linked
to the sight of something," the female genitals; and similarly "the
sight of Medusa's head makes the spectator stiff with terror, turns
him to stone," but at the same time offers him "consolation . . . the
stiffening reassures him."[42] This is what Cixous parodies in "The
Laugh of the Medusa," when she says: "[Men] need femininity to be
associated with death; it's the jitters that give them a hard-on! for
themselves!" (p. 255). "What then of the look of the woman?" asks
Heath. "The reply given by psychoanalysis is from the phallus. If the
woman looks, the spectacle provokes, castration is in the air, the Medusa's head is not far off; thus, she must not look, is absorbed herself
on the side of the seen, seeing herself seeing herself, Lacan's femininity." And he quotes the Lacanian analyst Eugénie Lemoine-
Luccioni: "In thus offering herself to the look, in giving herself for
sight, according to the sequence: see, see oneself, give oneself to be
seen, be seen, the girl—unless she falls into the complete alienation of
the hysteric—provokes the Other to an encounter and a reply which
give her pleasure."[43] Cixous's anti-Lacanian response is certainly more
encouraging, but only slightly more useful practically or theoretically:
"you only have to look at the Medusa straight on to see her. And she's
not deadly. She's beautiful and she's laughing" (p. 255). The problem
is that to look at the Medusa "straight on" is not a simple matter, for
women or for men; the whole question of representation is precisely

there. A politics of the unconscious cannot ignore the real, historical, and material complicities, even as it must dare theoretical utopias.

Freud may not have known it, but in that two-page paper he put forth the definitive theory of pornographic cinema and, some have argued, of cinema *tout court*.[44] Death at work. But whose death is it, whose work, and what manner of death? My question then, how did Medusa feel looking at herself being slain and pinned up on screens, walls, billboards, and other shields of masculine identity, is really a political question that bears directly upon the issues of cinematic identification and spectatorship: the relation of female subjectivity to ideology in the representation of sexual difference and desire, the positions available to women in film, the conditions of vision and meaning production, for women.

To succeed, for a film, is to fulfill its contract, to please its audiences or at least induce them to buy the ticket, the popcorn, the magazines, and the various paraphernalia of movie promotion. But for a film to work, to be effective, it *has* to please. All films must offer their spectators some kind of pleasure, something of interest, be it a technical, artistic, critical interest, or the kind of pleasure that goes by the names of entertainment and escape; preferably both. These kinds of pleasure and interest, film theory has proposed, are closely related to the question of desire (desire to know, desire to see), and thus depend on a personal response, an engagement of the spectator's subjectivity, and the possibility of identification.

The fact that films, as the saying goes, speak to each one and to all, that they address spectators both individually and as members of a social group, a given culture, age, or country, implies that certain patterns or possibilities of identification for each and all spectators must be built into the film. This is undoubtedly one of the functions of genres, and their historical development throughout the century attests to the need for cinema to sustain and provide new modes of spectator identification in keeping with social changes. Because films address spectators as social subjects, then, the modalities of identification bear directly on the process of spectatorship, that is to say, the ways in which the subjectivity of the spectator is engaged in the process of viewing, understanding (making sense of), or even *seeing* the film.

If women spectators are to buy their tickets and their popcorn, the work of cinema, unlike "the aim of biology," may be said to require women's consent; and we may well suspect that narrative cinema in particular must be aimed, like desire, toward seducing women into femininity. What manner of seduction operates in cinema to procure that consent, to engage the female subject's identification in the narrative movement, and so fulfill the cinematic contract? What manner of seduction operates in cinema to solicit the complicity of women spectators in a desire whose terms are those of the Oedipus? In the following pages I will be concerned with female spectatorship, and in particular the kinds of identification available to women spectators and the nature of the process by which female subjectivity is engaged in narrative cinema; thus I will reconsider the terms or positionalities of desire as constituted in cinema by the relations of image and narrative.

The cinematic apparatus, in the totality of its operations and effects, produces not merely images but imaging. It binds affect and meaning to images by establishing terms of identification, orienting the movement of desire, and positioning the spectator in relation to them.

> The film poses an image, not immediate or neutral, but posed, framed and centered. Perspective-system images bind the spectator in place, the suturing central position that is the sense of the image, that sets its scene (in place, the spectator *completes* the image as its subject). Film too, but it also moves in all sorts of ways and directions, flows with energies, is potentially a veritable festival of affects. Placed, that movement is all the value of film in its development and exploitation: reproduction of life and the engagement of the spectator in the process of that reproduction as articulation of coherence. What moves in film, finally, is the spectator, immobile in front of the screen. Film is the regulation of that movement, the individual as subject held in a shifting and placing of desire, energy, contradiction, in a perpetual retotalization of the imaginary (the set scene of image and subject).[45]

What Heath has called the "passage" of the spectator-subject through the film (the movement of the spectator taken up as subject, performing the film) is modulated on the movement of the film, its "regulation" of the flow of images, its "placing" of desire. The process of regulation, in the classical economy of film, is narrativization; and narrative, the "welding together" of space and spectator, is the form of that economy (p. 43). "Narrativization is then the term of film's entertaining: process and process contained, subject bound in that process and its directions of meaning. . . . The spectator is *moved,* and *related* as subject in the process and images of that movement" (p. 62). The formulation is forceful and convincing, though not unambiguous. While anyone who has watched movies and reflected on the experience of spectatorship would agree that, indeed, to watch is to be moved and, at the same time, held in a coherence of meaning and vision; yet that very experience is what must make us question whether—or better, how—women spectators are "related as subject" in the film's images and movement.

In the narrative film the spectator's movement or passage is subject to an orientation, a direction—a teleology, we might say, recalling Freud's word—that is the movement of narrative. Film narrative too, if Lotman's typology be credited, is a process by which the text-images distributed across the film (be they images of people, objects, or of movement itself) are finally regrouped in the two zones of sexual difference, from which they take their culturally preconstructed meaning: mythical subject and obstacle, maleness and femaleness. In cinema the process is accomplished in specific ways. The codes whereby cinema articulates and inscribes both the narrative movement and the subject's passage in the film, the codes which constitute the specificity of cinema as a semiotic practice, have been discussed elsewhere. But for the purposes of the present inquiry one crucial point may be usefully emphasized: the centrality of the system of the look in cinematic representation.

The look of the camera (at the profilmic), the look of the spectator (at the film projected on the screen), and the intradiegetic look of each character within the film (at other characters, objects, etc.) intersect, join, and relay one another in a complex system which structures vision and meaning and defines what Alberti would call the "visible things" of cinema. Cinema "turns" on this series of looks, writes Heath, and that series in turn provides the framework "for a pattern of multiply relaying identifications"; within this framework occur both "subject-identification" and "subject-process."[46] "It is the place of the look that defines cinema," specifies Mulvey, and governs its representation of woman. The possibility of shifting, varying, and exposing the look is employed both to set out and to contain the tension between a pure solicitation of the scopic drive and the demands of the diegesis; in other words, to integrate voyeurism into the conventions of storytelling, and thus combine visual and narrative pleasure. The following passage refers to two particular films, but could easily be read as paradigmatic of the narrative film in general:

> The film opens with the woman as object of the combined gaze of spectator and all the male protagonists in the film. She is isolated, glamorous, on display, sexualised. But as the narrative progresses she falls in love with the main male protagonist and becomes his property, losing her outward glamorous characteristics, her generalised sexuality, her show-girl connotations; her eroticism is subjected to the male star alone.[47]

If the female position in narrative is fixed by the mythical mechanism in a certain portion of the plot-space, which the hero crosses or crosses to, a quite similar effect is produced in narrative cinema by the apparatus of looks converging on the female figure. The woman is framed by the look of the camera as icon, or object of the gaze: an image made to be looked at by the spectator, whose look is relayed by the look of the male character(s). The latter not only controls the events and narrative action but is "the bearer" of the look of the spectator. The male protagonist is thus "a figure in a landscape," she adds, "free to command the stage . . . of spatial illusion in which he articulates the look and creates the action" (p. 13). The metaphors could not be more appropriate.

In that landscape, stage, or portion of plot-space, the female character may be all along, throughout the film, representing and literally marking out the place (to) which the hero will cross. There she simply awaits his return like Darling Clementine; as she indeed does in countless Westerns, war, and adventure movies, providing the "love interest," which in the jargon of movie reviewers has come to denote, first, the singular function of the female character, and then, the character itself.[48] Or she may resist confinement in that symbolic space by disturbing it, perverting it, making trouble, seeking to exceed the boundary—visually as well as narratively—as in film noir. Or again, when the film narrative centers on a female protagonist, in melodrama, in the "woman's film," etc., the narrative is patterned on a journey, whether inward or outward, whose possible outcomes are those outlined by Freud's mythical story of femininity. In the best of cases, that is, in the "happy" ending, the protagonist will reach the place (the space) where a modern Oedipus will find her and fulfill the promise of his (off-screen) journey. Not only, then, is the female position that of a given portion of the plot-space; more precisely, in cinema, it figures the (achieved) movement of the narrative toward that space. It represents narrative closure.

In this sense, Heath has suggested, narrative is a process of restoration that depends finally on the image of woman, generalized into what he calls the *narrative image*, a function of exchange within the terms of the film's contract. In *Touch of Evil*, specifically, "the narrative must serve to restore the woman as good object (the narrative image depends on this); which obliges it to envisage her as bad object (the other side of the restoration that it seeks to accomplish)." Of narrative cinema in general he writes:

> Narrative contains a film's multiple articulations as a single articulation, its images as a single image (the 'narrative image', which is a film's presence, how it can be talked about, what it can be sold and bought on, itself represented as—in the production stills displayed outside a cinema, for example).[49]

If narrative is governed by an Oedipal logic, it is because it is situated within the system of exchange instituted by the incest prohibition, where woman functions as both a sign (representation) and a value (object) for that exchange. And if we remark Lea Melandri's observation that the woman as Mother (matter and matrix, body and womb) is the primary measure of value, "an equivalent more universal than money," then indeed we can see why the narrative image on which the film, any film, can be represented, sold, and bought is finally the woman.[50] What the promotion stills and posters outside the cinema display, to lure the passers-by, is not just an *image of woman* but the image of her narrative position, the *narrative image* of woman—a felicitous phrase suggestive of the join of image and story, the interlocking of visual and narrative registers effected by the cinematic apparatus of the look. In cinema as well, then, woman properly represents the fulfillment of the narrative promise (made, as we know, to the little boy), and that representation works to support the male status of the mythical subject. The female position, produced as the end result of narrativization, is the figure of narrative closure, the narrative image in which the film, as Heath says, "comes together."

With regard to women spectators, therefore, the notion of a passage or movement of the spectator through the narrative film seems strangely at odds with the theories of narrative presented so far. Or rather, it would seem so if we assumed—as is often done—that spectators naturally identify with one or the other group of text-images, one or the other textual zone, female or male, according to their gender. If we assumed a single, undivided identification of each spectator with either the male or the female figure, the passage through the film would simply instate or reconfirm male spectators in the position of the mythical subject, the human being; but it would only allow female spectators the position of the mythical obstacle, monster or landscape. How can the female spectator be entertained as subject of the very movement that places her as its object, that makes her the figure of its own closure?

Clearly, at least for women spectators, we cannot assume identification to be single or simple. For one thing, identification is itself a movement, a subject-process, a relation: the identification (of oneself) with something other (than oneself). In psychoanalytic terms, it is succinctly defined as the "psychological process whereby *the subject* assimilates an aspect, property or attribute of the other and *is transformed,* wholly or partially, after the model the other provides. It is by means of a series of identifications that the personality is constituted and specified."[51] This last point is crucial, and the resemblance of this formulation to the description of the apparatus of the look in cinema cannot escape us. The importance of the concept of identification, Laplanche and Pontalis insist, derives from its central role in the formation of subjectivity; identification is "not simply one psychical mechanism among others, but the operation itself whereby the human subject is constituted" (p. 206). To identify, in short, is to be actively involved as subject in a process, a series of relations; a process that, it must be stressed, is materially supported by the specific practices—textual, discursive, behavioral—in which each relation is inscribed. Cinematic identification, in particular, is inscribed across the two registers articulated by the system of the look, the narrative and the visual (sound becoming a necessary third register in those films which intentionally use sound as an anti-narrative or de-narrativizing element).

Secondly, no one can really *see* oneself as an inert object or a sightless body; neither can one see oneself *altogether* as other. One has an ego, after all, even when one is a woman (as Virginia Woolf might say), and by definition the ego must be active or at least fantasize itself in an active manner.[32] Whence, Freud is led to postulate, the phallic phase in females: the striving of little girls to be masculine is due to the active aim of the libido, which then succumbs to the momentous process of repression when femininity "sets in." But, he adds, that masculine phase, with its libidinal activity, never totally lets up and frequently makes itself felt throughout a woman's life, in what he calls "regressions to the fixations of the pre-Oedipus phases." One can of course remark that the term "regression" is a vector in the field of (Freud's) narrative discourse. It is governed by the same mythical mechanism that underlies his story of femininity, and oriented by the teleology of (its) narrative movement: progression is toward Oedipus, toward the Oedipal stage (which in his view marks the onset of womanhood, the initiation to femininity); regression is away from Oedipus, retarding or even impeding the female's sexual development, as Freud would have it, or as I see it, impeding the fulfillment of the male's desire, as well as narrative closure.

The point, however, is made—and it is relevant to the present discussion—that "femininity" and "masculinity" are never fully attained or fully relinquished: "in the course of some women's lives there is a repeated alternation between periods in which femininity or masculinity gain the upper hand."[53] The two terms, femininity and masculinity, do not refer so much to qualities or states of being inherent in a person, as to positions which she occupies in relation to desire. They are terms of identification. And the alternation between them, Freud seems to suggest, is a specific character of female subjectivity. Following through this view in relation to cinematic identification, could we say that identification in women spectators alternates between the two terms put in play by the apparatus: the look of the camera and the image on the screen, the subject and the object of the gaze? The word alternation conveys the sense of an either/or, either one or the other at any given time (which is presumably what Freud had in mind), not the two together. The problem with the notion of an alternation between image and gaze is that they are not commensurable terms: the gaze is a figure, not an image. We see the image; we do not see the gaze. To cite again an often-cited phrase, one can "look at her looking," but one cannot look at oneself looking. The analogy that links identification-with-the-look to masculinity and identification-with-the-image to femininity breaks down precisely when we think of a spectator alternating between the two. Neither can be abandoned for the other, even for a moment; no image can be identified, or identified with, apart from the look that inscribes it as image, and vice versa. If the female subject were indeed related to the film in this manner, its division would be irreparable, unsuturable; no identification or meaning would be possible. This difficulty has led film theorists, following Lacan and forgetting Freud, practically to disregard the problem of sexual differentiation *in the spectators* and to define cinematic identification as masculine, that is to say, as an identification with the gaze, which both historically and theoretically is the representation of the phallus and the figure of the male's desire.[54]

That Freud conceived of femininity and masculinity primarily in narrative rather than visual terms (although with an emphasis on sight—in the traumatic apprehension of castration as punishment—quite in keeping with his dramatic model) may help us to reconsider the problem of female identification. Femininity and masculinity, in his story, are positions occupied by the subject in relation to desire, corresponding respectively to the passive and the active aims of the libido.[55] They are positionalities within a movement that carries both the male child and the female child toward one and the same destination: Oedipus and the Oedipal stage. That movement, I have argued, is the movement of narrative discourse, which specifies and even produces the masculine position as that of mythical subject, and the feminine position as mythical obstacle or, simply, the space in which that movement occurs. Transferring this notion by analogy to cinema, we could say that the female spectator identifies with both the subject and the space of the narrative movement, with the figure of movement and the figure of its closure, the narrative image. Both are figural identifications, and both are possible at once; more, they are concurrently borne and mutually implicated by the process of narrativity. This manner of identification would uphold both positionalities of desire, both active and passive aims: desire for the other, and desire to be desired by the other. This, I think, is in fact the operation by which narrative and cinema solicit the spectators' consent and seduce women into femininity: by a double identification, a surplus of pleasure produced by the spectators themselves for cinema and for society's profit.

In other words, if women spectators are "related as subject" in the film's images and movement, as Heath puts it, it is insofar as they are engaged in a twofold process of identification, sustaining two distinct sets of identifying relations. The first set is well known in film theory: the masculine, active, identification with the gaze (the looks of the camera and of the male characters) and the passive, feminine identification with the image (body, landscape). The second set, which has received much less attention, is implicit in the first as its effect and specification, for it is produced by the apparatus which is the very condition of vision (that is to say, the condition under which what is visible acquires meaning). It consists of the double identification with the figure of narrative movement, the mythical subject, and with the figure of narrative closure, the narrative image. Were it not for the possibility of this second, figural identification, the woman spectator would be stranded between two incommensurable entities, the gaze and the image. Identification, that is, would be either impossible, split beyond any act of suture, or entirely masculine. The figural narrative identification, on the contrary, is double; both figures can and in fact must be identified with at once, for they are inherent in narrativity itself. It is this narrative identification that assures "the hold of the image," the anchoring of the subject in the flow of the film's movement; rather than, as Metz proposes, the primary identification with the all-perceiving subject of the gaze.[56]

In fact, the order of priority borne by the words "primary cinematic identification" might be reversed: if the spectator can identify "with himself as look, as pure act of perception," it is because such identification is supported by a prior, narrative identification with the figure of narrative movement. When the latter is weak, or undercut by a concomitant and stronger identification with the narrative image—as is the case with female spectators more often than not—the spectator will find it difficult to maintain the distance from the image implicit in the notion of a "pure act of perception." Metz's formulation of primary cinematic identification, which comes from Lacan's concept of the mirror stage, has been criticized precisely for the strictly chronological implication of the word "primary."[57] In the psychoanalytic discourse, primary identification refers to an early or primitive mode of identification with the Other (usually the mother) not dependent upon the establishment of an object-relationship, that is to say, prior to the subject's awareness of the Other's autonomous existence.[58]

Freud's other and more fundamental concept of primary and sec-

ondary processes, however, sheds doubt on the usefulness of the notion of a primary or primitive identification, at least insofar as adult
spectators are concerned. Primary (unconscious) processes, one of the
two modalities of the psychic apparatus, never exist alone after the
formation of the ego, whose function is precisely that of inhibiting
them. They do continue to exist, nevertheless, but only in interplay
with or in opposition to the other modality, secondary (conscious-
preconscious) processes, such as operate in waking thought, reasoning, judgment, etc. While Metz obviously recognizes that his
analogy between the adult film spectator and the child at the mirror
stage is no more than that: an analogy—he does not fully work out its
limitations; a principal one being that if the child can be construed as
not (yet) gendered, the adult spectator cannot. The basic hypothesis
of psychoanalysis is that sexual differentiation occurs between 3 and 5
years of age, whereas the mirror phase is located between the ages of
6 and 18 months. But film spectators enter the movie theatre as either
men or women, which is not to say that they are simply male or female
but rather that each person goes to the movies with a semiotic history,
personal and social, a series of previous identifications by which she or
he has been somehow en-gendered. And because she and he are
historical subjects, continuously engaged in a multiplicity of signifying
practices which, like narrative and cinema, rest on and perpetuate the
founding distinction of culture—sexual difference—the film's images
for them are not neutral objects of a pure perception but already
"significant images," as Pasolini observed; already significant by virtue
of their relation to the viewer's subjectivity, coded with a certain potential for identification, placed in a certain position with respect to
desire. They already bear, even as the film begins, a certain "place of
the look."

This valence of images, the empirical fact of a certain "impact"
which certain images have on viewers, cannot be accounted for in
terms of a simple notion of referentiality; but even the more sophis-
ticated semiotic notion of image content as a cultural unit, proposed
by Eco (and Gombrich), needs to be further articulated in relation to
extratextual codes, such as narrative, which are nonspecific to the
particular form and matter of expression of the iconic sign. And while
narrative articulation in cinema has been examined, notably in Metz's
early work, I have argued that the semiological definition of narrative
was and remains inadequate, for it fails to address the working of

desire in both the movement of narrativity and the critical discourse. In order to present the problem more concretely, I will now make a digression and discuss a recent article by Seymour Chatman, whose comparative analysis of Renoir's *Une Partie de campagne* (A Day in the Country, 1936) with the Maupassant novella on which it is based demonstrates precisely how the value or the impact of the image is fully overdetermined by the narrative's inscription of desire. In chapter 3 such overdetermination was suggested in my reading of a nonnarrative film. Here I will restate the point by a detour through the reading of a narrative film by a critic highly skilled in semiotic analysis.[59]

To exemplify the differences between filmic and literary narrative, Chatman chooses two scenes for comparison. First, the description of the cart in the opening sequence introducing the Dufour family. He notes that despite the greater capacity of cinema for presenting visual details (he compares the great number of details available to us in the image of the cart with the few, merely three, given in the written text), the fixed temporality of viewing, in contradistinction to the self-determining pace of reading, paradoxically prevents our seeing them because we are more preoccupied with what is going to happen next. Thus cinema's specific asset, its capacity for visual over-specification, is overriden by a "narrative pressure" bearing on the images; and that pressure is defined in terms of story or sequence of events. Chatman's second example, the description of Mlle. Dufour, gives him a harder time. He is now obliged to resort to another canonical feature of narrative, point of view (which had not been necessary for the cart, where "description" was sufficient), for here the question is: how to present cinematically not just Mlle. Dufour but her character, or rather her seductiveness. Maupassant's text reads:

> Mademoiselle Dufour . . . . was a pretty girl of about eighteen; *one of those women who suddenly excite your desire when you meet them in the street, and who leave you with a vague feeling of uneasiness and of excited sense.* She was tall, had a small waist and large hips, with a dark skin, very large eyes, and very black hair. . . . Her hat, which a gust of wind had blown off, was hanging behind her, and as the swing gradually rose higher and higher, *she showed her delicate limbs* up to the knees at each time. . . .[60]

Since an actress to fit the measurements could be found without difficulty, the problem for Renoir, and now for Chatman, was all in the lines I italicize: how to convey the implications of "showed" (for Mlle. Dufour cannot be an exhibitionist, yet the verb "neither excludes nor includes conscious intention"); how to convey the ambiguity between innocence and seductiveness ("her unconsciously seductive innocence") capable of exciting in the spectator the same desire that it excited in Maupassant and allegedly his readers?

In a film, some shots will work and some won't. For instance, the shot of the young woman with her family—grandmother, father, and fiancé—serves "to background Henriette, to make her again just a bourgeois daughter and not the inducer of vague feelings of uneasiness and excited senses" (p. 134). Another shot, a close-up of her face, works better, as it "enhances the difference between the buoyant fresh girl, a product of nature, and the ponderous and torpid family" (p. 135). But a shot of her on the swing from the point of view of Rodolphe, the boatman, succeeds: it is "as if she were performing for him, although, of course, she is quite innocent of his existence [his watching her]." This kind of shot begins to render the ambiguity of the text: "Henriette will display herself without being aware of it, she will reveal, yet *malgré elle*" (p. 134). Naturally, then, Renoir repeats the shot, each time from the point of view of a different man or group of men. Chatman sums up the effect:

> The erotic effect of her appearance explicitly described by the narrator of Maupassant's story is only implicitly depicted in the film by the reaction shots. Something of her appeal is caught by the looks on the faces of four ages of gazing men—the pubescent peekers in the hedge, the seminarians, Rodolphe, and the older priest leading his students. [P. 139][61]

If I may put it in my own words, the male bond that united the author and the reader of Maupassant's text is now extended and generalized by the cinematic contract across the four ages of man. Renoir, a modern Oedipus, has solved the riddle of cinematic description. But that there was a riddle or a problem in the first place suggests that a woman in film, *pace* Lotman, is not a cart. The differential value of the two images, as Chatman's analysis demonstrates so well that it should be read as a companion piece to Mulvey's essay on visual pleasure, derives not from the pressure of narrative as sequence of events but from the pressure of narrative as Oedipal drama, which urges narrativity well before the spectators enter the theatre and the film begins. Had Chatman read Mulvey, however, he might have further advanced our understanding of narrative codes by elaborating his interesting notion of a narrative pressure bearing on the image not simply in terms of story, what happens next, but in the terms of Oedipal desire; which is obviously the reason why spectators *look at* Henriette and not the cart. He might have said, for instance, that the differential value of the two images rests not on their placement within a sequence of events but on their inscribing a different "place of the look," defining two distinct views and points of view for the spectator. And that the mastery of point of view by Renoir's camera—far from being "neutral," even as it detaches itself from Rodolphe's "libidinous thoughts"—consists in articulating, within the frame of reference of cinema and its specific and non-specific codes, a vision *for* the spectator; a picture of the world's "visible things," whose standard of meaning and measure of desire are inscribed, incorporated in the spectator's own vision. This is what produces the spectator as Oedipus, male subject, restoring to him, as to Oedipus at Colonus, a vision capable of exciting desire for the princess and the serpent, innocence and seductiveness, and thus allows him to cope with the contradictions of his increasingly difficult task in the patriarchal and capitalist state where cinema exists.

Willemen's notion of "the fourth look" appears most significant in this context. The possibility that the viewer may be "overlooked in the act of looking" is emphatically present in pornographic imagery (and film). Because of its "direct implication in the social and psychic aspects of censorship," the fourth look "introduces the social into the very activity of looking."[62] The recent proliferation of porn imagery of female pleasure, he argues, far from being a progressive development toward liberating the image of woman, "constitutes an emphatic insistence on the centrality of male pleasure and suggests that the male population in Western societies now requires to be reassured more often, more directly and more publicly than before" (p. 60). The crisis in male sexuality is a result of the changes in the definition of woman brought about by the women's struggle; and the porn imagery itself would "address women by representing back to them those changes, i.e., the crisis provoked within male sexuality"; it thus would acknowledge the presence of woman as "the subject of the fourth look for the male" (p. 63). Though Willemen's plea that the fight against pornography "is equally in the interests of both men and women" (p. 64) strikes no chord of enthusiastic agreement in me, I do concur with his effort to introduce the weight of the social and the wedge of actual practices into the reading of images.

In short, to end the digression, if images are already, from the beginning, implicated with narrativity and overdetermined by its inscription of the movement and positionalities of desire, there can be no earlier, primitive, primary, or purely imagistic identification; positions of identification, visual pleasure itself, would involve not only primary and secondary processes but personal and social practices as well. We should rather think of the subject's relation to the filmic image(s) as a figural-narrative relation: the spectator's identification with, as well as of, the film's images would be bound up with narrativity in the same way as dreams are with secondarization in analytic practice, or as Lacan's imaginary and Kristeva's "semiotic" are with the symbolic in actual practices of language.[63] For if the conception of cinema as a semiotic or signifying practice is to have any value at all, both filmmakers and spectators must be understood to be subjects in history.[64] And thus not only meaning but vision itself, the very possibility or impossibility of "seeing" the film, would depend on its engagement of a historically and socially constituted subjectivity.

An interesting hypothesis regarding female subjectivity in its present and historically specific constitution is offered by Kaja Silverman's reading of *Histoire d'O*. A classic of literary pornography attributed to the authorship of one Pauline Réage, *Story of O* owes equally to Sadean writing and to cinema. As Silverman acknowledges in her subtitle, "The Story of a Disciplined and Punished Body," this is no lesser story of femininity than Freud's own. The analysis of the text provides the occasion of a larger speculative argument: "The structuration of the female subject begins not with her entry into language, or her subordination to a field of cultural desire, but with the organization of her body" by means of a discourse which speaks for her and to which she has no access. The body "is charted, zoned and made to bear meaning, a meaning which proceeds entirely from external relationships, but which is always subsequently apprehended as an internal condition or essence."[65] That internal condition, the essence of femininity, is then a product of discourse. First, the female body is constructed as object of the gaze and multiple site of male pleasure— and so internalized, for this is the meaning it bears: female equals the body, sexuality equals the female body. Then, once her desire has been made congruent with the desire of the Other, the female, now woman, can gain access to speech and to that discourse. Silverman cites a passage, of particular interest with regard to cinema, in which O "confesses" the masochistic desires imputed to her by her master, and in so doing actually assumes those desires, makes them her own. Immediately thereafter O recalls a sixteenth-century picture she has seen long ago (she has, Freud would say, a screen memory) "in which the theme of female guilt is not only conspicuous but played out within the scenario of the family."

> Her eyes were closed, and an image she had seen several years before flashed across her mind: a strange print portraying a woman kneeling, as she was, before an armchair. The floor was of tile, and in one corner a dog and child were playing. The woman's skirts were raised, and standing close beside her was a man brandishing a handful of switches, ready to whip her. They were all dressed in sixteenth-century clothes, and the print bore a title which she had found disgusting: Family Punishment.[66]

Silverman observes:

> First of all, O recalls the image of female subjugation as something which belongs to a moment not only long ago in her own history, but that of her culture. . . . Secondly, it is available to her in the most elaborately mediated way; it is not only a memory, but a memory of a picture. It is thus the product of two levels of representation, the initial model of which is not recoverable. This doubly mediated representation structures and gives meaning to an "actual" event in the present moment, the whipping of O by Sir Stephen. However, the so-called memory comes into existence only as a consequence of the later event [the whipping by her master], one of whose functions would precisely seem to be to equip O with an Oedipal past. [Pp. 53–54; my emphasis]

It should be noted that, whereas in cinema, where the image predominates, narrativity has the greater burden of equipping the characters with an Oedipal past; here, in a pornographic (cinematographic?) novel, that function is relayed to the female character, and through her to the reader, via an image. The mutual implication of image and narrative is once again reaffirmed as a necessary complicity. But we must note further that the image is remembered and acquires its subjective meaning for O in connection with the whipping. In other words, the cultural meaning of the image, woman's subjection, is brought home to O and rendered subjective by its relation to her own body and by means of a social practice—the employ of corporal punishment to chastize and educate—in which the subject's body is materially involved.

I will come back to the link between subjectivity and practice(s) later on. For the moment I wish to stress that narrativity is what mediates or sublates physical sensation and image into the meaning, the semantic unit, "female guilt and subjugation," a meaning only too appropriately constructed within the scenario of the family, for it is itself no more than a narrative image produced by the bourgeois myth of origins.[67] O's "remembered" picture condenses and synthesizes the Oedipal drama for the female, placing the viewer (the character O) in the position or role that drama assigns her. But O, female protagonist, is herself meant to be a narrative image, a point of identification for the reader, a two-way mirror that would send back the image of female guilt, unchanged though now invested with desire. The two positionalities of figural identification, the narrative image and the figure of narrative movement, are thus collapsed into one: the masochist position, the (impossible) place of a purely *passive* desire.

In film, the specularization or *mise en abyme* of the woman image, which characterizes the representation of the female's Oedipal drama, is often correlated to the thematic centrality of the portrait, as Tania Modleski has shown in her analysis of Hitchcock's *Rebecca*.[68] There too the female body is constructed as site of pleasure and sexuality; Rebecca's image, suggested in the life-size portrait of the ancestor and in the verbal representations made of her, bears the weight of meaning and serves as the term of the heroine's identification with the Mother. Here again the woman position is that of narrative image, both in the diegesis and for the spectator, the title itself joining image and narrative, portrait and character into a single narrative image for the film. Unlike *Histoire d'O*, however, *Rebecca* is crossed by a twin parental gaze, the Mother's being the more insistent throughout the film. The heroine's double relation of desire for the Father and for the Mother (as image and as image internalized as self-image) is inscribed by the looks in what I have called a double figural identification: with the narrative image (Rebecca), and with the narrative movement of which the nameless heroine is the subject, the protagonist. This double set of identifying relations is relayed to the spectator via the figuration of the heroine, who then functions not as a mirror, a flat specular surface, but rather as a prism diffracting the image into the double positionality of female Oedipal desire and sustaining the oscillation between "femininity" and "masculinity." For this reason, I believe, in spite of the conventional Oedipal resolution, Modleski is able to argue that "the extent and power of woman's desire have been so forcefully expressed that we cannot rest secure in the film's 'happy' ending" (p. 41). Still, and all the more perhaps, the film is "determined to get rid of Rebecca," she comments, and nothing short of "massive destruction" will do. "Finally, there is nothing left for the heroine but to desire to kill the mother off, a desire which . . . entails killing part of herself" (p. 38).

Do we have to conclude that all representation of the female subject's desire is hopelessly caught in *this* nexus of image and narrative, in the web of a male Oedipal logic? That the Sphinx *must* kill herself in disgust and Medusa go on sleeping? That the little girl has no other prospect but to consent and be seduced into femininity? What Modleski's reading suggests to me, quite apart from any idea of the "correct" reading, goes beyond a critical textual practice devoted to seeking out ruptures, contradictions, or excess, which the text allows but also finally reintegrates, retotalizes or recaptures. It points, on the one hand, to the theoretical usefulness of re-examining the notion of specularization in the context of a figural narrative identification; and, on the other hand, to its implications for filmmaking practice and the politics of women's cinema.

If the narrative image of Rebecca, like O's screen memory, serves to equip the heroine with an Oedipal past inscribed in a pictorial history of female ancestry, this past is far richer in contradiction; and what the film articulates by intersecting the looks with a twin parental gaze is precisely the *duplicity* of this Oedipal scenario. On the contrary, the picture relayed through the heroine of the pornographic novel simplifies the female's Oedipal situation and reduces it to the simple obverse of the male's Oedipal drama, the Electra complex, which Freud himself discarded as an inadequate hypothesis, an all-too-facile answer to the question of female sexual development. The image of Rebecca that reaches us via a heroine acting as prism of the specularization is thereby diffracted into several images, or positionalities of narrative identification: "Rebecca," as self-image and rival, marks not only the place of the object of the male's desire, but also and more importantly, the place and object of a female active desire (Mrs. Danvers's). The "portrait" here is not, as in the *Story of O,* simply a mirror reflection of its viewer or the image the viewer must become, according to the ideological operation by which all women are represented as (reducible to) woman; for the film narrative works precisely to problematize, to engage and disengage, the heroine's—and through her, the spectator's—identification with that single image. What I am proposing, following through Modleski's critical insight and actually regardless of the particular text that may have prompted it, is this: if the spectator's identification is engaged and directed in each film by specific cinematic-narrative codes (the place of the look, the figures of narrative), it should be possible to work through those codes in order to shift or redirect identification toward the two positionalities of desire that define the female's Oedipal situation; and if the alternation between them is protracted long enough (as has been said of *Rebecca)* or in enough films (and several have already been made), the viewer may come to suspect that such duplicity, such contradiction cannot and perhaps even need not be resolved. In *Rebecca,* of course, it is; but it is not in *Les Rendez-vous d'Anna* by Chantal Akerman, for example, or in Bette Gordon's *Variety* (1983).

Let me be more precise, at the cost of some repetition. If the heroine of *Rebecca* is made to kill off the mother, it is not only because the rules of the drama and Lotman's "mythical mechanism" demand narrative closure; it is also because, like them, cinema works for Oedipus. The heroine therefore has to move on, like Freud's little girl, and take her place where Oedipus will find her awaiting *him.* What if, once he reached his destination, he found that Alice didn't live there anymore? He would promptly set out to find another, to find true woman or at least her truthful image. The Mrs. DeWinter Maxim wants in the place of Rebecca is one who is true to him; the image into which Scottie "remakes" Judy for himself (literally makes her up) in *Vertigo* must be the truthful image of Madeleine. With his uncommonly keen sense of cinematic convention, Hitchcock encapsulates this search for the true image—a search on the part of the hero, but equally a search on the part of the film itself—in a visual parable. When Scottie's one-time fiancée and now "good friend" Midge wants to offer herself as object of his desire, she paints a portrait of herself dressed as Carlotta Valdes, the presumed ancestor in the museum portrait who is the object of Madeleine's desire and identification. Scottie evidently rejects the offer; Midge has failed to understand that what attracts Scottie is not the simple *image* of woman (were it so, he would be in love with Carlotta) but her narrative image, in this case the desire for the (dead) Mother which Madeleine represents and mediates for him. Whence Hitchcock's comment: "I was intrigued by the hero's attempts to re-create the image of a dead woman through another one who's alive. . . . To put it plainly, the man wants to go to bed with a woman who's dead; he is indulging in a form of necrophilia."[69] Ostensibly, Hitchcock is referring here to the second part of the film and Scottie's efforts to remake Judy as Madeleine. But the film's construction *en abyme* supports, I think, this reading of the portrait sequence.

In the second part (the third reel) of *Vertigo*, after Madeleine's "death," Scottie essays to remake Judy in her image, to make her up, quite literally, to look like Madeleine. Ironically, it is exactly at the moment when he has achieved the transformation, and thus the identity of the two images (and just after a very long kiss sequence, ending in a fade, signals the moment of sexual consummation), that he discovered the hoax by which Judy had impersonated Madeleine; which renders both their images equally "untrue." But Judy has agreed to impersonate Madeleine *the second time* out of her love for Scottie; her desire is thus revealed at the same time as the hoax, concurrent and complicit with it. It is the same with Midge's portrait, only this time what is false is not merely the image (the portrait of Carlotta with Midge's face), but indeed the narrative image of the woman, for Judy-Madeleine turns out to be alive and real—and *thus* untrue. Unlike *Rebecca*, the different images and desires put in play by *Vertigo* are relayed through the male protagonist. Madeleine's desire for (and identification with) the dead Mother, mirroring Scottie's own desire, is impossible; the Mother is dead, and so does Madeleine die. Judy's and Midge's desires for Scottie are duplicitous. The film closes, appropriately, on the narrative image of Judy dead on the rooftop and Scottie looking.[70] Hitchcock says:

> I put myself in the place of a child whose mother is telling him a story. When there's a pause in her narration, the child always says, "What comes next, Mommy?" Well, I felt that the second part of the novel was written as if nothing came next, whereas in my formula, the little boy, *knowing* that Madeleine and Judy are the same person, would then ask, "And Stewart doesn't know it, does he? What will he do when he finds out about it?" [Pp. 184–85]

This is the question the film addresses, as do so many other films and as Freud's exploration of the psyche does. No story perhaps can be written "as if nothing came next." But the question of desire is always cast in these terms: "what will he do when he finds out?" the little boy asks of the man, or vice versa.

Such is the work of cinema as we know it: to represent the vicissitudes of his journey, fraught with false images (his blindness) but unerringly questing after the one true vision that will confirm the truth of his desire. So that even in the genre Molly Haskell aptly dubbed "the woman's film," which is supposed to represent a woman's fantasy or, like *Rebecca*, actually sets in play the terms of female desire, dominant cinema works for Oedipus.[71] If it stoops to the "old-fashioned psychological story," the tear-jerker from the "school of feminine literature," as Hitchcock lamented of his script for *Rebecca*, it is to conquer women's consent and so fulfill its social contract, the promise made to the little man.[72] Alas, it is still for him that women must be seduced into femininity and be remade again and again as woman. Thus when a film accidentally or unwisely puts in play the terms of a divided or double desire (that of the person Judy-Madeleine who desires both Scottie and the Mother), it must display that desire as impossible or duplicitous (Madeleine's and Judy's, respectively, in *Vertigo*), finally contradictory (Judy-Madeleine is split into Judy/Madeleine *for* Scottie); and then proceed to resolve the contradiction much in the same way as myths and the mythologists do: by either the massive destruction or the territorialization of women.

This sounds harsh, I realize, but it is not hopeless. Women are resisting destruction and are learning the tricks of making and reading maps as well as films. And what I see now possible for women's cinema is to respond to the plea for "a new language of desire" expressed in Mulvey's 1975 essay. I see it possible even without the stoic, brutal prescription of self-discipline, the destruction of visual pleasure, that seemed inevitable at the time. But if the project of feminist cinema—to construct the terms of reference of another measure of desire and the conditions of visibility for a different social subject—seems now more possible and indeed to a certain extent already actual, it is largely due to the work produced in response to that self-discipline and to the knowledge generated from the practice of feminism and film.

At the conclusion of her reading of *Story of O*, Silverman argues that only "an extreme immersion" in discourse can alter the female subject's relationship to the current monopoly held by the male "discursive fellowships," and make her participate in the production of meaning. For the theory and the practice of women's cinema, this would entail a continued and sustained work with and against narrative, in order to represent not just the power of female desire but its duplicity and ambivalence; or, as Johnston has insisted since the early days of feminist film theory, "women's cinema must embody the working through of desire." This will not be accomplished by (paraphrasing Schafer) another normative narrative wrapped around a thematics of liberation. The real task is to enact the contradiction of female desire, and of women as social subjects, in the terms of narrative; to perform its figures of movement and closure, image and gaze, with the constant awareness that spectators are historically engendered in social practices, in the real world, and in cinema too.

It may well be, however, that the story has to be told differently. Take Oedipus, for instance. Suppose: Oedipus does not solve the riddle. The Sphinx devours him for his arrogance; he didn't *have* to go to Thebes by that particular crossroads. Or, *he* kills himself in disgust. Or, he finally understands Tiresias' accusation ("You are the rotting canker in the state") to mean that patriarchy itself, which Oedipus represents as he represents the state, is the plague that wastes Thebes—and *then* he blinds himself; after which, possibly, Artemis would grant that he become a woman, and here the story of Oedipus could end happily.[73] Or, it could start over and be exactly like Freud's story of femininity, and this version could end with a freeze-frame of him as a patient of Charcot at the Salpêtrière. Or. . . . But in any case if Oedipus does not solve the riddle, then the riddle is no longer a riddle; it remains an enigma, structurally insoluble because undecidable, like those of the Oracles and the Sybils. And men will have to imagine other ways to deal with the fact that they, men, are born of women. For this is the ultimate purpose of the myth, according to Lévi-Strauss: to resolve that glaring contradiction and affirm, by the agency of narrative, the autochthonous origin of man.[74] Or perhaps they will have to accept it *as* a contradiction, by which in any case they will continue to be born. And in this remake of the story the Sphinx does not kill herself in self-hatred (women do that enough as it is); but continues to enunciate the enigma of sexual difference, of life and death, and the question of desire. Why, asks Ursula LeGuin in her essay-fiction "It Was a Dark and Stormy Night: Why Are We

Huddling about the Campfire?", why do we tell one another stories? Probably, she answers, just in order to exist, or to sustain desire even as we die from it.[75] The Sphinx, which according to the *Los Angeles Times* of March 2, 1982, is dying of cancer, as Freud was when he wrote the never-delivered lecture on femininity, is the enunciator of the question of desire as precisely enigma, contradiction, difference not reducible to sameness by the signification of the phallus or to a body existing outside discourse; an enigma which is structurally undecidable but daily articulated in the different practices of living. And this could be the end of my Oedipus story, but I had rather end it with a hopeful footnote.[76]

As for *Rebecca*, it too could be remade in several ways, some of which may actually be already available as films: *Les Rendez-vous d'Anna* or *Jeanne Dielman* (Chantal Akerman), *Thriller* (Sally Potter), probably many others. *Marnie* could be interestingly remade as *Sigmund Freud's Dora: A Case of Mistaken Identity* (McCall, Pajaczkowska, Tyndall, Weinstock); and *Vertigo* definitely should be remade as *Bad Timing: A Sensual Obsession* (Nicolas Roeg). And so on. This list of remakes and rereadings should suggest that I am not advocating the replacement or the appropriation or, even less, the emasculation of Oedipus. What I have been arguing for, instead, is an interruption of the triple track by which narrative, meaning, and pleasure are constructed from his point of view. The most exciting work in cinema and in feminism today is not anti-narrative or anti-Oedipal; quite the opposite. It is narrative and Oedipal with a vengeance, for it seeks to stress the duplicity of that scenario and the specific contradiction of the female subject in it, the contradiction by which historical women must work with and against Oedipus.

> Long afterward, Oedipus, old and blinded, walked the roads. He smelled a familiar smell. It was the Sphinx. Oedipus said, "I want to ask one question. Why didn't I recognize my mother?" "You gave the wrong answer," said the Sphinx. "But that was what made everything possible," said Oedipus. "No," she said. "When I asked, What walks on four legs in the morning, two at noon, and three in the evening, you answered, Man. You didn't say anything about woman." "When you say Man," said Oedipus, "you include women too. Everyone knows that." She said, "That's what you think."[77]

Semiotics and Experience

6

THERE IS A FAMOUS PASSAGE TOWARD THE BEGINNING of *A Room of One's Own,* in which Woolf's fictional "I," sitting on the banks of the Oxbridge river to meditate on the topic of women and fiction, is suddenly seized by a great excitement, a tumult of ideas. No longer able to sit still, though lost in thought, "I" starts walking rapidly across the campus lawn.

> Instantly a man's figure rose to intercept me. Nor did I at first understand that the gesticulations of a curious-looking object, in a cut-away coat and evening shirt, were aimed at me. His face expressed horror and indignation. *Instinct rather than reason came to my help; he was a Beadle; I was a woman.* This was the turf; there was the path. Only the Fellows and Scholars are allowed here; the gravel is the place for me.[1]

The irony of the passage, with its exaggerated contrast and the emphatic disproportion of the two figures, "I" and the enforcer of academic patriarchy, comes into sharp focus in the sentences I underline. For what Woolf calls "instinct rather than reason" is in fact not instinct but inference, that is, the very process on which reasoning is based; reasoning which (this is the point of the passage) is neither admitted of, nor allowed to, women. And yet, to call it "instinct" is not quite so inaccurate, for what is instinct but a kind of knowledge internalized from daily, secular repetition of actions, impressions, and meanings, whose cause-and-effect or otherwise binding relation has been accepted as certain and even necessary? But since "instinct" carries too strong a connotation of automatic, brute, mindless response, it may be best to find a term more suggestive of the particular manner of knowledge or apprehension of self which leads Woolf's "I"

158

to the gravel, to know that such is her place, and that she is not just *not* a Fellow or *not* a Scholar, but positively a woman. What term, other than "instinct" or "reason," can best designate that process of "understanding," of which the walk across the campus (rapid, excited, though "lost in thought") is the fictional analogue, the objective correlative; that process of self-representation which defines "I" as a woman or, in other words, en-genders the subject as female? Peirce might have called it "habit," as we shall see. But I will propose, at least provisionally, the term "experience."

"Experience" is a word widely recurrent in the feminist discourse, as in many others ranging from philosophy to common conversational speech. My concern here is only with the former. Though very much in need of clarification and elaboration, the notion of experience seems to me to be crucially important to feminist theory in that it bears directly on the major issues that have emerged from the women's movement—subjectivity, sexuality, the body, and feminist political practice. I should say from the outset that, by experience, I do not mean the mere registering of sensory data, or a purely mental (psychological) relation to objects and events, or the acquisition of skills and competences by accumulation or repeated exposure. I use the term not in the individualistic, idiosyncratic sense of something belonging to one and exclusively her own even though others might have "similar" experiences; but rather in the general sense of a *process* by which, for all social beings, subjectivity is constructed. Through that process one places oneself or is placed in social reality, and so perceives and comprehends as subjective (referring to, even originating in, oneself) those relations—material, economic, and interpersonal—which are in fact social and, in a larger perspective, historical.² The process is continuous, its achievement unending or daily renewed. For each person, therefore, subjectivity is an ongoing construction, not a fixed point of departure or arrival from which one then interacts with the world. On the contrary, it is the effect of that interaction—which I call experience; and thus it is produced not by external ideas, values, or material causes, but by one's personal, subjective, engagement in the practices, discourses, and institutions that lend significance (value, meaning, and affect) to the events of the world.

But if it is to further our critical understanding of how the female subject is en-gendered, which is also to say, how the relation of women to woman is set up and variously reproduced (endlessly, it would seem), the notion of experience must be elaborated theoretically. It must be confronted, for one thing, with relevant theories of meaning or signification and, for another, with relevant conceptions of the subject. The following pages discuss the most urgent questions brought up by such a confrontation, and sketch out something of a direction for feminist theory.

In recent years the problem of the subject has come to be seen as fundamental for any inquiry, be it humanistic or social scientific, aimed at what may be broadly called a theory of culture. The terms in which the question of the subject was to be cast and recast in various disciplines, especially semiotics and film theory, had been set since the fifties and the well-known debate between Sartre and Lévi-Strauss, when the former accused the nascent structuralist method in the human sciences of doing away with the concrete, existential, historical subject in favor of ahistorical structures immanent in the mind. The reply of Lévi-Strauss, whose position on the matter was to weigh heavily not only on semiotics but on Lacanian psychoanalysis and Althusser's theory of ideology, was stated in the last volume of his *Mythologiques*. Its title was *L'homme nu, Naked Man*.[3] Thus whether one accepted the structuralist or the existential definition, the human subject was theoretically inscribed—hence solely conceivable—in the terms of a patriarchal symbolic order; and of that subject, women represented the sexual component or counterpart. The unstated assumption became explicit in Lévi-Strauss's paradoxical thesis that women are both like men and unlike men: they are human beings (like men), but their special function in culture and society is to be exchanged and circulated among men (unlike men). His theory stands on the premise that, because of their "value" as means of sexual reproduction, women are the means, objects, and signs, of social communication (among human beings).[4] Nevertheless, as he is unwilling to renounce humanism altogether, he cannot exclude women from humanity or "mankind." He therefore compromises by saying that women are also human beings, although in the symbolic order of culture they do not speak, desire, or produce meaning *for themselves*, as men do, by means of the exchange of women. One can only conclude that, insofar as women are human beings, they are (like) men. In short, be he naked or clothed by culture and history, this human subject is male.

A similar paradox was found to be concealed in the "grammatical" argument that "man" was the generic term for humankind. As studies in language-usage demonstrate, if "man" includes women (while the obverse is not true, for the term "woman" is always gendered, i.e., sexually connoted) it is only to the extent that, in the given context, women are (to be) perceived as non-gendered "human beings," and therefore, again, as man.[5] The feminist efforts to displace this assumption have been more often than not caught in the logical trap set up by the paradox. Either they have assumed that "the subject," like "man," is a generic term, and as such can designate equally and at once the female and the male subjects, with the result of erasing sexuality and sexual difference from subjectivity.[6] Or else they have been obliged to resort to an oppositional notion of "feminine" subject defined by silence, negativity, a natural sexuality, or a closeness to nature not compromised by patriarchal culture.[7] But such a notion— which simply reverts woman to the body and to sexuality as an immediacy of the biological, as nature—has no autonomous theoretical grounding and is moreover quite compatible with the conceptual framework of the sciences of man, as Lévi-Strauss makes clear. This feminine subject is not a different subject, one engendered or semiotically constituted as female by a specific kind of experience, but instead can easily continue to be seen as merely the sexual component or counterpart of the generic (masculine or male) subject. And indeed the maleness of that human subject and of his discourse is not only affirmed but universalized by theorizing woman as its repressed, its "negative semantic space," or its imaginary fantasy of coherence.

Another debate, not less important to our ends than the more illustrious one already mentioned, may serve to bring home the difficulty of constructing a notion of female subject from current discourses, as well as its vital theoretical necessity. The debate took place around the work of the British film journal *Screen*, whose special issue on Brecht (15 [Summer 1974]) marked the beginning of a project the journal was to develop over the next several years: a critique of the ideological structures of representational, classical narrative cinema. The debate was prompted by an American marxist-feminist film critic's response to *Screen*'s introduction of psychoanalytic concepts such as fetishism and (symbolic) castration into film theory.

Despite the journal's usefulness in making available "Continental Marxist-oriented studies" to American film students, Julia Lesage charged, *Screen* writers "use certain premises from orthodox Freudianism as the basis for their political arguments about narrative form: premises . . . which are not only false but overtly sexist and as such demand political refutation."[8] Lesage's argument develops along two lines. First, she takes issue with the employ of what she calls "orthodox Freudianism" in a critical project that would otherwise be politically sound; and second, she objects to the textual interpretations offered by the *Screen* contributors, which she considers misreadings or distortions of the texts in question, one of them being Barthes's *S/Z*. In the latter case, too, the misreading is attributed to "a strictly Freudian interpretation of Barthes's use of the term 'fetishism' [which] finally undermines Heath's whole political argument in his reading of Brecht" (pp. 80–81).

While the two lines of the argument proceed from a single objection, the critic's aversion to "Freudian orthodoxy," they do not intersect again to produce the expected "refutation." I shall discuss them separately, beginning with the second.

> The major theoretical point made in the Brecht issue of *Screen* is that representational art—either a fictional narrative where there is an omniscient point of view or a feature film where we are given a superior viewpoint from which to judge the characters—makes us into 'subjects'. We consume the knowledge offered by the narrative, and as spectators, we get a sense of ourselves as unified, not as living in contradiction. [P. 81]

The alternative proposed by *Screen*, and supported by Lesage as politically correct, is "a Brechtian cinema," such as Godard's, in which "the spectator's very position is no longer one of pseudo-dominance; rather, it is given as critical and contradictory" (pp. 81–82). So far so good. But for the feminist critic the difficulties begin when the theoretical premises of this analysis (and of Godard's cinema, I would insinuate) are made explicit. For the conception of the subject underlying this critique of classical representation and *its* unified subject comes not from orthodox Freudianism, as Lesage thinks, but from Lacan's rereading of Freud, and *there* the notion of castration (and consequently fetishism) is not only central but absolutely determining of subject processes.[9] In other words, the split, non-coherent subject that may be engaged or produced by a "Brechtian" cinema, as understood by the *Screen* contributors, is a subject constituted by the symbolic function of castration. And only with respect to this (Lacanian) subject, can it be said that representation is a structure of fetishism, serving to guarantee the subject's imaginary self-coherence, the delusion of one's stable identity. This, Lesage cannot accept: "Fetishism is described solely in phallic terms. . . . For Heath spectators are all the same—all male" (p. 83). Thus, she concludes, the "profound political implications" of the *Screen* critique of classical narrative cinema are severely undermined by positing the subject "as a monolith without contradictions: that is as male" (p. 82).

The problem here is that, for better or for worse, fetishism can only be "described" in phallic terms, at least by psychoanalysis. Any non-phallic description—assuming one were possible—would simply hide the term's discursive ground, the semantic network in which it takes its meaning, its conceptual basis in a certain epistemology; and at best we would be back with the humanistic subject, male but pretending to be "the human being." As the *Screen* contributors point out in their response, "if 'phallic' is *simply* made to mean 'masculine' and hence 'repressive', and then pushed back onto psychoanalysis as a monolithic orthodoxy, it will be easy to dismiss Freud, but what gets dismissed along with this is, again, the whole question of the process of the subject" (p. 89). The exchange is an excellent example of how discourse (including "political" discourse) is not just laden with pitfalls but is itself a pitfall. Lesage's argument falls into the very "trap" she accuses Heath of falling into; that is to say, the trap of representational coherence (Woolf's "reason"?), the pressure to collapse distinct orders of discourse into a single discourse that will account for contradictions and resolve them. "Phallic terms" and "male spectators," for example, cannot sit side by side; the political as practice (e.g., consciousness-raising groups) cannot be reduced to the adjective "political" used to mean a marxist or materialist textual interpretation; nor can the term "psychoanalysis," referring to the elaboration of a theory of the unconscious, be immediately compared and contrasted with "Freudianism," designating several popular and heterogeneous discourses on sexuality, from Karen Horney to Kate Millett to Masters and Johnson, which Lesage cites against "Freudian orthodoxy." Finally, if her argument fails to produce a refutation of the *Screen* critique or of its premises, it is because Lesage is unwilling to throw away the "political" baby (the "Brechtian" cinema and its divided subject) with the "sexist" bath water (the phallic order of the Lacanian symbolic) in which it is immersed.

The bind of theoretical feminism in its effort to work through the discourses of psychoanalysis and marxism is sharply focused in the writers' reply to Lesage's criticism of their use of the pronoun "he" in reference to the subject. Her point is well taken, they admit, but what pronoun should be used?

> What is probably needed in English is a movement between 'it', the subject in psychoanalysis, male and female (remember the importance of the thesis of bisexuality), and 'she', the subject defined as exchange value in the ideological assignation of discourse in so far as this is the positioning of a 'masculinity' in which 'femininity' is placed and displaced. [P. 86]

As noted in previous chapters, while psychoanalysis recognizes the inherent bisexuality of the subject, for whom femininity and masculinity are not qualities or attributes but positions in the symbolic processes of (self)-representation, psychoanalysis is itself caught up in "the ideological assignation of discourse," the structures of representation, narrative, vision, and meaning it seeks to analyze, reveal, or bring to light. Whence the tendency toward "he" in psychoanalytic writings, or indeed "she," with femininity *sous rature* (as Derrida would have it).[10] Lacan's statement "The woman does not exist," Jacqueline Rose explains, "means, not that women do not exist, but that her status as an absolute category and guarantor of fantasy (exactly *The* woman) is false (The)." In his theory of psychoanalysis, therefore, the question then becomes not so much the 'difficulty' of feminine sexuality consequent on phallic division, as what it means, given that division, to speak of the 'woman' at all."[11] However, although it is often stressed that "femininity" is not the same as "femaleness," just as "woman" is not the same as "women" (or the phallus is not the same as the penis), the two sets of terms continually overlap and slide onto each other, even in the writings of those who would insist that the distinction, tenuous as it is, is absolute. I think they should be taken at their word.[12]

That femininity *is* but the underside of masculinity—that is what taking them at their word implies—is no less evident in the practice of Freud's research than in the theory it has since produced: his work with Breuer on hysteria and the evidence collected from female patients were cast aside until the full elaboration of the Oedipus theory would require, toward the end of his life's work, a direct inquiry into female sexuality. This is well known. Why are we still surprised or unwilling to accept that, like the *Screen* discourse on the subject, psychoanalytic theory can only speak of women as woman, "she," or "the woman"? Quite correctly Rose points out: "The description of feminine sexuality is, therefore, an exposure of the terms of its definition, the very opposite of a demand as to what that sexuality should be."[13] This definition is obviously inadequate to the current task of feminist theory, which, I believe, must address women, not woman, and question precisely that specific relation to sexuality which constitutes femaleness as the experience of a female subject. But this inadequacy, this inability of psychoanalytic theory to provide a satisfactory answer (which no other theory, by the way, provides), is not sufficient cause for dismissing Freud, who, unlike Jung or Horney, to say nothing of Masters and Johnson, does account for the continued existence and the functioning of patriarchy as a structure of subjectivity; in the same way as Marx accounts for the socioeconomic relations of capital that inform patriarchy in our times. Unless we too want to toss the baby along with the bath water, both Marx and Freud must be retained and worked through at once. And this has been the insistent emphasis of *Screen,* and its extraordinarily important contribution to film theory and, beyond it, to feminism.

That patriarchy exists concretely, in social relations, and that it works precisely through the very discursive and representational structures that allow us to recognize it, is the problem and the struggle of feminist theory. It is also, and more so, a problem of women's life. Thus, the relevance of this debate on the subject extends beyond its immediate context—the introduction of psychoanalytic terms into film studies in the early seventies—to the present impasse in the theoretical and political struggle. For the feminist critique of ideology, it is still the first line of Lesage's argument that carries its critical weight: her reaction of "political and intellectual rage." It is most appropriately a rage, an intensely personal response, grounded in the historical experience of both psychoanalytic and feminist practices in the United States. As she tells it,

> As child of the 50's in the US, I lived in a milieu where I interpreted all personal relations and most literature I read in Freudian terms, where psychoanalysis promised the middle class solutions to their identity problems and angst, and where vulgarised Freudian concepts were

part of daily life in the childbearing advice of Spock and Gessell, the advice columns of Dear Abby, and the sentimental filmic melodramas of Douglas Sirk. . . . In the 60's one of the first victories of the women's movement in the US was to liberate ourselves both academically and personally from the Freud trap. On the personal level, we stopped seeing ourselves as sick people who needed to be *cured* of masochism or of not having vaginal orgasms. We saw that the definition of an arrival at womanhood could not come through orthodox psychotherapy but rather through an understanding of the mechanisms of socialisation, which are inherently oppressive to women. [Pp. 77–78]

If her argument fails to refute, and in fact corroborates, her opponents' contention that theory must be argued against in theoretical terms and at its own level of conceptual abstraction, the fundamental political (this time without quotation marks) validity of her intervention is summed up in the statement: "We not only have to recognize differences of class but *entirely different social experiences* based on the fact of sex, the fact of the oppression of one sex" (p. 83, my emphasis). The real difficulty, but also the most exciting, original project of feminist theory remains precisely this—how to theorize that experience, which is at once social and personal, and how to construct the female subject from that political and intellectual rage.

Women, writes Catharine MacKinnon, acquire gender identification "not so much through physical maturation or inculcation into appropriate role behavior as through the experience of sexuality."[14] Sex means both sexuality and gender, and the two are usually defined in terms of each other, in a vicious circle. But it is sexuality that determines gender, not vice versa; and sexuality, she says, is "a complex unity of physicality, emotionality, identity, and status affirmation." This is her description of how one "becomes a woman":

Socially, femaleness means femininity, which means attractiveness to men, which means sexual attractiveness, which means sexual availability on male terms. What defines woman as such is what turns men on. Good girls are "attractive," bad girls "provocative." Gender socialization is the process through which women come to identify themselves as sexual beings, as beings that exist for men. It is that process through which women internalize (make their own) a male image of their sexuality *as* their identity as women. It is not just an illusion. [Pp. 530–31]

Brilliant as this insight is in its dazzling concision, we still need to be more precise as to the ways in which the process works and how the experience of sexuality, in en-gendering one as female, does effect or construct what we may call a female subject. In order to begin to articulate, however tentatively, the relation of experience to subjectivity, we must make a detour through semiotics, where the question of the subject, as it happens, has become more prominent and more urgent.

In the last decade or so, semiotics has undergone a shift of its theoretical gears: a shift away from the classification of sign systems—their basic units, their levels of structural organization—and toward the exploration of the modes of production of signs and meanings, the ways in which systems and codes are used, transformed or transgressed in social practice. While formerly the emphasis was on studying sign systems (language, literature, cinema, architecture, music, etc.), conceived of as mechanisms that generate messages, what is now being examined is the work performed through them. It is this work or activity which constitutes and/or transforms the codes, at the same time as it constitutes and transforms the individuals using the codes, performing the work; the individuals who are, therefore, the subjects of semiosis.

"Semiosis," a term borrowed from Charles Sanders Peirce, is expanded by Eco to designate the process by which a culture produces signs and/or attributes meanings to signs. Although for Eco meaning production or semiosis is a social activity, he allows that subjective factors are involved in each individual act of semiosis. The notion then might be pertinent to the two main emphases of current, or poststructuralist, semiotic theory. One is a semiotics focused on the subjective aspects of signification and strongly influenced by Lacanian psychoanalysis, where meaning is construed as a subject-effect (the subject being an effect of the signifier). The other is a semiotics concerned to stress the social aspect of signification, its practical, aesthetic, or ideological use in interpersonal communication; there, meaning is construed as semantic value produced through culturally shared codes. I am referring in particular, for the first emphasis, to the work of Julia Kristeva and Christian Metz (the Metz of *The Imaginary Signifier*), who maintain an affiliation with semiotics, though strongly influenced by psychoanalytic theory and, in Kristeva's case, intent on redefining in that perspective the very field and theoretical object of semiotics. The second emphasis is that of the work of Umberto Eco, whose attitude toward psychoanalysis has been consistently one of non-collaboration.

I will contend that there is, between these two emphases of semiotics, an area of theoretical overlap, a common ground; and there one ought to pose the question of the subject, locating subjectivity in the space contoured by the discourses of semiotics and psychoanalysis, neither in the former nor in the latter, but rather in their discursive intersection. Whether, or to what extent, the notion of semiosis may be stretched to reach into that common ground and to account for the subjective and the social aspects of meaning production, or whether indeed it can be said to mediate between them, will determine its usefulness in mapping the relations of meaning to what I have proposed to call experience.

At the end of *A Theory of Semiotics,* in a short, hasty chapter entitled "The Subject of Semiotics," Eco asks:

> Since it has been said that the labor of sign production also represents a form of social criticism and of social practice, a sort of ghostly presence, until now somewhat removed from the present discourse, finally makes an unavoidable appearance. What is, in the semiotic framework, the place of the *acting subject* of every semiosic act?[13]

From the answer given, it is clear that by "acting subject" he means the sender of the message, the subject of enunciation or of a speech act, not its addressee or receiver; not the reader but the speaker/writer. Moreover such a subject, insofar as it is presupposed by its statements, must be "'read' as an element of the conveyed content" (*TS*, p. 315). And although he grants that "a theory of the relationship of sender-addressee should also take into account the role of the 'speaking' subject not only as a communicational figment but as a concrete historical, biological, psychic subject, as it is approached by psychoanalysis and related disciplines," nevertheless, for Eco, semiotics can approach the subject only by semiotic categories—and these exclude all pre-symbolic or unconscious processes. He professes awareness, however, that some attempts have been made, within semiotics, to specify the subjective determinants of a text, or the "creative activity of a semiosis-making subject"; and in a footnote we find the reference to, and a long quotation from, Julia Kristeva. As the quotation sets out the other term of Eco's argument and identifies his interlocutor (Kristeva's "speaking subject" is ostensively the only notion of the subject against which he debates), it is necessary to cite it in its entirety here. Kristeva writes:

> One phase of semiology is now over: that which runs from Saussure and Peirce to the Prague School and structuralism, and has made possible the systematic description of the social and/or symbolic constraint within each significant practice. . . . A critique of this "semiology of systems" and of its phenomenological foundations is possible only if it starts from a theory of meaning which must necessarily be a theory of the speaking subject. . . . The theory of meaning now stands at a crossroads: either it will remain an attempt at formalizing meaning-systems by increasing sophistication of the logico-mathematical tools which enable it to formulate models on the basis of a conception (already rather dated) of meaning as the act of a *transcendental ego*, cut off from its body, its unconscious, and also its history; or else it will attune itself to the theory of the speaking subject as a divided subject (conscious/ unconscious) and go on to attempt to specify the types of operations characteristic of the two sides of this split: thereby exposing them . . . on the one hand, to bio-physiological processes (themselves already an inescapable part of signifying processes; what Freud labelled "drives"), and, on the other hand, to social constraints (family structures, modes of production, etc.).[16]

With these words, Kristeva defines (and Eco implicitly accepts her definition) a fork in the path of semiotic research, a "cross-roads" where the theory of meaning encounters the "ghost" of the subject. After abandoning the path of the transcendental ego to follow the divided subject, a critical semiotics itself finds the way ahead divided, like that subject, split into conscious and unconscious, social constraints and pre-symbolic drives. And while Kristeva's work will increasingly inscribe itself on the "side of the split" investigated by the science of the unconscious, Eco's situates itself squarely on the other side. Thus, in his response, he concedes that the subjective determinants and the "individual material subjects" of a text are part of the signifying process, but at the same time excludes them from the semiotic field of inquiry: "either [the subjects] can be defined in terms of semiotic structures or—from this point of view—they do not exist at all" (*TS*, p. 316). For just as the subjective determinants can only be studied semiotically "as contents of the text itself," so can the subject be affirmed or known only as a textual element. "Any other attempt to introduce a consideration of the subject into the semiotic discourse would make semiotics trespass on one of its 'natural' boundaries" (*TS*, p. 315).[17] And it is not by chance, he adds slyly, that Kristeva calls her work not "semiotics" but "*sémanalyse*."

Something of a territorial struggle transpires from these remarks of Eco's, and I will return to it later on; however, he is not alone in maintaining the "split," if not the disciplinary distinction, between discourses which take as their theoretical objects, respectively, the conscious and the unconscious. Of Metz's attitude toward this question, something has been said in chapter 1. Kristeva herself, who pinpointed the problem exactly, in the essay just cited, seems to be exclusively concerned with the operations of the unconscious insofar as they exceed or escape the symbolic; this was already clear in her strategy of shifting the ground of the term "semiotic" (*le sémiotique*) to the domain of bio-physiological or pre-symbolic processes, a strategy that does not appear to have been successful. For my present purposes, the advantage of Eco's stance with regard to what comprises the object, field, and method of semiotics is that his position is unambiguously spelled out, and thus offers us the possibility not only of assessing its limits, but also of engaging it constructively, of working through it, and displacing its "boundaries."

Unlike Kristeva's, the boundaries which Eco imposes on the field and on the theoretical object of semiotics are postulated methodologically and are not to be ascribed to an ontology. His boundaries are posed as terms of a cultural process and a perspective from which to understand it, with no claim whatsoever as to their being substantive (hence the quotation marks he puts around the word "natural"). Yet one cannot help observing that they do coincide almost too neatly with a pre-Freudian perspective that reproposes a dichotomous idea of body and mind, matter and intellect, physis and reason. On one side is the area of stimuli and what Eco calls "physical information," thus suggesting its non-significant, mechanical nature—for example, the salivation of the dog in Pavlov's famous experiment. These constitute "the lower threshold" of the semiotic domain, before which there is no semiosis, signification, or culture. On the other side, at the "upper threshold," are those phenomena which, universally shared by all societies, must therefore be taken as the very foundation of culture, its institutive moment: kinship, tool production, and the economic exchange of goods. But these latter too are communicative exchanges, says Eco after Marx and Lévi-Strauss, no less productive of meanings and social relations than is language itself. Thus all of culture and its laws can be studied semiotically, as a system of systems of signification. In other words, the semiotic perspective would subsume the fields of cultural anthropology and political economy—the upper threshold extending all the way to the vanishing point—but exclude the entire area of human physicality, the body, instincts, drives, and their representations (it is no coincidence that the single example of "stimulus" to be found in *A Theory of Semiotics*, Pavlov's dog, is derived from the non-human world). Eco's semiotics excludes, that is, the very area in which human physicality comes to be represented, signi-fied, assumed in the relations of meaning, and thus productive of subjectivity—the area delineated and sketched out by the work of Freud.

The "methodological" decision to exclude this no man's land between nature and culture (a no man's land, exactly, where Lévi-Strauss had stumbled and found himself bogged down) amounts to a political gesture: to declare it a demilitarized zone, a theoretical Berlin Wall. This gesture has many advantages for a theory of meaning production that wants to be scientific and uncompromisingly historical-materialist, as Eco's does.

> By accepting this limit, semiotics fully avoids any risk of idealism. On the contrary semiotics recognizes as the only testable subject matter of its discourse the social existence of the universe of signification, as it is revealed by the physical testability of interpretants—which are, to reinforce this point for the last time, *material expressions*. [*TS*, p. 317]

To escape the idealist danger is doubtless of the utmost importance, given the historical context of Eco's work and the philosophical tradition to which he may be the last innovative contributor—the Italian tradition of secular, progressive, democratic rationalism, that in our century has included Croce as well as Gramsci. It remains to be seen, however, whether another, equally serious danger can be avoided, a risk against which no methodological disclaimer can insure: that of elaborating a historical-materialist theory of culture which must deny the materiality and the historicity of the subject itself, or rather the *subjects* of culture. For it is not just the "speaking subject" of Kristeva's narrowly linguistic, or language-determined, perspective that is at issue, but subjects who speak and listen, write and read, make and watch films, work and play, and so forth; who are, in short, concurrently and often contradictorily engaged in a plurality of heterogeneous experiences, practices, and discourses, where subjectivity and gender are constructed, anchored, or reproduced.

Eco's project is the outline of a materialist, nondeterministic theory of culture, one in which aesthetics can be founded in social communication, and creativity integrated in human work; semiosis being a work by and through signs, and signs being—he unequivocally asserts—social forces. This is the sense of his rereading of Peirce, of what he calls Peirce's "not ontological but pragmatic realism": Peirce was not only interested in "objects as ontological sets of properties," but more importantly he conceived of objects as "occasions and results of active experience. To discover an object means to discover the way by which we operate upon the world, producing objects or producing practical uses of them."[18] Eco's debt to Peirce is extensive. The latter's concepts of interpretant and unlimited semiosis are pivotal to *A Theory of Semiotics,* which turns on the notion of a dialectic interaction between codes and modes of sign production. They serve to bridge the gap between discourse and reality, between the sign and its referent (the empirical object to which the sign refers); and so they usher in a theory of meaning as a continual cultural production that is not only susceptible of ideological transformation, but materially based in historical change.

When Eco redefines the classical notion of sign as a sign-function, and proposes it to be the complex, but temporary and even unstable correlation between a sign-vehicle and a sign content, rather than a fixed, though arbitrary, relationship between a signifier and a signified; and when he further allows that the correlation is dependent on the context, including the conditions of enunciation and reception in actual communicative situations, he is following a trail marked out in Peirce's famous definition:

> A sign, or representamen, is something which stands to somebody for something in some respect or capacity. It addresses somebody, that is, it creates in the mind of that person an equivalent sign, or perhaps a more developed sign. That sign which it creates I call the *interpretant* of the first sign. The sign stands for something, its *object.* It stands for that object, not in all respects, but in reference to a sort of idea, which I have sometimes called the *ground* of the representation.[19]

Peirce greatly complicates the picture in which a signifier would immediately correspond to a signified. As Eco notes, the notions of meaning, ground, and interpretant all pertain in some degree to the area of the signified, while interpretant and ground also pertain in some degree to the area of the referent (Object). Moreover, Peirce distinguishes a Dynamic Object and an Immediate Object, and it is the notion of ground that sustains the distinction. The Dynamic Object is external to the sign: it is that which "by some means contrives to determine the sign to its representation" (4.536). On the contrary, the Immediate Object ("the object as the sign itself represents it") is internal; it is an "Idea" or a "mental representation." From the analysis of the notion of "ground" (a sort of context of the sign, which makes pertinent certain attributes or aspects of the object and thus is already a component of meaning), Eco argues that not only does the sign in Peirce appear as a textual matrix; the object too, "is not necessarily a thing or a state of the world but a rule, a law, a prescription: it appears as the operational description of a set of possible experiences" (*RR*, p. 181).

> Signs have a direct connection with Dynamic Objects only insofar as objects determine the formation of a sign; on the other hand, signs only "know" Immediate Objects, that is, meanings. There is a difference between *the object of which a sign is a sign* and the *object of a sign*: the former is the Dynamic Object, a state of the outer world; the latter is a semiotic construction. [*RR*, p. 193]

But the Immediate Object's relation to the representamen is established by the interpretant, which is itself another sign, "perhaps a more developed sign." Thus, in the process of unlimited semiosis the nexus object-sign-meaning is a series of ongoing mediations between "outer world" and "inner" or mental representations. The key term, the principle that supports the series of mediations, is the interpretant. However, cautions Eco, the potentially endless succession of interpretants is not to be construed as infinite semiotic regression, a free circulation of meaning: for the pragmatist, reality is a construction, "more a Result than a mere Datum" and "the idea of *meaning* is such as to involve some reference to a *purpose*" (5.175). Hence the crucial notion, for both Eco and Peirce, is that of a final or "ultimate" interpretant.

As Peirce puts it, "the problem of what the 'meaning' of an intellectual concept is can only be solved by the study of the interpretants, or proper significate effects, of signs" (5.475). He then describes three general classes. 1. "The first proper significate effect of a sign is a *feeling* produced by it." This is the *emotional* interpretant. Although its "foundation of truth" may be slight at times, often this remains the only effect produced by a sign such as, for example, the performance of a piece of music. 2. When a further significate effect is produced, however, is it "through the mediation of the emotional interpretant"; and this second type of meaning effect he calls the *energetic* interpretant, for it involves an "effort," which may be a muscular exertion but is more usually a mental effort, "an exertion upon the Inner World." 3. The third and final type of meaning effect that may be produced by the sign, through the mediation of the former two, is "a *habit-change*": "a modification of a person's tendencies toward action, resulting from previous experiences or from previous exertions." This is the "ultimate" interpretant of the sign, the effect of meaning on which the process of semiosis, in the instance considered, comes to rest. "The real and living logical conclusion *is* that habit," Peirce states, and designates the third type of significate effect, the *logical* interpretant. But immediately he adds a qualification, distinguishing this logical interpretant from the concept or "intellectual" sign:

> The concept which is a logical interpretant is only imperfectly so. It somewhat partakes of the nature of a verbal definition, and is as inferior to the habit, and much in the same way, as a verbal definition is inferior to the real definition. The deliberately formed, self-analyzing habit—self-analyzing because formed by the aid of analysis of the exercises that nourished it—is the living definition, the veritable and final logical interpretant. [5.491]

The final interpretant, then, is not "logical" in the sense in which a syllogism is logical, or because it is the result of an "intellectual" operation like deductive reasoning. It is "logical" in the sense that it is "self-analyzing" or, put another way, that it "makes sense" of the emotion and muscular/mental effort that preceded it, by providing a conceptual representation of that effort. Such a representation is implicit in the notion of habit as a "tendency toward action" and in the solidarity of habit and belief.[20]

This logical interpretant is precisely illustrated, I submit, in the passage cited from Woolf's text. What she calls "instinct rather than reason" is semiosis as Peirce describes it: the process by which the "I" interprets the sign (the "curious-looking object, in cut-away coat and evening shirt") to mean a Beadle, and his gesticulations to convey the patriarchal prohibition well known to her as a result of habit, of previous emotional and muscular/mental effort; their ultimate "significate effect" being the "logical" representation, "I was a woman." Having so understood the sign, the "I" acts accordingly—she moves over to the gravel path. ("The real and living logical conclusion *is* that habit," as Peirce said.) This notion of semiosis, therefore, need not be stretched to reach into the two semiotic territories marked out, by their respective proponents, as the biophysiological and the social operations of signification. It is already so stretched to span them both and to connect them, though obviously, in Peirce, it has no purchase on the unconscious, no hold on unconscious processes. And whether it may even venture, so to speak, into that side of the "split" must remain in question for the time being. But with regard to the more immediate problem of articulating the relation of meaning production to experience, and hence to the construction of subjectivity, Peirce's semiosis appears to have a usefulness that Eco vehemently denies and that I, on the contrary, will attempt to demonstrate further.

The importance of Peirce's formulation of the ultimate interpretant for Eco's own theory is that it provides him with the link between semiosis and reality, between signification and concrete action. The final interpretant is not a Platonic essence or a transcendental law of signification but a result, as well as a rule: "to have understood the sign as a rule through the series of its interpretants means to have acquired the habit to act according to the prescription given by the sign. . . . The action is the place in which the *haecceitas* ends the game of semiosis" (*RR*, pp. 194–95). This theory of meaning does not incur the risk of idealism because the system of systems of signs which makes human communication possible is translatable into habits, concrete action upon the world; and this action then rejoins the universe of signification by converting itself into new signs and new semiotic systems. At this point in his theory, however, Eco again needs to distance or to ward off the possibility that something of a subjective order might enter the semiotic field, specifically through the energetic interpretant.

> In order to make the interpretant a fruitful notion, one must first of all free it from any psychological misunderstanding. . . . According to [Peirce] even ideas are signs, in various passages the interpretants appear also as mental events. I am only suggesting that from the point of view of the theory of signification, *we should perform a sort of surgical*

operation and retain only a precise aspect of this category. Interpretants are the testable and describable correspondents associated *by public agreement* to another sign. In this way the analysis of content becomes a cultural operation which works only on physically testable cultural products, that is, other signs and their reciprocal correlations. [*RR*, p. 198; my emphasis]

On the one hand, then, the rereading of Peirce allows Eco to find the "missing link" between signification and physical reality, that link being human action. On the other, that human action must be excised (by a "surgical operation") of its psychological, psychic, and subjective component. This paradoxical situation is most evident in Eco's subsequent work, in particular the title essay of the volume *The Role of the Reader* (1979), where the essay on Peirce I have been discussing is also published, though it was written in 1976, at the time of *A Theory of Semiotics,* and thus constitutes a bridge between the two works. Published in Italy in a book-length version, with the Latin title *Lector in fabula* ("The Reader in the Fable")—but that title is a pun on the proverb "*lupus in fabula*," speak of the devil—the later book is logically, all too logically, devoted to the Reader. It provides a painstakingly detailed account of the "role" of the reader in interpreting the text; interpretation being the manner in which the reader cooperates with the text's own construction of meaning, its "generative structure."

More pointedly than "the subject of semiotics," Eco's Model Reader is presented as a *locus* of logical moves, impervious to the heterogeneity of historical process, to difference or contradiction. For the Reader is already contemplated by the text, is in fact an element of its interpretation. Like the Author, the Reader is a textual strategy, a set of specific competences and felicitous conditions established by the text, which must be met if the text is to be "fully actualized" in its potential content (*RR*, p. 11). Such a theory of textuality, in short, at one and the same time invokes a reader who is already "competent," a subject fully constituted prior to the text and to reading, *and* poses the reader as the term of the text's production of certain meanings, as an effect of its structure.[21] The circularity of the argumentation and the reappearance of terms and concerns recurrent in structuralist writers like Lévi-Strauss and Greimas suggest a kind of retrenchment on Eco's part to the positions which he himself was among the very first to criticize in *La struttura assente* (1968), and which his *Theory of Semiot-*

ics subsequently argued to be untenable.[22] Why, then, such retrenchment? I will offer two reasons, not unrelated to one another and to the purpose that has led me to consider Eco's rereading of Peirce.

Firstly, it seems to me that the problem, and the limit, of Eco's theory of reading is once again the subject, much more pressing now behind the reader, not merely *in* the text or simply *outside* the text, but as an instance of textuality. As the earlier book ended by posing the question of the subject, almost off-handedly and with reference to Kristeva, so does *Lector in fabula* begin. Both the English and the Italian introductions allude more or less explicitly to Kristeva and Barthes, two writers for whom the centrality of the subject, or the process of the subject, in language goes hand in hand with the exploration of textuality, and whose theories and practices of reading necessitate an attention to the discourse of psychoanalysis. It is Eco's defensiveness toward the latter, I suspect, and his determination to keep semiotics "free" of it, that forces him to perform on the reader a surgical operation analogous to the one auspicated for the interpretant, and so deprive him of a body as well as subjectivity. I said "deprive *him* of a body," because there is no doubt that Eco's reader is masculine in gender. And is not gender in fact usually construed as the addition of feminine markers to the morphological form of the masculine, and the concomitant attribution of the body to the feminine?

Secondly and less speculatively, even perhaps in greater fairness to Eco, we may be reminded that his productivist emphasis has its roots in the philosophical tradition of historical materialism. The priority of the sphere of production, of the work or text as artifact over the conditions of its enunciation and reception, and the priority given to artistic creativity ("invention") over other modes of sign production derive, as I suggest elsewhere in this volume, from his theoretical grounding in classical aesthetics and marxism.[23] Whence, too, the confident image of *homo faber* which emerges as the protagonist of his *Theory:* the subject of semiotics is the materialist subject of history. Thus, while no one could deny Eco's awareness of the social and dialogic nature of all communicative intercourse, and the active participation in it of both "producers" and "users" of signs, one cannot but recognize in his work an emphasis, a sharper focus, a special attention paid to one of the two poles of the communicative exchange, the moment of enunciation, of production: "the moment of production"—so-called with all the ideological connotations that the words "production" and "productivity" carry. Among them, first and foremost, is the implication of a creative and enriching "activity" (one makes art and history, one makes oneself or another, one has made it, etc.) as opposed to the "passivity" of reception, consumption, entertainment and enjoyment, whether hedonistic or economic. For example, Eco does not rule out the possibility that other forms of social practice may effect a transformation of the codes, and hence of the universe of meaning, as much as or more than artistic practice. Nevertheless his definition of "invention" as a "creative" use of the codes that produces new meanings and percepts seems to exclude all practices which do not result in actual texts, or "physically testable cultural products." And yet there are such practices—political or more often micropolitical: consciousness-raising groups, alternative forms of labor organization, familial or interpersonal relations, and so on—which produce no texts as such, but by shifting the "ground" of a given sign (the conditions of pertinence of the representamen in relation to the object), effectively intervene upon the codes, codes of perception as well as ideological codes. What these practices do produce, in Peirce's terms, is a habit-change; consequently, for their "users" or practitioners—their subjects—they are rather interpretants than texts or signs, and as interpretants they result in "a modification of consciousness" (5.485).

Let us go back to Peirce, then, whose view of semiotics as the study of the varieties of possible semiosis appears to be less restrictive than Eco's.[24] When Peirce speaks of habit as the result of a process involving emotion, muscular and mental exertion, and some kind of conceptual representation (for which he finds a peculiar term: self-analysis), he is thinking of individual persons as the subjects of such process. If the modification of consciousness, the habit or habit-change, is indeed the meaning effect, the "real and living" conclusion of each single process of semiosis, then where "the game of semiosis" ends, time and time again, is not exactly in "concrete action," as Eco sees it, but in a disposition, a readiness (for action), a set of expectations. Moreover, if the chain of meaning comes to a halt, however temporarily, it is by anchoring itself to somebody, some body, an individual subject.[25] As we use or receive signs, we produce interpretants. Their significate effects must pass through each of us, each body and each consciousness, before they may produce an effect or an action upon the world. *The individual's habit as a semiotic production is both the result and the condition of the social production of meaning.*

With regard to Eco's view of the dialectic of codes and modes of sign production, this puts into question the corollary opposition, between producers and users of signs, that seems integral to it. But to question the theoretical validity of that opposition is not to counter it with the identity of writer and reader, to say that filmmaker and spectator, or speaker and listener are interchangeable positions. For this would abolish the important distinction between enunciation and reception, and thus preempt any critical analysis of their context and of the political nature of address: the relations of power involved in enunciation and reception, which sustain the hierarchies of communication; the control of the means of production; the ideological construction of authorship and mastery; or more plainly, who speaks to whom, why, and for whom. If I question the necessity of a theoretical opposition, albeit dialectical, between producers and users, it is with another objective: to shift its ground and its focus, to say that the interpreter, the "user" of the sign(s), is also the producer of the meaning (interpretant) because that interpreter is the place in which, the body in whom, the significance effect of the sign takes hold. That is the subject in and for whom semiosis takes effect.

It might be interesting here to reconsider Peirce's definition (1897),

> A sign, or representamen, is something which stands to somebody for something in some respect or capacity. It addresses somebody, that is, it creates in the mind of that person an equivalent sign, or perhaps a more developed sign [the interpretant],

and bring it face to face with Lacan's equally famous, and ostensibly antithetical, formula: "a signifier represents a subject for another signifier."[26] In light of Peirce's later elaboration of the notion of interpretant (dated ca. 1905), as I have discussed it, the doubt crops up whether the two formulations of the relation of subject and sign are so antithetical, worlds apart, irreconcilable, or whether, after all, they may be more compatible than they are made out to be. We may keep in mind that the essay in which Lacan's statement appears, "Position de l'inconscient" (1964), makes a direct if nameless reference to Peirce's, with the clear intent to oppose it.[27]

The second sentence in Peirce's statement, which is more often than not omitted when the definition is quoted, shifts the emphasis from the sign or representamen (the signifier) to the subject, the person for whom the interpretant represents "perhaps *a more developed sign.*" Peirce's subject is thus actually placed between the two signs, as Lacan's is between two signifiers. The difference is in the orientation of the movement, the sense of the representation as expressed by the word "for": Peirce's signs represent *for* a subject, Lacan's subject represents *for* the signifiers. Lacan's formula is intended to stress the "causation" of the subject in language (the "discourse of the Other") and the subject's inadequacy, its "lack-in-being" vis-à-vis the Other; for in the very moment and by the very fact of its utterance, the subject of the enunciation is split from itself as subject of the enounced. Consequently, the speaking subject and the subject of its, or rather *the*, statement are never one; the subject does not own its statement, the signifier, which is in the domain of the Other. In the process of signification conceived of as a chain of signifiers, then, the relation of the subject to the chain of its discourse is always of the order of a near-miss. As Lacan puts it, the signifier plays and wins *(joue et gagne)* before the subject is aware of it. For Lacan, the division or alienation of the subject in language is constitutive *("originaire")* and structural, a-temporal.

In Peirce's formula, the subject's division from itself occurs in a temporal dimension ("in the flow of time" [5.421]), but it also occurs by means of its relation to the chain of interpretants. As each interpretant results in habit or habit-change, the process of semiosis comes to a stop, provisionally, by fixing itself to a subject who is but *temporarily* there.[28] In Lacanian terms, this fixing might be designated by the term "suture," which carries the implication of delusion, "pseudo-identification," imaginary closure, even false consciousness, as the product of the operations of ideology. And in the general critical discourse based on Lacanian psychoanalysis and Althusser's theory of ideology, "suture" is bad.[29] Peirce, on the other hand, does not say whether the habit that provisionally joins the subject to social and ideological formations is good or bad. But this, there should be no need to point out, is hardly the same as claiming a transcendental reality for the subject or for the world. It seems to me, in short, that in opposing the truth of the unconscious to the illusion of an always already-false consciousness, the general critical discourse based on Lacanian psychoanalysis subscribes too easily, as Eco does, to the territorial distinction between subjective and social modes of signification and the cold war that is its issue.

If one looks up the word "desire" in the index of subjects of Peirce's *Collected Papers,* one finds it in volume 5, cross-referenced with "Effort." In 5.486, it is mentioned as one of the four categories of mental facts that are of general reference: desires, expectations, conceptions, and habits. Unlike habit, which is the effect of effort (or more exactly of the combined action of semiosis through the three types of interpretants), desire for Peirce "is cause, not effect, of effort." That is to say, desires—the plural is significant—are something of a conceptual nature, like expectations and conceptions. In Laplanche and Pontalis's *Vocabulaire de la psychanalyse,* published in English as *The Language of Psycho-Analysis,* the word "Desire" appears in parentheses behind the title of the entry "Wish." The authors explain that Freud's term, *Wunsch,* corresponds rather to "wish" than to "desire," and that although *Wunsch* refers primarily to unconscious wishes, Freud did not always use the word strictly in that sense. At any rate, Freud did not use the word "desire." Lacan did, as he "attempted to re-orientate Freud's doctrine around the notion of desire," distinguishing it from the adjacent concepts of need (directed toward specific objects and satisfied by them) and demand (addressed to others and, regardless of its object, essentially a demand for love or recognition by the other). "Desire appears in the rift which separates need and demand." Like the subject, whose division it signifies, desire is an alienation in language.

The caption definition of "Wish (Desire)," however, states:

> [In Freud] unconscious wishes tend to be fulfilled through the restoration of signs which are bound to the earliest experiences of satisfaction; this restoration operates according to the laws of primary processes.... Wishes, in the form of compromises, may be identified in symptoms.[30]

I do not think it preposterous to read the definition as bearing the possible meaning that (unconscious) wishes are the effect of unconscious effort and indeed habit; thereby to speculate that, if such a thing as unconscious habit (unconscious in Freud's sense, habit in Peirce's) can be theoretically conceivable, wishes—whether conscious or unconscious—may be thought of as both the effect and the cause of effort and habit; and then finally to suggest that a cautious, very

cautious journey into the terrain of subjectivity as conscious *and* unconscious might begin here for someone not willing to accept Eco's or
Kristeva's boundaries, heedless of the territorial claims of either discourse, semiotics or psychoanalysis, someone refusing to choose between instinct and reason.[31]

I started out, in this chapter, from a question only implicit in the
irony of Woolf's "instinct rather than reason" quip, but explicitly
posed as the very project of her book, *A Room of One's Own*—a book
and a question, furthermore, explicitly addressed to women: how
does "I" come to know herself as "a woman," how is the speaking/
writing self en-gendered as a female subject? The answer rendered in
the passage is only a partial answer. By certain signs, Woolf says; not
only language (no words are exchanged between "I" and the Beadle)
but gestures, visual signs, and something else which establishes their
relation to the self and thus their meaning, "I was a woman." That
something, she calls "instinct" for lack of a better word. In order to
pursue the question, I have proposed instead the term "experience"
and used it to designate an ongoing process by which subjectivity is
constructed semiotically and historically. Borrowing Peirce's notion of
"habit" as the issue of a series of "significate effects," or meaning
effects, produced in semiosis, I have then sought to define experience
more accurately as a complex of habits resulting from the semiotic
interaction of "outer world" and "inner world," the continuous engagement of a self or subject in social reality. And since both the
subject and social reality are understood as entities of a semiotic nature, as "signs," semiosis names the process of their reciprocally constitutive effects.

The question can now be rephrased in this way: is the female subject one constituted in a particular kind of relation to social reality? by
a particular kind of experience, specifically a particular experience of
sexuality? And if we answer that, yes, a certain experience of sexuality
does effect a social being which we may call the female subject; if it is
that experience, that complex of habits, dispositions, associations and
perceptions, which en-genders one as female, then *that* is what remains to be analyzed, understood, articulated by feminist theory. The
point of my return to Peirce, rereading him through Eco, was to
restore the body to the interpreter, the subject of semiosis. That subject, I have argued, is the place in which, the body in whom, the

significate effect of the sign takes hold and is real-ized. It should not be inferred, however, that Peirce ever so much as suggests what kind of body it is, or how the body is itself produced as a sign *for* the subject and variously represented in the mutually constitutive interaction of inner and outer worlds. In this question, Peirce is no help at all. Nevertheless, the notion of habit as "energetic" attitude, a somatic disposition at once abstract and concrete, the crystallized form of past muscular/mental effort, is powerfully suggestive of a subject touched by the practice of signs, a subject physically implicated or bodily engaged in the production of meaning, representation and self-representation.

We may recall, in this context, the observations made in the previous chapter on the basis of Kaja Silverman's assertion that the female body "is charted, zoned and made to bear . . . a meaning which proceeds entirely from external relationships, but which is always subsequently apprehended as an internal condition or essence."[32] In her textual example, the heroine's recollection of a picture of a woman about to be beaten by a man, is prompted by an identical actual event, the whipping of the heroine by her master. The cultural meaning of the image, woman's subjugation, acquires its subjective meaning (guilt and pleasure) for the heroine through her identification with the image, an identification resulting from the identical behavior of the two men. As Silverman notes, the representation structures and gives meaning to the present event (her whipping by her master), and yet the "memory" of the picture occurs as a consequence of that very event. The nexus sign-meaning, in other words, is not only significant *for* a subject, the heroine in whose body the muscular/mental effort produces the "logical" significate effect (her identification with the "guilty woman"), the memory and the habit (woman's subjection and masochistic pleasure). But the significance of the sign could not take effect, that is to say, the sign would not be a sign, without the existence or the subject's experience of a *social practice* in which the subject is physically involved; in this case, the employ of corporal punishment to chastise and educate, or rather, chastise and educate to give pleasure.

The intimate relationship of subjectivity to practices is recognized by psychoanalysis and semiotics in the expression "signifying practice(s)," but seldom analyzed outside of verbal or literary textual practices, cinema being the notable exception. The dominance of linguistic determination in theories of the subject, and the objectivist or logico-mathematical bias of most semiotic research have made the notion of signifying practice restrictive and over-specialized, forcing it into what amounts to theoretical obsolescence. This could have severe consequences for feminism, a critical discourse that begins as a reflection on practice and only exists as such in conjunction with it. Feminist theory constitutes itself as a reflection on practice and experience: an experience to which sexuality must be seen as central in that it determines, through gender identification, the social dimension of female subjectivity, one's personal experience of femaleness; and a practice aimed at confronting that experience and changing women's lives concretely, materially, and through consciousness.

The relevance to theoretical feminism of the notion of semiosis, such as I have outlined it, seems undeniable. In the first place, semiosis specifies the mutual overdetermination of meaning, perception, and experience, a complex nexus of reciprocally constitutive effects between the subject and social reality, which, in the subject, entail a continual modification of consciousness; that consciousness in turn being the condition of social change. In the second place, the notion of semiosis is *theoretically* dependent on the intimate relationship of subjectivity and practices; and the place of sexuality in that relationship, feminism has shown, is what defines sexual difference *for women*, and gives femaleness its meaning as the experience of a female subject.

If, as Catharine MacKinnon states in the essay cited earlier on, "sexuality is to feminism what work is to marxism: that which is most one's own, yet most taken away" (p. 515), that which is most personal and at the same time most socially determined, most defining of the self and most exploited or controlled, then to ask the question of what constitutes female sexuality, for women and for feminism (the emphasis is important), is to come to know things in a different way, and to come to know them as political. Since one "becomes a woman" through the experience of sexuality, issues such as lesbianism, contraception, abortion, incest, sexual harassment, rape, prostitution, and pornography are not merely social (a problem for society as a whole) or merely sexual (a private affair between "consenting adults" or within the privacy of the family); for women, they are political and epistemological. "To feminism, the personal is epistemologically the political, and its epistemology *is* its politics" (p. 535). This is the sense in which it is possible to argue, as MacKinnon does, that consciousness raising is a "critical method," a specific mode of apprehension or "appropriation" of reality. The fact that today the expression "consciousness raising" has become dated and more than slightly unpleasant, as any word will that has been appropriated, diluted, digested and spewed out by the media, does not diminish the social and subjective impact of a practice—the collective articulation of one's experience of sexuality and gender—which has produced, and continues to elaborate, a radically new mode of understanding the subject's relation to social-historical reality. Consciousness raising is the original critical instrument that women have developed toward such understanding, the analysis of social reality, and its critical revision. The Italian feminists call it "*autocoscienza*," selfconsciousness, and better still, self consciousness. For example, Manuela Fraire: "the practice of self consciousness is the way in which women reflect politically on their own condition."[33]

I have been struck by the resonance of this word, self consciousness (which in the re-translation seems to lose its popular sense of uneasiness or excessive preoccupation with one's manner or looks, and to revert to the more literal sense of "consciousness of self"), with the curious adjective, "self-analyzing," that Peirce saw fit to use as modifier of "habit" in his description of the ultimate meaning-effect of signs: "The deliberately formed self-analyzing habit—self-analyzing because formed by the aid of analysis of the exercises that nourished it—is the living definition, the veritable and final logical interpretant" (5.491). This statement occurs in the context of an example Peirce gives to illustrate the process of semiosis. The point of the example is to show how one acquires a demonstrative knowledge of the solution of a certain problem of reasoning. A few lines above those just quoted we read: "the activity takes the form of experimentation in the inner world; and the conclusion (if it comes to a definite conclusion), is that under given conditions, the interpreter will have formed the habit of acting in a given way whenever he may desire a given kind of result. The real and living logical conclusion *is* that habit; the verbal formulation merely expresses it." I am again struck by the coincidence, for the feminist mode of analyzing self and reality has also been a mode of acting politically, in the public as well as in the private sphere. As a form of political critique or critical politics, feminism has not only "invented" new strategies, new semiotic contents and new signs, but more importantly it has effected a habit-change in readers, spectators, speakers, etc. And with that habit-change it has produced a new social subject, women. The practice of self consciousness, in short, has a constitutiveness as well as a constituency.

This is where the specificity of a feminist theory may be sought: not in femininity as a privileged nearness to nature, the body, or the unconscious, an essence which inheres in women but to which males too now lay a claim; not in a female tradition simply understood as private, marginal and yet intact, outside of history but fully there to be discovered or recovered; not, finally, in the chinks and cracks of masculinity, the fissures of male identity or the repressed of phallic discourse; but rather in that political, theoretical, self-analyzing practice by which the relations of the subject in social reality can be rearticulated from the historical experience of women. Much, very much, is still to be done, therefore. "Post-feminism," the *dernier cri* making its way across the Atlantic into feminist studies and the critical establishment, "is not an idea whose time has come," Mary Russo remarks, and then goes on to show how indeed "it is not an idea at all."[34]

From a city built to represent woman, but where no women live, we have come to the gravel path of the academic campus. We have learned that one becomes a woman in the very practice of signs by which we live, write, speak, see. . . . This is neither an illusion nor a paradox. It is a real contradiction—women continue to become woman. The essays collected here have attempted to work through and with the subtle, shifting, duplicitous terms of that contradiction, but not to reconcile them. For it seems to me that only by knowingly enacting and re-presenting them, by knowing us to be both woman and women, does a woman today become a subject. In this 1984, it is the signifier who plays and wins before Alice does, even when she's aware of it. But to what end, if Alice doesn't?

NOTES

Introduction

1. Lewis Carroll, *The Annotated Alice*, with an introduction and notes by Martin Gardner (Cleveland and New York: The World Publishing Company, 1963), p. 269. The other passages cited below are on pp. 261, 262, and 270.

2. M. Bakhtin, *The Dialogic Imagination*, ed. Michael Holquist (Austin and London: University of Texas Press, 1981), p. 294.

3. J. Hillis Miller, "Ariadne's Thread: Repetition and the Narrative Line," *Critical Inquiry* 3, no. 1 (Autumn 1976), suggests that Ariadne's thread "maps the whole labyrinth, rather than providing a single track to its center and back out. The thread is the labyrinth, and at the same time it is the repetition of the labyrinth" (p. 70). Thus the Minotaur or spider at the center of the maze is the "weaver of a web which is herself, and which both hides and reveals an absence, the abyss" (p. 73). Miller does not refer to Humpty Dumpty, but I submit that the latter's "web" of words is much more appropriate to Miller's point about literature and literary criticism than is the reference chosen by Miller, Arachne, the spider "who devours her mate." In the politics of literary reference, Carroll here comes out ahead.

4. Anthony Wilden, *System and Structure: Essays in Communication and Exchange* (London: Tavistock, 1972), p. 294.

5. Claire Johnston, ed., *Notes on Women's Cinema* (London: SEFT, 1974), pp. 28–29.

6. Virginia Woolf, *A Room of One's Own* (New York and London: Harcourt Brace Jovanovich, 1929), p. 35; Laura Mulvey, "Visual Pleasure and Narrative Cinema," *Screen* 16, no. 3 (Autumn 1975): 6–18.

7. Luce Irigaray, "La tache aveugle d'un vieux rêve de symétrie," in *Speculum de l'autre femme* (Paris: Minuit, 1974), pp. 7–162.

1. Through the Looking-Glass: Woman, Cinema, and Language

1. Italo Calvino, *Invisible Cities*, trans. William Weaver (New York: Harcourt Brace Jovanovich, 1974) from Italo Calvino, *Le città invisibili* (Turin: Einaudi, 1972). I have slightly altered Weaver's translation of p. 52 of the Italian edition.

2. I have discussed this at length in "Semiotic Models, *Invisible Cities*," *Yale Italian Studies* 2 (Winter 1978): 13–37.

3. Teresa de Lauretis and Stephen Heath, eds., *The Cinematic Apparatus* (London: Macmillan, and New York: St. Martin's Press, 1980), p. 6.

4. "Motivate" here is to be understood not as intentionality or design on the part of individuals who promote those discourses, but rather in the sense in which Marx describes the social determinations by which the capitalist, for example, is not a "bad" person but a function in a specific system of social relations.

5. Roman Jakobson, "Closing Statement: Linguistics and Poetics," in *Style in Language*, ed. Thomas A. Sebeok (Cambridge, Mass: The MIT Press, 1960), p. 368.

6. Claude Lévi-Strauss, *Structural Anthropolopgy* (Garden City, New York: Doubleday, 1967), p. 60. My emphasis.

7. Claude Lévi-Strauss, *The Elementary Structures of Kinship* (Boston: Beacon Press, 1969), p. 496.

8. Elizabeth Cowie, "Woman as Sign," *m/f*, no. 1 (1978), p. 57.

9. Jean Baudrillard, *The Mirror of Production* (St. Louis: Telos Press, 1975).

10. Lévi-Strauss, *Elementary Structures of Kinship*, p. 496.

11. Lévi-Strauss, *Structural Anthropology*, pp. 198–99. In this essay, entitled "The Effectiveness of Symbols," Lévi-Strauss interprets a Cuna incantation performed by the shaman to facilitate childbirth. Several of the terms used here by Lévi-Strauss return as metaphors in the language of Lacan's reading of the child's *fort-da* game described by Freud: "It is with his object [the spool, the object little a] that that infant leaps the boundaries of his domain transformed into holes, shafts, and with which he commences his incantation." Jacques Lacan, *Le Seminaire IX;* quoted by Constance Penley, "The Avant-Garde and Its Imaginary," *Camera Obscura*, no. 2 (Fall 1977), p. 30.

12. Gayle Rubin, "The Traffic in Women: Notes on the 'Political Economy' of Sex," in *Toward an Anthropology of Women*, ed. Rayna R. Reiter (New York: Monthly Review Press, 1975), pp. 191–92.

13. Jacques Lacan, "Pour une logique du fantasme," *Scilicet*, no. 2/3 (1970), p. 259; quoted by John Brenkman, "The Other and the One: Psycho-analysis, Reading, the *Symposium*," *Yale French Studies*, no. 55/56 (1977): 441; my emphasis.

14. "Where the conception of the symbolic as movement and production of difference, as chain of signifiers in which the subject is effected in division, should forbid the notion of some presence from which difference is then derived; Lacan instates the visible as the condition of symbolic functioning, with the phallus the standard of visibility required: seeing is from the male organ." Stephen Heath, "Difference," *Screen* 19, no. 3 (Autumn 1978): 52 and 54. See also Luce Irigaray's critique of this seminar, "Cosi fan tutti," in *Ce sexe qui n'en est pas un* (Paris: Minuit, 1977), pp. 84–101.

15. Heath, "Difference," pp. 54 and 66. The ambiguity in the phallus/penis relation is emphasized by J. Laplanche and J.–B. Pontalis in *The Language of Psycho-Analysis*, trans. Donald Nicholson-Smith (New York: Norton, 1973), pp. 312–14. See also Anthony Wilden, "The Critique of Phallocentrism," in *System and Structure* (London: Tavistock, 1972).

16. Lea Melandri, *L'infamia originaria* (Milan: Edizioni L'Erba Voglio, 1977), p. 25. My translation.

17. Christian Metz, *Le signifiant imaginaire* (Paris: UGE, 1977). All page references hereafter are to the English translation by Ben Brewster, "The Imaginary Signifier," *Screen* 16, no. 2 (Summer 1975): 14–76, now reprinted in *The Imaginary Signifier* (Bloomington: Indiana University Press, 1981).

18. Laplanche and Pontalis, p. 313.

19. After stating that "the psychoanalytic itinerary is *from the outset a semiological one*" (p. 14), Metz then singles out linguistics and psychoanalysis as the sciences of the symbolic *par excellence*, "the only two sciences whose immediate and sole object is the fact of signification as such," which specifically explore, respectively, the secondary and the primary processes, and "between them . . . cover the whole field of the *signification-fact*" (p. 28). Where, then, does semiotics (or semiology) stand in relation to the fact of signification?

What distinguishes the theoretical project of semiotics from those of linguistics and psychoanalysis?

20. Yann Lardeau, "Le sexe froid (du porno au dela)," *Cahiers du cinéma,* no. 289 (June 1978), pp. 49, 52, and 61. My translation.

21. Ibid., pp. 51 and 54.

22. Stephen Heath, *Questions of Cinema* (Bloomington: Indiana University Press, 1981), p. 154.

23. See, in particular, Stephen Heath, "Narrative Space," in *Questions of Cinema,* pp. 19–75.

24. *"Empire of the Senses* is crossed by that possibility of a nothing seen, which is its very trouble of representation, but that possibility is not posed, as it were, from some outside; on the contrary, it is produced as a contradiction within the given system of representation, the given machine" (Heath, *Questions of Cinema,* p. 162). The thought is further developed in the following passage: "The order of the look in the work of the film is neither the thematics of voyeurism (note already the displacement of the look's subject from men to women) nor the binding structure of a classic narrative disposition (where character look is an element at once of the form of content, the definition of the action in the movement of looks exchanged, and of the form of expression, the composition of the images and their arrangement together, their 'match'). Its register is not that of the 'out of frame', the *hors-champ* to be recaptured in the film by the spatially suturing process of 'folding over' of which field/reverse-field is the most obvious device, but that of the edging of every frame, of every shot, towards a *problem* of 'seeing' for the spectator" (ibid., p. 150).

25. Judith Mayne, in "Women and Film: A Discussion of Feminist Aesthetics," *New German Critique,* no. 13 (Winter 1978), p. 86.

26. Metz, "The Imaginary Signifier," pp. 51 and 52.

27. Stephen Heath, "Questions of Property," *Cine-Tracts,* no. 4 (Spring-Summer 1978), p. 6.

28. See, for example, Maureen Turim, "The Place of Visual Illusions"; Peter Gidal, "Technology and Ideology in/through/and Avant-Garde Film: An Instance"; and Jacqueline Rose, "The Cinematic Apparatus: Problems in Current Theory"; all in de Lauretis and Heath, pp. 143–86.

29. Ruby Rich, in "Women and Film: A Discussion of Feminist Aesthetics," p. 87. Rich here refers to Laura Mulvey, "Visual Pleasure and Narrative Cinema," *Screen* 16, no. 3 (Autumn 1975): 6–18; and to Pam Cook and Claire Johnston, "The Place of Women in the Cinema of Raoul Walsh," in *Raoul Walsh,* ed. Phil Hardy (Edinburgh: Edinburgh Film Festival, 1974), pp. 93–109.

30. Melandri, p. 27. My translation.

31. Many have argued for Lacan's project as a materialist theory of language, and in particular a materialist rewriting of the idealist discourse on love from Plato on (see John Brenkman, "The Other and the One: Psychoanalysis, Reading, the *Symposium"*). But where a dialectic is certainly the movement of the subject's passage through language, and thus of its "personal" history, it is not at all clear to me whether that dialectic is a materialist or a Hegelian one; in a preestablished structural order, a logic of the signifier, that is always already determined for each entering subject, the personal history comes very close to being written with a capital H.

32. Heath, *Questions of Cinema*, pp. 19–75.

33. See Paul Willemen, "Reflections on Eikhenbaum's Concept of Internal Speech in the Cinema," *Screen* 15, no. 4 (Winter 1974/5): 59–70; and "Cinematic Discourse: The Problem of Inner Speech," *Screen* 22, no. 3 (1981): 63–93; and Stephen Heath, "Language, Sight and Sound" in *Questions of Cinema*, pp. 194–220.

34. Metz, in *The Cinematic Apparatus*, p. 23.

35. Heath, *Questions of Cinema*, p. 107.

36. Paul Willemen, "Notes on Subjectivity," *Screen* 19, no. 1 (Spring 1978): 43.

37. Umberto Eco, *A Theory of Semiotics* (Bloomington: Indiana University Press, 1976), p. 49.

38. Ibid., p. 78. This is one reason why translation presents problems and why a film can be read so differently in different cultures or viewing situations; for example, Antonioni's controversial documentary on China, *Chung Kuo*, discussed by Eco in an interview with William Luhr in *Wide Angle* 1, no. 4 (1977): 64–72.

39. Eco, *A Theory of Semiotics*, pp. 65–66. The quotation has been slightly edited.

40. Sheila Rowbotham, *Woman's Consciousness, Man's World* (Harmondsworth: Penguin Books, 1973).

2. Imaging

1. A compact and fully articulated formulation of these concepts with regard to cinema may be found in Stephen Heath, *Questions of Cinema* (Bloomington: Indiana University Press, 1981), especially chapter 1, "On Screen, In Frame: Film and Ideology," and chapter 10, "The Cinematic Apparatus: Technology as Historical and Cultural Form." On the notion of signifying practice, see also Julia Kristeva, "Signifying Practice and Mode of Production," *Edinburgh '76 Magazine* (London: British Film Institute, 1976), pp. 64–76.

2. While some works assume that cinema and film make up and circulate certain images of women, and accordingly examine and classify them, others start from the premise that cinema and film construct woman as image, and take as their task the understanding of that process in relation to, or as it affects, female spectators. As even a basic list of bibliographical references would be too extensive, only a few will be cited. In the first category, see Marjorie Rosen, *Popcorn Venus: Women, Movies and the American Dream* (New York: Avon Books, 1973); Joan Mellen, *Women and Their Sexuality in the New Film* (New York: Horizon Press, 1974); Molly Haskell, *From Reverence to Rape: The Treatment of Women in the Movies* (New York: Holt, Rinehart and Winston, 1974). The notion of images of women is critically discussed in the following: Claire Johnston, "Feminist Politics and Film History," *Screen* 16, no. 3 (Autumn 1975): 115–24; Griselda Pollock, "What's Wrong with Images of Women," *Screen Education*, no. 23 (Summer 1977), pp. 25–33; Elizabeth Cowie, "Women, Representation and the Image," *Screen Education*, no. 23 (Summer 1977), pp. 15–23. As for the second category, which I refer to as the feminist critique of representation, the following are general and/or survey works which provide additional and specific references: Claire Johnston, ed., *Notes on Women's Cinema* (London: SEFT, 1974); Julia Lesage, "Feminist Film

Criticism: Theory and Practice," *Women and Film,* no. 5/6 (1974), pp. 12–14; "Feminism and Film: Critical Approaches," editorial, *Camera Obscura,* no. 1 (Fall 1976), pp. 3–10; Karyn Kay and Gerald Peary, eds., *Women and Cinema: A Critical Anthology* (New York: Dutton, 1977); Christine Gledhill, "Recent Developments in Feminist Criticism," *Quarterly Review of Film Studies* 3, no. 4 (1978): 457–93; Laura Mulvey, "Feminism, Film and the Avant-Garde," *Framework,* no. 10 (1979), pp. 3–10; Annette Kuhn, *Women's Pictures* (London: Routledge & Kegan Paul, 1982); E. Ann Kaplan, *Women and Film: Both Sides of the Camera* (London and New York: Methuen, 1983).

3. Basic works in these areas, with regard to cinema, include Teresa de Lauretis and Stephen Heath, eds., *The Cinematic Apparatus* (London: Macmillan, and New York: St. Martin's Press, 1980); Christian Metz, *Film Language: A Semiotics of the Cinema,* trans. Michael Taylor (New York: Oxford University Press, 1974), *Language and Cinema* (The Hague and Paris: Mouton, 1974), and *The Imaginary Signifier* (Bloomington: Indiana University Press, 1981); *Screen Reader 1* (London: SEFT, 1980) and *Screen Reader 2* (London: SEFT, 1981); Bill Nichols, *Ideology and the Image* (Bloomington: Indiana University Press, 1981).

4. "The linguistic sign unites, not a thing and a name, but a concept and a sound-image *[image acoustique].* The latter is not the material sound, a purely physical thing, but the psychological imprint of the sound, the impression that it makes on our sense. The sound-image is sensory, and if I happen to call it 'material', it is only in that sense, and by way of opposing it to the other term of the association, the concept, which is generally more abstract." Ferdinand de Saussure, *Course in General Linguistics* (New York: Philosophical Library, 1959), p. 12.

5. For the redefinition of the sign as sign-function, see Umberto Eco, *A Theory of Semiotics* (Bloomington: Indiana University Press, 1976). All further references to this work will be cited in the text.

6. The debate is succinctly summarized in Eco, *La struttura assente* (Milan: Bompiani, 1968), pp. 149–60, and in Stephen Heath, "Film/Cinetext/Text," *Screen* 14, no. 1/2 (Spring/Summer 1973): 102–27, now in *Screen Reader 2.* This *Reader* as a whole is a useful document of the first impact of semiology (though primarily French works) on British film culture.

7. "The expressiveness of the world (of the landscape or face) and the expressiveness of art (the melancholy sound of the Wagnerian oboe) are ruled essentially by the same semiological mechanism: *'Meaning' is naturally derived from the signifier as a whole, without resorting to a code.* It is at the level of the signifier, and only there, that the difference occurs: In the first case the author is nature (expressiveness of the world) and in the second it is man (expressiveness of art)." Christian Metz, *Film Language,* p. 79. My emphasis.

8. Pier Paolo Pasolini, *Empirismo eretico* (Milan: Garzanti, 1972), p. 207. All references to this work, in my translation, will be cited in the text.

9. Eco's own analysis of cinematic articulation, which I now discuss, may be found in *La struttura assente,* pp. 154–58.

10. Emilio Garroni, *Semiotica ed estetica* (Bari: Laterza, 1968), p. 17. My translation.

11. Cf. Joseph and Barbara Anderson, "Motion Perception in Motion Pictures"; and Susan Lederman and Bill Nichols, "Flicker and Motion in Film," both in de Lauretis and Heath.

12. Precisely this spatiotemporal relation is what Pasolini was concerned to identify, and tentatively called "ritmema" in a short paper of 1971 entitled "Teoria delle giunte" (A Theory of Splicing), now in *Empirismo eretico*.

13. Eco, *La struttura assente*, p. 159.

14. "If language is everywhere, it is not as simple system but, exactly, as practice. One encounters not 'language' or 'a language' but practices of language; language exists only as signifying practice—'discursive formations' are signifying practices of language—and itself offers no unity to which subject and signification can be returned." Stephen Heath, "The Turn of the Subject," *Cine-Tracts*, no. 7/8 (Summer/Fall 1979), p. 43.

15. Claire Johnston, "The Subject of Feminist Film Theory/Practice," *Screen* 21 (Summer 1980): 30.

16. Eco's thesis that the presumed similarity of iconic signs to their referents is also a matter of cultural convention ("similarity does not concern the relationship between the image and its object but that between the image and a previously culturalized content," p. 204) is buttressed with examples from Gombrich, *Art and Illusion*. The function of iconic conventions as "standards of truth" will taken up later, as I discuss Gombrich's views in greater detail. For the notion of pertinence as it relates to purposeful human activity in the marxian sense, see Luís Prieto, *Pertinence et pratique* (Paris: Minuit, 1975).

17. For example, Eco cites Dürer's drawing of a rhinoceros covered with scales and imbricated plates, an image that reappeared unchanged in the books of explorers and zoologists for over two centuries; although the latter had seen actual rhinoceroses and knew better, the imbricated plates were the conventional graphic sign to denote the roughness of the skin. However ridiculous the drawing might seem today, when compared to the photograph of an actual rhinoceros in which the skin appears uniform and almost smooth, Dürer's exaggerated representation is more effective in rendering the impression of the skin's roughness (in comparison, say, with human skin) that one would have in looking at the rhinoceros close by. Thus, he concludes, "Dürer's rhinoceros is more successful in portraying, if not actual rhinoceroses, at best our cultural conception of a rhinoceros. Maybe it does not portray our visual experience, but it certainly does portray our semantic knowledge or at any rate that shared by its addressees" (p. 205). The problem with Eco's analysis is obvious: he assumes that viewers—the "addressees" of the image, constitute a homogeneous category and therefore share not only a common "semantic knowledge" but the same "visual experience" as well. The difficulty becomes insuperable if we simply replace the image of a rhinoceros with an image of woman, which in the history of Western iconography is certainly a more frequent occurrence. If we admit (how is it possible not to?) that women and men do not have the same visual experience in looking at an image of woman, and even less the same knowledge of women, what happens then to the communion of meaning and experience on which "our cultural conception" of woman is supposedly founded? The problem, however, is not only in Eco's analysis but, more to the immediate point, in our society's modes of image-production, where indeed all viewers are addressed as male, or, insofar as they are known to be female, they are expected and obliged to share the male's "cultural" conception of woman.

18. As often happened with Pasolini's political positions, in which he will-

fully assumed the role of an extremist critic of bourgeois culture. A negative evaluation of his theoretical work may be found in Antonio Costa, "The Semiological Heresy of Pier Paolo Pasolini," in *Pier Paolo Pasolini*, ed. Paul Willemen (London: British Film Institute, 1977), originally published in 1974. On the other hand Geoffrey Nowell-Smith accurately points out that "Pasolini n'était pas un cinéaste théorique, à la manière de Godard, de Straub/ Huillet ou de Mulvey/Wollen mais il était, parmi ses autres activités intellectuelles, un théoricien de cinéma" ("Pasolini dans le cinéma," in *Pasolini: Séminaire dirigé par Maria Antonietta Macciocchi* [Paris: Grasset, 1980], pp. 91–92).

19 . Pasolini, pp. 209–10. The Italian verb *rappresentare* denotes both to represent and to perform or enact.

20. "*Un complesso mondo di immagini significative*—sia quelle mimiche o ambientali che corredano i linsegni, sia quelle dei ricordi e dei sogni—*che prefigura e si propone come fondamento 'strumentale' della comunicazione cinematografica*" (ibid., p. 172).

21. See Sergei Eisenstein, *Film Form*, ed. and trans. Jay Leyda (New York: Harcourt Brace Jovanovich, 1949), pp. 130–31; Boris Eikhenbaum, "Problems of Film Stylistics," in Poetika Kino (1927), trans. in *Screen* 15 (Autumn 1974), discussed by Paul Willemen (see note 33, chapter 1).

22. Compare, for instance, Pasolini's statement "In our actions, in practical existence, we represent/perform/enact ourselves. Human reality is this double representation in which we are at once actors and spectators" with Heath's notion of film performance: "Cinema is founded as the memory of reality, the spectacle of reality captured and presented. All presentation, however, is representation—a production, a construction of positions and effects—and all representation is performance—the time of that production and construction, of the realization of the positions and effects. Which is why . . . an avant-garde—and political—practice of film is involved necessarily at least in an attention to the real functioning of representation and is involved directly thereby in a problematic of performance, of film performance" (*Questions of Cinema*, p. 115).

23. In *The Role of the Reader* (Bloomington: Indiana University Press, 1979) and *Lector in fabula* (Milan: Bompiani, 1979).

24. As noted by G. C. Ferretti in *La letteratura del rifiuto* (Milan: Mursia, 1968, p. 209), Pasolini in effect poses the problem of how to grasp and become fully conscious of the new social facts which are misunderstood or not accepted by the organized movements aligned with official marxism, and "sees cinema as the only possibility fully to realize the 'expressive needs' which those very facts produce or bring about."

25. *The Book of Progress*, ed. Alfred A. Hopkins (New York, 1915), quoted by Stuart and Elizabeth Ewen, *Channels of Desire: Mass Images and the Shaping of American Consciousness* (New York: McGraw-Hill, 1982), p. 36.

26. Colin Blakemore, "The Baffled Brain," in *Illusion in Nature and Art*, ed. R. L. Gregory and E. H. Gombrich (New York: Scribner's, 1973), p. 26. All further page references in the text are to this edition.

27. Cf. Hermann von Helmholtz, *Handbook of Physiological Optics*, trans. and ed. J. P. Southhall (London and New York, 1963).

28. R. L. Gregory, "The Confounded Eye," in *Illusion in Nature and Art*, p. 61.

29. For example, the word /cinema/: in linguistic terms, when one utters the word /cinema/ one merely reproduces it from the language; one does not invent it, one cannot be creative by changing the phonemes or the morphological aspects of the word. See Eco, *A Theory of Semiotics*, pp. 182–83.

30. The critique of cinema, of course, is not limited to critical discourses on cinema but includes, and to some extent depends on, feminist film practices. A short list of filmmakers whose work has been important to the feminist critique of representation would include Chantal Akerman, Dorothy Arzner, Liliana Cavani, Michelle Citron, Marguerite Duras, Valie Export, Bette Gordon, Bonnie Klein, Babette Mangolte, Laura Mulvey, Ulrike Ottinger, Sally Potter, Yvonne Rainer, Jackie Raynal, Helke Sander.

31. Laura Mulvey, "Visual Pleasure and Narrative Cinema," *Screen* 16, no. 3 (Autumn 1975): 17–18. The passages cited above are on p. 11. On alternative film practice see also Claire Johnston, "Women's Cinema as Counter-Cinema," in *Notes on Women's Cinema*, pp. 24–31.

32. Quoted in E. H. Gombrich, "Illusion and Art," in *Illusion in Nature and Art*, p. 193. This essay is a concise and revised statement of Gombrich's views on illusion, which were initially put forth in his well known *Art and Illusion: A Study in the Psychology of Pictorial Representation* (London, 1960). All further references cited in the text, unless otherwise indicated, are to the 1973 essay, "Illusion and Art."

33. The possibility of anticipating events, the capacity for making some kind of inference from evidence "must sometimes make the difference between life and death. A capacity for anticipatory reactions must therefore be one of the greatest assets evolution can bestow on an organism." Thus, Gombrich suggests, the strict behaviorist notion of learning by automatic trigger actions or stimulus-response conditioning is just as untenable as the Platonic separation between cognition and perception, which it reiterates. Had Pavlov's dog not been "confined in an apparatus," hunger would have made it search its environment for food. And, in a situation not controlled, it would be practically impossible to distinguish which scents and sights might trigger an inborn reaction and which have been learned. We should then rather "picture the organism as scanning the world for meaningful configurations—meaningful, that is, in relation to its chances of survival" ("Illusion and Art," p. 210).

34. Christian Metz, "The Imaginary Signifier," trans. Ben Brewster, *Screen* 16, no. 2 (Summer 1975): 67–76. Cf. Metz's formula (borrowed from Octave Mannoni), "Je sais bien, mais quand même," with Gombrich's Italian idiom, "Non è vero, ma ci credo" ("Illusion and Art," p. 223).

35. See E. H. Gombrich, "Standards of Truth: The Arrested Image and the Moving Eye," in *The Language of Images*, ed. W. J. T. Mitchell (Chicago and London: The University of Chicago Press, 1980), pp. 181–217.

36. Joel Snyder, "Picturing Vision," in ibid., p. 222. All further references to this work will be cited in the text.

37. For a critical history of the camera and the cinematic apparatus, see Jean-Louis Baudry, "Ideological Effects of the Basic Cinematographic Apparatus," *Film Quarterly* 28, no. 2 (Winter 1974–75), and "The Apparatus," *Camera Obscura*, no. 1 (Fall 1976); Jean-Louis Comolli, "Technique and Ideology: Camera, Perspective, Depth of Field," *Film Reader*, no. 2 (1977), pp. 132–38 [a translation of the first part of Comolli's "Technique et idéologie"

published in several issues of *Cahiers du cinéma* beginning with no. 229 (May–June 1971) and continuing through no. 241]. See also Comolli, "Machines of the Visible" and Peter Wollen, "Cinema and Technology: A Historical Overview," both in de Lauretis and Heath.

38. The formal account of vision given in the theoretical system of *perspectiva* "required that what we see be understood as the product of a construction, initiated by the impression, but informed at the level of imagination. The rules of perspective construction are, for Alberti, the same rules employed by the imagination in attending to the visible world" (Snyder, p. 231). Moreover, the system contained its own standards of truth: only unified or "certified" judgments about things grasped by the senses are capable of establishing objects as having existence apart from perception; these judgments alone "achieve the purpose of vision. The depiction of incomplete and shifting appearances would imply an inability to act rationally and harmoniously" (p. 236).

39. According to Panofsky, "artistic practice in Italy during the two centuries prior to Alberti was, in fact, tending toward an equation of perception with depiction, and this equation was [essential] for the development of linear perspective" (Snyder, p. 237). And the *camera obscura* described in print for the first time by Cesariano in 1521, nearly a century after the publication of Alberti's text, "is in all essentials the same kind of instrument used by the medieval *perspectiva* theorists" (p. 232). Like cinema, then, perspective was not the invention of a single mind or genius but the point of coalescence of many practices and discourses into one hegemonic social technology.

40. Again, for these crucial formulations film theory is indebted to the work of Stephen Heath; see in particular "Narrative Space," in *Questions of Cinema*. For the notion of *vérité romanesque* or truth of the novel, as opposed to the Romantic lie of triangular desire, see René Girard, *Desire, Deceit, and the Novel* (Baltimore: The Johns Hopkins Press, 1965).

41. On these strategies of materialist avant-garde cinema see Stephen Heath, "Repetition Time" in *Questions of Cinema,* and Constance Penley, "The Avant-Garde and Its Imaginary," *Camera Obscura*, no. 2 (Fall 1977), pp. 3–33. Basic works on structural-materialist cinema to which both essays refer are Peter Gidal, ed., *Structural Film Anthology* (London: British Film Institute, 1976) and Malcolm Le Grice, *Abstract Film and Beyond* (London: Studio Vista and Cambridge, Mass.: MIT Press, 1977). In this sense and with this emphasis, I agree with Willemen's criticism of "Visual Pleasure and Narrative Cinema": "Mulvey overlooks the fact that in so-called non-narrative films exactly the same mechanisms are at play: scopophilia, fetishism and sadism. Mulvey's article ends with what appears to be an error prompted by her concern to relate a feminist politics to an avant garde orthodoxy. Undoubtedly, the kind of voyeuristic pleasure which involves sadistic/fetishistic pleasure at the expense of an objectification of the image of women must be attacked and destroyed. But this does not mean that it is possible, or indeed, desirable, to expel these drives from the filmic process altogether, as such a move would simply abolish cinema itself. It is essential if cinema is to continue to exist that the scopophilic drive be granted some satisfaction. *What matters is not whether this pleasure is present or absent, but the positioning of the subject in relation to it.*" Paul Willemen, "Voyeurism, the Look and Dwoskin," *Afterimage*, no. 6 (1976), pp. 44–45; my emphasis.

3. Snow on the Oedipal Stage

1. "Michael Snow," in *Structural Film Anthology*, ed. Peter Gidal (London: BFI, 1978), p. 37.

2. Stephen Heath, "Narrative Space," in *Questions of Cinema* (Bloomington: Indiana University Press, 1981).

3. "The Question Oshima," in ibid., p. 148. All further references to this work will be cited in the text.

4. *Film Comment* (May–June 1981), p. 37.

5. Julia Kristeva, "Interview," trans. Claire Pajaczkowska, *m/f*, no. 5/6 (1981), p. 166.

6. Peter Wollen, "Manet: Modernism and Avant-Garde," *Screen* 21, no. 2 (Summer 1980): 22.

7. "I am tired of men arguing amongst themselves as to who is the most feminist, frustrated by an object feminism becoming the stakes in a displaced rivalry between men because of a refusal to examine the structure of the relations between themselves," writes Claire Pajaczkowska; and "insofar as this homosexuality . . . is also primarily a history, or more precisely that consistently unspoken process by which the production of history is displaced from its discursive contradictions, it remains the issue that men must now address—that of men's sexualities, the problem of their own desire, the problem of their theory." "The Heterosexual Presumption: A Contribution to the Debate on Pornography," *Screen* 22, no. 1 (1981): 92.

8. "Primary cinematic identification [for Metz] entails not only the spectator's identification *with* the camera but his identification *of* himself as the condition of the possibility of what is perceived on the screen. The film viewer, according to Metz, is positioned by the entire cinematic apparatus as the site of an organization—the viewer lends coherence to the image and is simultaneously posited as a coherent entity. [But] in the realm of artistic practice, identification on the part of the female reader or spectator cannot be, as it is for the male, a mechanism by means of which mastery is assured. On the contrary, if identification is even 'provisionally' linked with the woman (as Irigaray does), it can only be seen as re-inforcing her submission." Mary Ann Doane, "Misrecognition and Identity," *Cine-Tracts*, no. 11 (Fall 1980), pp. 28 and 30. See also Kaja Silverman's discussion of masochism in Freud and in Cavani's film, *The Night Porter*, in "Masochism and Subjectivity," *Framework*, no. 12 (n.d.), pp. 2–9.

9. "Misrecognition and Identity," pp. 31, 29, and 30. The essay by Laura Mulvey referred to is "Visual Pleasure and Narrative Cinema," *Screen* 16, no. 3 (Autumn 1975): 6–18.

10. A.-J. Greimas, *Sémantique structurale* (Paris, 1966); V. Propp, *Morphology of the Folktale* (Austin: University of Texas Press, 1968), p. 79; Claude Lévi-Strauss, *The Raw and the Cooked: Introduction to a Science of Mythology*, vol. I (New York, 1969); Paul Bouissac, "Poetics in the Lion's Den: The Circus Act as a Text," *Modern Language Notes* 86, no. 6 (December 1971): 845–57.

11. J. M. Lotman, "The Discrete Text and the Iconic Text: Remarks on the Structure of Narrative," *New Literary History* 6, no. 2 (Winter 1975): 337.

12. "Snow Drift," *The Village Voice*, April 22–28, 1981, p. 48.

13. "It is through sex—in fact, an imaginary point determined by the deployment of sexuality—that each individual has to pass in order to have access to his own intelligibility . . . to the whole of his body . . . to his identity." Michel

Foucault, *The History of Sexuality, Volume I: An Introduction,* trans. Robert Hurley (New York: Vintage, 1980), pp. 155–56.

4. Now and Nowhere: Roeg's *Bad Timing*

1. By spectatorship I mean that particular relation of viewers to the film text and to cinema as an apparatus of representation which engages the spectators as subjects. Representation, as Stephen Heath puts it, "names the process of the engagement of subjectivity in meaning, the poles of which are the signifier and the subject but which is always a complex, specifically historical and social production. . . . The ideological is not in or equivalent to representation—which, precisely, is this complex process of subjectivity—but is the constant political institution of the productive terms of representation in a generalised system of positions of exchange." "The Turn of the Subject," *Cine-Tracts*, no. 8 (Summer-Fall 1979), pp. 44–45.

2. Michel Foucault, *The History of Sexuality, Volume I: An Introduction,* trans. Robert Hurley (New York: Vintage, 1980), pp. 94–96.

3. When Foucault states, "It is doubtless the strategic codification of these points of resistance that makes a revolution possible" (p. 96), one is reminded of Bloch's notion of an "expectant tendency" in human history which at certain times becomes concrete, as in the French revolution, the Paris commune, the October revolution, etc. At these times, "the objective-real possibilities are acted out," and "the 'potency of human hope' links up with the potentialities within the world" (Ernst Bloch, *On Karl Marx* [New York: Herder and Herder, 1971], p. 136). For Bloch, this utopian tendency was to find concrete expression in marxism, which can account for it in terms of the totality, "as the process latency of a still unfinished world." While the utopian-teleological drift appears to be absent from Foucault's discontinuous "histories," where the world is always both finished and in process, the concern with totality (that according to Bloch characterizes "all authentic philosophy") is not abandoned but transferred to discourse, recast in purely discursive terms.

4. Foucault, p. 97.

5. Fernando Solanas and Octavio Getino, "Toward a Third Cinema," *Cinéaste* 4, no. 3 (Winter 1970–71): 1–11.

6. See Foucault's analysis of "the perverse implantation" by which "unnatural" sexual behaviors were, first, medically categorized and labeled as sexual perversions, then given juridical status as individual personality types, in *The History of Sexuality*, pp. 36–49. The above excerpts from the dialogue of *Bad Timing*, and all the subsequent ones, are from the actual film soundtrack. I am deeply grateful to Yale M. Udoff for his generosity in discussing the film with me and for allowing me to see his original screenplay as well as the script, bearing the title "Nicolas Roeg's Film *ILLUSIONS*" and dated February 27, 1979 (copyright 1978, Recorded Picture Co., London).

7. It is not accidental that the police(man)'s role is central in narrative cinema. Foucault speaks of *police*, in the broad sense the word had in the sixteenth and seventeenth centuries, to designate the activity or systematic intervention of public institutions, especially the state, in social life for the purpose of steering it toward an ideal order: "The house of confinement in the classical age constitutes the densest symbol of that 'police' which conceived of itself as the civil equivalent of religion for the edification of a perfect city"

(*Madness and Civilization: A History of Insanity in the Age of Reason* [New York: Random House, 1965], p. 63). Insofar as such policing was dependent upon the systematic gathering of information and thus required an organization of knowledge, Gianna Pomata suggests, Foucault's later concept of power/knowledge can be seen as "the abstract formulation of that notion of 'police': an ordering of social reality which constantly sets up for itself new areas of knowledge and control" ("Storie di 'police' e storie di vita: note sulla storiografia foucaultiana," *Aut aut,* 170–71 [marzo-giugno 1979], p. 53; my translation).

8. Foucault, *History of Sexuality,* p. 157.

9. Ibid., p. 96.

10. See *I, Pierre Rivière, having slaughtered my mother, my sister, and my brother . . . A Case of Parricide in the Nineteenth Century* (New York: Pantheon Books, 1975) and Colin Gordon, ed., *Power/Knowledge: Selected Interviews and Other Writings, 1972–1977* (New York: Pantheon Books, 1980).

11. "The proletarian public sphere can best be understood as a necessary form of mediating, as the center of a production process in the course of which the varied and fragmented experiences of social contradictions and social interests can be combined into a theoretically mediated consciousness and life style directed towards a transforming praxis. Thus, the concept of the 'proletarian public sphere' designates the contradictory and non-linear process of development towards class consciousness . . . a form of interaction which expresses the vital interests of the working class in a specific form while relating them to the entire society . . . mediating between social being and consciousness" (Eberhard Knoedler-Bunte, "The Proletarian Public Sphere and Political Organization: An Analysis of Oskar Negt and Alexander Kluge's *The Public Sphere and Experience,*" *New German Critique,* no. 4 (Winter 1975), p. 56. The reference is to Oskar Negt und Alexander Kluge, *Oeffentlichkeit und Erfahrung: Zur Organisationsanalyse von buergerlicher und proletarischer Oeffentlichkeit* (Frankfurt am Main, 1973).

12. "The genealogical discourse on power appears to merge into a sort of mysticism of indetermination. Hence the impression of weakness Foucault's discourse produces, its paradoxical 'conservatism', in spite of its apparent revolutionary charge: on the one hand it falls into a kind of anarchy; on the other, in the absence of a determinate alternative, the analysis of the mechanisms of power becomes merely a description of the universal modalities of the construction of reality" (Franco Crespi, "Foucault o il rifiuto della determinazione," *Aut aut,* 170–71 [marzo-giugno 1979], p. 107; my translation).

13. "On Popular Justice: A Discussion with Maoists," in Gordon, pp. 8–9; my emphasis.

14. Ibid., p. 23.

15. Ibid., pp. 14–15.

16. Foucault, *History of Sexuality,* pp. 31–32.

17. "Interview" (1974, reprinted in *Polylogue,* Paris, 1977), trans. Claire Pajaczkowska, *m/f,* no. 5/6 (1981), p. 166.

18. Heath, *Questions of Cinema* (Bloomington: Indiana University Press, 1981), p. 145. An immediate instance of such "impossibilities" is obvious in the descriptions of Milena's character given by reviewers and casual spectators alike. For example, "a mysterious young woman . . . whose neurotic, demanding behavior feeds and frustrates his own anxieties" (Howard Kissel, "The Fragmented Figments of Nicholas [*sic*] Roeg," *W,* September 12–19,

1980, p. 20); or "the occasional wife of a retired Czech Colonel, Stefan Vognic (Denholm Elliott), many years her senior and vastly tolerant of her unfaithful, unpredictable sexuality (she leaves him whenever she feels like it, has affairs)" (Ian Penman, "*Bad Timing,* a Codifying Love Story," *Screen* 21, no. 3 [1980]: 108). Such descriptions not only proceed from an enunciative perspective entirely congruent with Alex's and Netusil's point of view, and all but disregard the film's work to disrupt that "vision" (through montage, sound-image mismatch, the final "Brechtian" epilogue, etc.); but in their moralizing ("unfaithful, unpredictable sexuality") and easy psychologizing ("neurotic, demanding"), they assume the very categories of female definition produced by classical narrative discourse, which have man (husband, lover, and male spectator) as their single term of reference. In short, they assume and take for granted that which in the film is, precisely, at issue.

19. The connection between this image and its libidinal investment is made several times in the film and, most explicitly, in the nightclub scene where a female performer, naked but for a "choker" and leather straps, bounces in a net suspended above the audience.

20. For Jakobson, see "Linguistics and Poetics," in *Style in Language,* ed. Thomas Sebeok (Cambridge, Mass.: The MIT Press, 1960), p. 358. See also Jacques Lacan, *Ecrits: A Selection,* trans. Alan Sheridan (New York: Norton, 1977), pp. 147–71.

21. The actual dialogue, from the film's soundtrack is as follows:

> Alex: I say we go back, we get married, we build something solid together.
> Milena: What about now?
> Alex: What do you mean now?
> Milena, Here, right now, this minute, this second, what we are . . .
> Alex: Milena, did you miss that I just asked you to marry me?
> Milena: No!
> Alex: But what are you talking about? I'm asking you to marry me.
> Milena: I love these days . . .
> Alex: I don't get it. Weren't you happy? You had to be happy. I felt it.
> Milena: I am happy . . . I was happy . . . I am happy. When I'm with you, I'm with you . . . I love being with you.
> Alex: What does that mean "with me," "not with me"? You have a husband you don't want, but you . . .
> Milena: My own life, my own time. You can be a part of it, the biggest part of it, you *are* the biggest part of it, I love you . . . C'mon . . . look where we are!

22. Cf. the brief dialogue between Feathers and Sheriff Chance in *Rio Bravo* quoted at the beginning of this chapter, where the man speaks as "I," and the woman as "you." Only to the extent that the logical subject of discourse is one—a unity grammatically ensured by the dialogical opposition of I and you—and thus a masculine one, is the *dialogue* possible between them, and everything that dialogue represents: love, marriage, the happy ending, the "sense" of the story, narrative itself.

23. Perhaps every movie about woman should be set in Vienna. The resemblance to *Letter from an Unknown Woman* goes further than the name Stefan (Lisa's lover and son), the marital triangle, the Prater waltz heard in the background of two conversations, the diegetic time span of a few hours, from late evening to early morning, during which are revisited an entire relationship and a lifetime. As Heath has suggested of *In the Realm of the*

Senses, Roeg's film is also *Letter*'s "ruinous remake." Lisa is exactly where Milena is not, squarely in the center of the Oedipal trajectory, the narrative time of masculine vision and desire; her disembodied voice only partially outside the story, finally contained in it by the film's circular temporality. But both women are unknown, except as figures of an obsession, memory traces around which Ophuls' flowing camera constructs a full narrative space, a perfect memory, and Roeg's disjunctive montage the shadow of a doubt, a fragmentary memory of difference. And perhaps it is not pure coincidence that Cavani's *The Night Porter*, that perfect scenario of masochism, is also set in Vienna. See Kaja Silverman's very interesting reading of Freud and of the film in "Masochism and Subjectivity," *Framework*, no. 12, (n.d.), pp. 2–9.

24. Tom Waits's "Invitation to the Blues," sung over the opening credit sequence with a slurred jazz cadence which only allows a few key words (Cagney, Rita Hayworth) to be comprehended, goes like this:

> Well she's up against the register,
> With an apron and a spatula,
> With yesterday's deliveries,
> And tickets for the bachelors.
> She's a moving violation
> From her conk down to her shoes,
> But it's just an invitation to the blues.
> And you feel just like Cagney.
> Looks like Rita Hayworth
> At the counter of Schwab's drugstore. . . .

Hearing this song, who does not "see" Lana Turner in *The Postman Always Rings Twice*, a story surely proven to be worth telling, and not "just once more"?

5. Desire in Narrative

1. Laura Mulvey, "Visual Pleasure and Narrative Cinema," *Screen* 16, no. 3 (Autumn 1975): 14.

2. Roland Barthes, "Introduction to the Structural Analysis of Narratives" in *Image-Music-Text*, trans. Stephen Heath (New York: Hill and Wang, 1977), p. 79. All further references to this volume will be cited in the text.

3. Contributors to the volume included Claude Bremond, A.-J. Greimas, and Tzvetan Todorov (on whose work Barthes draws heavily for his model); plus Umberto Eco and Christian Metz, whose paper "La grande syntagmatique du film narratif" virtually opened up the area of structural-semiotic analysis of cinema.

4. Metz's work on narrative structuration in classical cinema—*Film Language: A Semiotics of the Cinema*, trans. Michael Taylor (New York: Oxford University Press, 1974), and *Language and Cinema* (The Hague and Paris: Mouton, 1974)—had a great impact on the development of film theory (see, for example, Stephen Heath, "The Work of Christian Metz" in *Screen Reader 2* [London: SEFT, 1981], pp. 138–61); but was soon overshadowed by Metz's own subsequent work, *The Imaginary Signifier*, trans. Ben Brewster et al. (Bloomington: Indiana University Press, 1981), which shifted attention in the direction of psychoanalysis and questions of spectatorship.

5. Claire Johnston, "Women's Cinema as Counter-Cinema," in Claire Johnston, ed., *Notes on Women's Cinema* (London: SEFT, 1974), pp. 28 and 31.

6. "In *Visual Pleasure* my argument was axed around a desire to identify a pleasure that was specific to cinema, that is the eroticism and cultural conventions surrounding the look. Now, on the contrary, I would rather emphasise the way that popular cinema inherited traditions of story telling that are common to other forms of folk and mass culture, with attendant fascinations other than those of the look." Laura Mulvey, "Afterthoughts on 'Visual Pleasure and Narrative Cinema' inspired by *Duel in the Sun* (King Vidor, 1946)," *Framework*, no. 15/16/17 (1981), p. 13.

7. Roland Barthes, *The Pleasure of the Text*, trans. Richard Miller (New York: Hill and Wang, 1975), p. 10.

8. Robert Scholes, *Fabulation and Metafiction* (Urbana: University of Illinois Press, 1979), p. 26. The following quotes are from p. 27.

9. H. J. Rose, *The Handbook of Greek Mythology* (New York: Dutton, 1959), p. 183. On the representation of difference in ancient Greek society, and the shift it underwent in the transition from literary-mythic to philosophical discourse between the fifth and the fourth centuries B.C., see Page du Bois, *Centaurs and Amazons: Women and the Pre-History of the Great Chain of Being* (Ann Arbor: The University of Michigan Press, 1982).

10. Rose, p. 30.

11. Ibid, p. 188.

12. Hélène Cixous, "The Laugh of the Medusa," trans. Keith Cohen and Paula Cohen, in *New French Feminisms*, ed. Elaine Marks and Isabelle de Courtivron (Amherst: The University of Massachusetts Press, 1980), pp. 245–64. All further references to this work will be cited in the text.

13. Shoshana Felman, "Rereading Feminity," *Yale French Studies*, no. 62 (1981), pp. 19 and 21. The text she quotes from is Freud, "Femininity," in *New Introductory Lectures on Psychoanalysis*, trans. James Strachey (New York: Norton, 1965), p. 112. In his biography of Freud, Ernest Jones states: "There is little doubt that Freud found the psychology of women more enigmatic than that of men. He said once to Marie Bonaparte: 'The great question that has never been answered and which I have not yet been able to answer, despite my thirty years of research into the feminine soul, is "What does a woman want?"'" (*Sigmund Freud: Life and Work*, vol. 2, London, 1955, p. 468).

14. See note 10 in chapter 3.

15. V[ladimir] Propp, *Morphology of the Folktale*, second edition revised and edited by Louis A. Wagner (Austin and London: University of Texas Press, 1968), p. 79. The first English translation of Propp's *Morfológija skázki* (originally published in 1928) by Laurence Scott, ed. Svatava Pirkova-Jakobson (Bloomington, Ind., 1958) caused much stir in folklore and narrative studies. Already in 1960, Lévi-Strauss responded with what amounted to a charge of formalism and reductivism, to which Propp rejoined on the occasion of the Italian translation (*Morfologia della fiaba*, trans. Gian Luigi Bravo [Turin: Einaudi, 1966]), as mentioned by Alan Dundes in his introduction to the second edition cited above, p. xii. In setting forth the differences between Lévi-Strauss and Propp, however, Dundes himself reiterates the former's critique by stating that "Propp made no attempt to relate his extraordinary morphology to Russian (or Indo-European) culture as a whole" (p. xiii). The irony of this grossly erroneous assessment of Propp's work is also a sobering

proof on the ethnocentrism of Western scholarship: Propp's work since 1928 had been precisely devoted to the social and historical foundations of folk narratives, and indeed as methodologically far as is possible from "structural analysis [as] an end in itself." That his *Istoricheskie korni volshebnoĭ skázki* [The Historical Roots of the Fairy Tale] (Leningrad, 1946) was not translated into English by 1968—nor has it yet been, to my knowledge—is not Propp's deficiency but ours; the fact that it did exist in Italian translation since 1949 (*Le radici storiche dei racconti di fate,* trans. Clara Coisson, [Turin: Einaudi, 1949]) compounds the problem of ethnocentrism in ethnography.

16. This essay, "Edip v svete fol'klora," first published in *Serija filologičeskich nauk* 9, no. 72 (1944): 138–75, is also unavailable in English translation, so far as I know. My own deficiency, inadequate knowledge of Russian, obliges me therefore to quote, retranslating, from the Italian version, *Edipo alla luce del folclore,* ed. Clara Strada Janovič (Turin: Einaudi, 1975), pp. 85–87.

17. Which is not to repropose unchanged the terms of the old debate between evolutionism and functionalism in anthropology on the issue of a transition and/or a struggle from mother-right matriarchal systems to patri-archy, although Propp's view must have been closer to that of Bebel and Engels (*The Origin of the Family, Private Property, and the State,* New York: Pathfinder Press, 1972) than to that of a Fromm (see "The Oedipus Myth," in Eric Fromm, *The Forgotten Language* [New York: Holt, Rinehart, and Winston 1951]). On the contrary, the value of Propp's work for us is to be seen in its emphasis that symbolic practices (in folk narratives) are overdetermined, not unilaterally caused by (hence a reflex of) economic social relations. That is also the value of the tension in Freud's theory between an evolutionist, phy-logenetic account of the Oedipus structure in the history of the human race (his story of the primitve horde in *Totem and Tabu* and *Moses and Monotheism*) and the subsequent recasting of the Oedipus as a formative structure (the function of castration) that initiates the possibility of representation. This latter point, put forth in the Lacanian rereadings of Freud, is particularly well made by Rosalind Coward, "On the Universality of the Oedipus Complex: Debates on Sexual Divisions in Psychoanalysis and Anthropology," *Critique of Anthropology* 14, no. 15 (Spring 1980): 8–12.

18. Jurij M. Lotman, "The Origin of Plot in the Light of Typology," trans. Julian Graffy, *Poetics Today* 1, no. 1–2 (Autumn 1979): 161–84; originally published in 1973. All further references to this work will be cited in the text.

19. René Girard, *Violence and the Sacred,* trans. Patrick Gregory (Baltimore and London: The Johns Hopkins University Press, 1977), pp. 74–75. My emphasis underscores the proximity of Lévi-Strauss ("an *object* . . . belonging to the father and *formally* forbidden the son"; the Saussurian notion of "dif-ference," etc.) and the distance of Propp ("*it* [metaphysical "violent reciproc-ity"] has chosen as the basis of *their* rivalry *an object* . . . belonging to the father"). Propp speaks of princesses and donors; Lotman and Girard, of obstacles and objects.

20. "Plot represents a powerful means of making sense of life. Only as a result of the emergence of narrative forms of art did man learn to distinguish the plot aspect of reality, that is, to break down the non-discrete flow of events into discrete units, to connect them to certain meanings (that is, to interpret them semantically) and to organize them into regulated chains (to interpret them syntagmatically). It is the isolation of events—discrete plot units—and

the allotting to them, on the one hand, of a particular meaning, and, on the other, a particular temporal, cause-result or other regulatedness that makes up the essence of plot" (Lotman, pp. 182–83).

21. Cf. Mia Campioni and Elizabeth Gross, "Little Hans: The Production of Oedipus," in *Language, Sexuality and Subversion*, ed. Paul Foss and Meaghan Morris (Darlington, Australia: Feral Publications, 1978), pp. 99–122. This reading of Freud's famous case history owes to Gilles Deleuze and Félix Guattari, *Anti-Oedipus: Capitalism and Schizophrenia*, trans. Robert Hurley et al. (New York: Viking, 1977); my extension of the argument to Lotman's analysis of plot owes to Campioni and Gross.

22. Claude Lévi-Strauss, *Structural Anthropology*, trans. C. Jacobson and B. G. Schoepf (Garden City, N.Y.: Doubleday, 1967), pp. 192 and 196. All further references to this volume will be cited in the text.

23. "The effectiveness of symbols would consist precisely in this 'inductive property,' by which formally homologous structures, built out of different materials at different levels of life—organic processes, unconscious mind, rational thought—are related to one another. Poetic metaphor provides a familiar example of this inductive process, but as a rule it does not transcend the unconscious level. Thus we note the significance of Rimbaud's intuition that metaphor can change the world" (ibid., p. 197). The "inductive property" which allows a two-way connection between "formally homologous structures" is the symbolic function, i.e., the specifically human ability for indirect or symbolic representation, whose laws are a-temporal and identical for all humans. As the organ of the symbolic function, "the unconscious merely imposes structural laws upon inarticulated elements which originate elsewhere—impulses, emotions, representations, and memories." This elsewhere is the preconscious, "a reservoir of recollections and images amassed in the course of a lifetime," "the individual lexicon where each of us accumulates the vocabulary of his personal history." But that vocabulary becomes significant, he adds, "only to the extent that the unconscious structures it according to its laws and thus transforms it into language" (p. 198–99).

24. This view that "women are body," as Cixous puts it, that their nearness to the sensory and the somatic through identification with the maternal body makes it at best difficult to articulate it symbolically and thus to separate self from body, is one prevalent in French theories of the feminine; and clearly not by chance, given the influence of Lacanian psychoanalysis (whose link with Lévi-Strauss has been already pointed out on several occasions) on contemporary discourses in France. See Hélène Cixous, "The Laugh of the Medusa," op. cit.; Luce Irigaray, "Women's Exile," *Ideology and Consciousness*, no. 1 (May 1977), pp. 62–76; Michèle Montrelay, "Inquiry into Femininity," *m/f*, no. 1 (1978), pp. 83–101; Sarah Kofman, "Ex: The Woman's Enigma," *Enclitic* 4, no. 2 (Fall 1980): 17–28.

25. Axel Ingelman-Sundberg and Claes Wirsen, *The Everyday Miracle: A Child Is Born*, trans. Britt and Claes Wirsen, Annabelle MacMillan (London: The Penguin Press, 1967), p. 26. [Original copyright: Albert Bonniers Forlag, Stockholm, 1965; English translation copyright: Dell Publishing Co., New York, 1966] I am indebted to Anne Scott of the University of British Columbia, Vancouver, for suggesting the example as well as providing the reference.

26. Sigmund Freud, "Femininity," in *The Standard Edition of the Complete*

Psychological Works of Sigmund Freud, ed. James Strachey (London: Hogarth Press, 1955), vol. 22, p. 114. All further references to the Standard Edition will be indicated by *SE* followed by the volume number.

27. In a very short paper with the very long title "On the Reduction and Unfolding of Sign Systems (The Problem of 'Freudianism and Semiotic Culturology')," in *Semiotics and Structuralism: Readings from the Soviet Union* ed. Henryk Baran (White Plains, N.Y.: International Arts and Sciences Press, 1974), pp. 301–309, Lotman argues that the complex of sexual motifs underlying Freud's psychoanalytic model and his notion of the unconscious is not a primary but a secondary fact; it arises as "the result of *translation* of complex texts, received by the child from the world of adults, into the considerably simpler language of specifically child ideas" (p. 301). Consequently, "the notorious 'Oedipus complex' is not something spontaneously engendered as the expression of the child's own sexual attractions and aggressive drives but is the fruit of the recoding of a text with a large alphabet into a text with a small one" (p. 304). The argument seems to be based entirely on the Little Hans case history, virtually the only case in which Freud dealt with a child patient; though, even there, one might well wonder where in Freud a justification could be found for what Lotman calls "the *spontaneous* texts of the child's consciousness" (p. 305; my emphasis). As for Freud's notion of the unconscious (here called "subconscious"), it "is astounding in its straightforward rationalism. . . . The Freudian subconscious is a masked conscious." Not only is it "totally translatable into the language of consciousness," but actually "*it is constructed* by the investigator's metamodels and, naturally, is translated into them" (p. 304). All the more surprising, in this context, are the names of Lacan, Benveniste, Green, and Kristeva (in addition to Voloshinov and Bakhtin) in the footnote reference to critiques of Freud "from the standpoint of semiotic theory."

28. Victor Turner, "Social Dramas and Stories About Them" *Critical Inquiry* 7, no. 1 (Autumn 1980): 149. All further references to this work will be cited in the text.

29. P. 167. As an example of the relation between folk narrative and political structure in west central African societies, Turner cites a story in which "the drunken king Yala Mwaku was derided and beaten by his sons but cared for tenderly by his daughter Lweji Ankonde, whom he rewarded by passing on to her, on his death, the royal bracelet, the *lukanu* . . . thus rendering her the legitimate monarch of the Lunda. Another story tells how the young queen [falls in love with] a handsome young hunter, Chibinda. . . . He marries Lweji out of love and, in time, receives from her the *lukanu*—she has to go into seclusion during menstruation and hands Chibinda the bracelet lest it become polluted—making him the ruler of the Lunda nation. Lweji's turbulent brothers refuse to recognize him and lead their people away to carve out new kingdoms for themselves and consequently spread the format of political centralization among stateless societies" (p. 148). The point of telling the story is to show how folk narrative reflects history, the establishment of the Lunda nation and the subsequent diaspora of its groups. What Turner does not think of asking, but Propp would have, is: what do we make of a queen who menstruates only at the time of marriage?

30. Hayden White, "The Value of Narrativity in the Representation of

Reality," *Critical Inquiry* 7, no. 1 (Autumn 1980): 8–9. All further references to this work will be cited in the text.

31. "It is the State which first presents subject-matter that is not only adapted to the prose of History, but involves the production of such history in the very progress of its own being" (G. W. F. Hegel, *The Philosophy of History*, trans. J. Sibree, New York: 1956, pp. 60–61, quoted by White, p. 16).

32. When White writes that the form of historical representation provided by Hegel's philosophy of history is held in universal disdain because "it consists of nothing but plot" (and thus gives to reality an "odor of the ideal" embarrassing to historians who believe plot—meaning—must be found in the events themselves), one cannot but think of the near-universal disdain in which Lévi-Strauss is held, and not by anthropologists alone, much for the same reason. In a similar vein one might remark that the Lacanian symbolic, in which each subject's personal history is written, is more akin to Hegel's History than to any instance of historical materialism. The congruence of many current critical discourses on narrative with narrativity itself has been broadly intimated in the preceding pages.

33. If I may be allowed to offer a miniature tropological mapping of my own on the discourse of the author of *Tropics of Discourse* (Baltimore: Johns Hopkins University Press, 1978): in the passage I cite, Freud's term, *Wunsch*, translated by Lacan as *désir* and greatly expanded through the notion of the unconscious as "le désir de l'Autre," generates the two English terms, wish and desire, used here as synonyms. Thus, in the context of the essay, the statement "In the enigma of this wish, this desire, we catch a glimpse of the cultural function of narrativizing discourse" can be read as follows: "narrativizing discourse" (or narrativity) is the Hegelian law recast as the Lacanian symbolic. This then must correspond to the third term of Lacan's famous triad—real, imaginary, symbolic—which does not otherwise appear in the essay.

34. See note 2 above; and Roland Barthes, *S/Z*, trans. Richard Miller (New York: Hill and Wang, 1974).

35. An often-cited text, in this respect, is Freud's 1919 paper "A Child Is Being Beaten: A Contribution to the Study of the Origin of Sexual Perversion," *SE*, vol. 17, pp. 177–204. Freud's analysis of the beating fantasy shows that the subject's narrativized self-representation shifts under the twin pressures of desire and repression. Thus, while Freud again reasserts the central role of the Oedipus complex in the formation of neuroses and perversions, the essay lends itself to anti-Oedipal readings such as Jean-François Lyotard, "The Unconscious as Mise-en-scène," in *Performance in Postmodern Culture*, ed. Michel Benamou and Charles Caramello (Madison, WI: Coda Press, 1977), pp. 87–98. For other examples of readings focused on the inscription of desire in the text, within the critical tradition I have traced to Barthes, see *Yale French Studies*, special issue on *Literature and Psychoanalysis: The Question of Reading: Otherwise*, ed. Shoshana Felman, no. 55/56 (1977); and Felman's "Rereading Femininity."

36. Roy Schafer, "Narration in the Psychoanalytic Dialogue," *Critical Inquiry* 7, no. 1 (Autumn 1980), pp. 29–30. All further references to this work will be cited in the text.

37. As Hayden White puts it, the demand for closure in the historical story

is a demand "for moral meaning, a demand that sequences of real events be assessed as to their significance as elements of a moral drama" (p. 24).

38. Sigmund Freud, *Dora: An Analysis of a Case of Histeria,* ed. Philip Rieff (New York: Collier Books, 1963), p. 73.

39. Freud, "Femininity," p. 118. In recent readings of this essay, of the kind devoted to examining primarily what the text does *not* say and therefore *ipso facto* represses, as they would have it, it has been repeatedly noted how Freud, in quoting four lines from Heine's *The North Sea,* has omitted, elided, displaced, disguised, deceived, concealed, pretended, even "castrated the stanza"—in short, repressed together with Heine's name the context and the content of his poem's question ("Tell me, what signifies Man?"); this is adduced as evidence that Freud has repressed (the) Man. I think the point that Freud is finally concerned with *man* and *his* position in the universe and in society is rather evident on the manifest level of the text. The rhetorical overkill deployed in such readings, therefore, only affirms the attraction that psychoanalysis exercises on us who work with language—with good reasons.

40. The phrase has been widely debated; see discussion by Stephen Heath, "Difference," *Screen* 19, no. 3 (Autumn 1978): 50–112, in particular pp. 73–76. The script of *Riddles of the Sphinx* is published in *Screen* 18, no. 2 (Summer 1977): 61–77.

41. Seymour Chatman, "What Novels Can Do That Films Can't (and Vice Versa)," *Critical Inquiry* 7, no. 1 (Autumn 1980): 139.

42. Sigmund Freud, "Medusa's Head," *SE,* vol. 18, pp. 273–74.

43. Eugénie Lemoine-Luccioni, *Partage des femmes* (Paris, 1976), quoted by Stephen Heath, "Difference," p. 85.

44. For example Yann Lardeau, see note 20 in chapter 1.

45. Stephen Heath, *Questions of Cinema* (Bloomington: Indiana University Press, 1981), p. 53.

46. Ibid., pp. 119–20. "The shift between the first and second looks sets up the spectator's identification with the camera (rigorously constructed, placing heavy constraints, for example, on camera movement). The look at the film is an involvement in identifying relations of the spectator to the photographic image (the particular terms of position required by the fact of the photograph itself), to the human figure presented in image (the enticement and the necessity of a human presence 'on the screen'), to the narrative which gives the sense of the flow of photographic images (the guide-line for the spectator through the film, the ground that must be adopted for its intelligible reception). Finally, the looks of the characters allow for the establishment of the various 'point of view' identifications (the spectator looking with a character, from near to the position of his or her look, or as a character, the image marked in some way as 'subjective')" (p. 120).

47. Mulvey, "Visual Pleasure and Narrative Cinema," p. 13. In this connection should be mentioned the notion of a "fourth look" advanced by Willemen: a form of direct address to the viewer, an "articulation of images and looks which brings into play the position and activity of the viewer. . . . When the scopic drive is brought into focus, then the viewer also runs the risk of becoming the object of the look, of being overlooked in the act of looking. The fourth look is the *possibility* of that look and is always present in the wings, so to speak." (Paul Willemen, "Letter to John," *Screen* 21, no. 2 [Summer 1980]: 56.) I will return to this notion later on.

48. See Claire Johnston, "Women's Cinema as Counter-Cinema," p. 27; and Pam Cook and Claire Johnston, "The Place of Women in the Cinema of Raoul Walsh," in *Raoul Walsh*, ed. Phil Hardy (Edinburgh: Edinburgh Film Festival, 1974).

49. Heath, *Questions of Cinema*, p. 121. The reference to *Touch of Evil* is on p. 140.

50. Lea Melandri, *L'infamia originaria* (Milan: Edizioni L'Erba Voglio, 1977), see notes, 16 and 30 of chapter 1.

51. J. Laplanche and J.–B. Pontalis, *The Language of Psycho-Analysis*, trans. Donald Nicholson-Smith (New York: Norton, 1973), p. 205; my emphasis.

52. This point is also made by Mulvey, "Afterthoughts . . . inspired by *Duel in the Sun*" (see note 6 above), who, on the basis of Freud's view of femininity, proposes that female spectators have access to the (film's) fantasy of action "through the metaphor of masculinity"; the character of Pearl (Jennifer Jones), by dramatizing the oscillation of female desire between "passive" femininity and "regressive masculinity," encapsulates the position of the female spectator "as she temporarily accepts 'masculinization' in memory of her 'active' phase." However, Mulvey concludes, as Pearl's story illustrates, masculine identification for the female spectator is always "at cross purposes with itself, restless in its transvestite clothes" (p. 15). Although my discussion will develop in rather different ways, I fully share her concern to displace the active-passive, gaze-image dichotomy in the theory of spectatorship and to rethink the possibilities of *narrative* identification as a subject-effect in women spectators, an effect that is persistently denied by the prevailing notion of women's narcissistic over-identification with the image. See Mary Ann Doane, "Film and the Masquerade: Theorising the Female Spectator," *Screen* 23, no. 3–4 (September/October 1982): 74–87.

53. Freud, "Femininity," p. 131. It may be worth repeating, however, that Freud's view of the female's Oedipus situation underwent considerable transformation. In "The Dissolution of the Oedipus Complex" (1924) he held that "the girl's Oedipus complex is much simpler than that of the small bearer of the penis . . . it seldom goes beyond the taking of her mother's place and the adopting of a feminine attitude towards her father." In two subsequent papers, "Some Psychical Consequences of the Anatomical Distinction Between the Sexes" (1925) and "Female Sexuality" (1931), this situation became progressively more complex as Freud began to stress and to articulate the nature of the female's pre-Oedipal attachment to the mother. His last paper on "Femininity" (1933) was further informed by analytical accounts of adult female patients provided by women analysts.

54. See Jacqueline Rose, "The Cinematic Apparatus: Problems in Current Theory" in *The Cinematic Apparatus*, ed. Teresa de Lauretis and Stephen Heath (London: Macmillan and New York: St. Martin's Press, 1980), pp. 172–86. See also Heath, "Difference," and note 43 above.

55. This is particularly clear in Freud's analysis of the beating fantasy in males and females. See "A Child is Being Beaten," op. cit.

56. Metz, *Imaginary Signifier*, p. 51.

57. See Mary Ann Doane, "Misrecognition and Identity," *Cine-Tracts*, no. 11 (Fall 1980), pp. 28–31 and my discussion thereof in the context of Snow's *Presents* in chapter 3.

58. Laplanche and Pontalis, p. 336. They also note, incidentally, that Freud

differs from this recent view in that the other who serves as model for the subject is usually the father.

59. Seymour Chatman, "What Novels Can Do That Films Can't" cited in note 41 above. All further references to this work will be cited in the text.

60. Guy de Maupassant, "Une Partie de campagne," *Boule de Suif* (Paris, n.d.), cited by Chatman, pp. 130–131, my emphasis.

61. This passage is followed by the concluding paragraph of the article. "One final difference between the film and the story: the features of Henriette's appearance that Maupassant's narrator asserts are given an order. First he mentions her height, then her shape, her skin, eyes, hair, then her shape again, her arms, her bosom, her hat, and finally her legs. The order itself seems at once clinical and caressing, going up and down her body, confirming our impression of the narrator as a sensualist. There is no such implication in Renoir's shots. The camera *could* have scanned her body in a cliché shot in the Hollywood mode accompanied by an offscreen wolf whistle. Renoir elected not to compromise the camera: it would have spoiled the whole effect of unconsciously seductive innocence. The camera is not required to share its viewpoint with Rodolphe and the three other groups of voyeurs. It maintains a clear distinction between shots from Rodolphe's point of view and those from a neutral point of view" (p. 139). As must by now be clear to the reader, I do not share Chatman's view of the camera's neutrality, in this case or any other. Renoir could not elect to compromise or not to compromise the camera because the cinematic apparatus, as a social technology that transcends the work of individual directors, was and is fully compromised in the ideology of vision and sexual difference founded on woman as image, spectacle, object and *locus* of sexuality.

62. Paul Willemen, "Letter to John" (cited in note 47 above), p. 57. All further references to this work will be cited in the text.

63. For a concise and useful explanation of the distinction between Kristeva's notion of "the semiotic" and Lacan's "the imaginary," see Jane Gallop, *The Daughter's Seduction: Feminism and Psychoanalysis* (Ithaca, N.Y.: Cornell University Press, 1982), pp. 124–25.

64. As Claire Johnston states, underscoring the need at the present moment to pose the question of subjectivity in historical and social terms within feminist film theory: "Feminist film practice can no longer be seen simply in terms of the effectivity of a system of representation, but rather as a production of and by subjects already in social practices which always involve heterogeneous and often contradictory positions in ideologies. In other words, feminist film practice is determined by the conjuncture of discursive, economic and political practices which produce subjects in history." "The Subject of Feminist Film Theory/Practice," *Screen* 21, no. 2 (Summer 1980): 30.

65. Kaja Silverman, "*Histoire d'O*: The Story of a Disciplined and Punished Body," manuscript, p. 6. All further references to this work will be cited in the text.

66. Pauline Réage, *Story of O*, trans. Sabine d'Estrée (New York: Grove Press, 1965), p. 77.

67. In *The Age of Desire: Reflections of a Radical Psychoanalyst* (New York: Pantheon Books, 1981), pp. 17–18, Joel Kovel examines his discomfort, as a theorist and practicing analyst, with the stifling atmosphere of academic psychoanalysis, what he calls "the smell of the discourse," and describes his

musings: "Why did so much psychoanalytic writing, even the most seemingly abstract theory, read like a string of complaints directed by a boy against his mother: the subject always a 'he,' the offending parent, who does too much or too little, a 'she'? It was not enough to pass off such usage as a necessity imposed by language or reflective of actual social structure. The analysts were always trying to do this. . . . Lost in an ideology of passive contemplation, they saw social practice as an automatic fixed structure, not as a dialectical play of forces within which their own activity and the choices they made sustained one side or another. And one side that analysts always seemed to sustain was patriarchy: the vector of their work invariably pointed to a 'nature' represented by woman who nourishes the human represented by the male and against which he is to struggle and eventually dominate."

68. Tania Modleski, "Never To Be Thirty-Six Years Old: *Rebecca* as Female Oedipal Drama," *Wide Angle* 5, no. 1 (1982): 34–41. All further references to this work will be cited in the text.

69. François Truffaut, *Hitchcock* (New York: Simon & Schuster, 1967), pp. 184, 186. All further references to this work will be cited in the text. The lead roles in *Vertigo* (1958) are James Stewart (Scottie), Kim Novak (Madeleine and Judy), and Barbara Bel Geddes (Midge).

70. Actually, we do not *see* Judy's body on the rooftop, but rather we imagine it, seeing Scottie's look. More precisely, the film imagines it for us by calling up the visual memory of Madeleine's body on the rooftop in an earlier shot from the same camera position now occupied by Scottie. This is one example, among many that could be brought, of the working of narrativity in the filmic text to construct a memory, a vision, and a subject position for the spectator. It is an especially clear example of the distinction made earlier between image and figure. While Scottie is the image we spectators look at, and Judy is not in the image at all, what we see (envision and understand) is the object of his look; what we are seeing is not the woman but her narrative image. Scottie is the figure of narrative movement, his look and his desire define what is visible or can be seen; Judy/Madeleine is the figure of narrative closure, on whom look and desire and meaning converge and come to rest. Thus it is only by considering the narrative and figural dimension embedded in vision, in our reading of an image, that the notion of "woman as image" can be understood in its complexity.

71. This is admirably demonstrated by Linda Williams in her extended review of *Personal Best*, Robert Towne's very popular film about two women pentathletes who are both friends and lovers, and competitors in the 1980 Olympics. While asserting a new ethic of support and cooperation among athletes who are female, the film denies or at least forcefully undercuts the significance of their lesbian relation and thus banishes one woman from its narrative conclusion in favor of reasserting the correct, adult heterosexuality of the other. Williams concludes: "This allows the film to recuperate their (unnamed) sensual pleasure into its own regime of voyeurism. Ultimately, the many nude scenes and crotch-shots can be enjoyed much the way the lesbian turn-ons of traditional heterosexual pornography are enjoyed—as so much titillation before the penis makes its grand entrance." Linda Williams, "*Personal Best:* Women in Love," *Jump Cut*, no. 27 (July 1982), p. 12.

72. Despite the film's success and its winning an Oscar, Hitchcock himself does not like *Rebecca*. Asked by Truffaut whether he is satisfied with his first

Hollywood film, the director answers: "Well, it's not a Hitchcock picture; it's a novelette, really. The story is old-fashioned; there was a whole school of feminine literature at the period, and though I'm not against it, the fact is that the story is lacking in humor. . . . [The film] has stood up quite well over the years. I don't know why." (*Hitchcock*, pp. 91–93).

73. Marie Balmary's reading of the Oedipus myth in *Psychoanalyzing Psychoanalysis: Freud and the Hidden Fault of the Father*, trans. Ned Lukacher (Baltimore and London: The Johns Hopkins University Press, 1982) stresses the role of the father in the son's destiny as a function of identification. Balmary's reading is against Freud's own, and indeed takes place in the context of her reevaluation of the theory of the Oedipus complex in light of Freud's biography: as Oedipus was doomed to repeat unwittingly, by his crimes of incest and patricide, the faults of Laius (sexual violation of another's son and intended murder of his own), so did Freud repress the knowledge of his father's sexual incontinence (Jakob Freud's relationships with Rebecca, his mysterious second wife, and then with Sigmund's mother, his third wife). According to Balmary, it was Sigmund's repression of Jakob's "fault" that caused Freud to repudiate his first seduction theory, namely, that hysteria was the result of sexual overtures or actual seduction by the patient's father; and to discount the massive clinical evidence he had collected in the ten years prior to Jakob's death (1896) in favor of a seduction-fantasy theory based on the sudden "discovery" in 1897 that the Oedipus complex was a universal psychic structure. That latter, "idealist" model, she argues, was but a projection of Freud's own psychic reality, his symbolic identification with the father; and that has been the price to psychoanalytic theory of his complicity with the Law. Regrettably Balmary's analysis, contained within a Lacanian framework, draws no larger critical implications than those of a vaguely anti-Oedipal ethics.

74. See Lévi-Strauss, *Structural Anthropology*, pp. 212 and 226; "The myth has to do with the inability, for a culture which holds the belief that mankind is autochthonous . . . to find a satisfactory transition between this theory and the knowledge that human beings are actually born from the union of man and woman. Although the problem obviously cannot be solved, the Oedipus myth provides a kind of logical tool which relates the original problem—born from one or born from two?—to the derivative problem: born from different or born from same?" (p. 212) And "since the purpose of myth is to provide a logical model capable of overcoming a contradiction (an impossible achievement if, as it happens, the contradiction is real), a theoretically infinite number of slates will be generated, each one slightly different from the others. Thus, myth grows spiral-wise *until the intellectual impulse which has produced it is exhausted*" (p. 226; my emphasis).

75. Ursula K. Le Guin, "It Was a Dark and Stormy Night; or, Why Are We Huddling about the Campfire?" *Critical Inquiry* 7, no. 1 (Autumn 1980): 191–99.

76. The fact that at this moment in history, it is women, feminists, who speak from the place of the Sphinx, and who look at Perseus while Medusa is being slain, may not be inconsistent with the structural-Hegelian paradigm. But then, that would mean that the moral order of meaning and the rule of law of patriarchy are no longer those in relation to which woman is being constituted as subject. It would mean, in short, that our moment in history

does mark the beginning of what Kristeva has called "the passage of patriarchal society." I said, a hopeful footnote.

77. Muriel Rukeyser, "Myth," in *The Collected Poems* (New York: McGraw-Hill, 1978), p. 498.

6. Semiotics and Experience

1. Virginia Woolf, *A Room of One's Own* (New York and London: Harcourt Brace Jovanovich, 1929), p. 6. My emphasis.

2. The process I here call experience might have been called ideology by others. The reasons for my choice of word, if not already apparent, must become clearer later on.

3. Claude Lévi-Strauss, *Mythologiques, IV: L'homme nu* (Paris: Plon, 1971); *The Naked Man*, trans. John and Doreen Weightman (New York: Harper and Row, 1981), in particular, "Finale," pp. 625–95.

4. See chapter 1 above.

5. See Dale Spender, *Man Made Language* (London: Routledge & Kegan Paul, 1980). In explaining the asymmetrical position of women and men in the semantic space of the English language ("the meanings available within the language"), Spender argues that the assumption of (male) grammarians that English is a language based on natural, rather than grammatical, gender has gone hand in hand with another, unstated, assumption: that the male is the norm of what is natural. Thus gender distinctions in language are constructed by the semantic markers "plus male" or "minus male" (i.e., female), with the result that the "positive" space is reserved for males. After surveying an impressive amount of sociolinguistic research conducted from the premise that both language and language research are slanted against women, Spender convincingly makes the point that all mixed-group linguistic interaction tends, not just to devalue women's speech, but to "construct women's silence"; and this tendency is further enforced by the institutionalized inaccessibility of women to one another's speech, since the places and occasions for "women's talk" have been severely restricted. Hence, she contends, the vital importance to women of consciousness raising groups and the feminist intervention in language, spoken and written, as a "politics of naming."

6. This is a rather marginal position within American feminism, but see, for example, Ursula K. Le Guin, "Is Gender Necessary?" in *The Language of the Night* (New York, 1979).

7. For example, Susan Griffin, *Woman and Nature: The Roaring Inside Her* (New York: Harper and Row, 1978). This is the dominant position, not only within American feminism, and is too extensive to be documented here.

8. Julia Lesage, "The Human Subject—You, He, or Me? (Or, The Case of the Missing Penis)," *Jump Cut*, no. 4 (November–December 1974), reprinted in *Screen* 16, no. 2 (Summer 1975): 73. A "Comment" by the writers in question, Ben Brewster, Stephen Heath, Colin MacCabe, follows on pp. 83–90. All further references to this work will be cited in the text.

9. One should actually be more precise and say that the conception of the subject defended by Brewster, Heath and MacCabe in their reply to Lesage actually comes from *their reading* of Lacan's rereading of Freud and from their historical materialist perspective, which brings them to claim for Lacan something that may not be his due: "Lacan's restitution of Freudian analysis as 'materialist theory of language'" (p. 86). At any rate, the "attempt to articu-

late the process of the subject within historical materialism" for film theory is not Lacan's or Althusser's but, admittedly, their own.

10. On Derrida's views of femininity, see Gayatri Chakravorty Spivak, "Displacement and the Discourse of Woman," in *Displacement: Derrida and After,* ed. Mark Krupnick (Bloomington and London: Indiana University Press, 1983).

11. Jacqueline Rose, "Introduction—II," in Jacques Lacan and the *école freudienne, Feminine Sexuality,* trans. Jacqueline Rose, ed. Juliet Mitchell and Jacqueline Rose (New York and London: W. W. Norton, 1982), p. 48.

12. So, for example, I believe Rose's other explanation, offered a couple of pages later in defense of Lacan against the "demands" of feminist analysts: "When Lacan says that women do not know, while, at one level, he relegates women outside, and against, the very mastery of his own statement, he was [*sic*] also recognising the binding, or restricting, of the parameters of knowledge itself ('masculine knowledge irredeemably an erring')" (p. 51). Woman is indeed nothing more and nothing less than "a 'symptom' for the man," his aching rib.

13. Rose, p. 44. Kaja Silverman, *The Subject of Semiotics* (New York: Oxford University Press, 1983), the most recent and systematic effort to argue for the centrality of the subject in theories of meaning, proposes that psychoanalysis be seen as, in effect, a branch of semiotics; and further, that if "semiotics as a self-conscious theory emerged only at the beginning of this century, in the writings of Charles Sanders Peirce and Ferdinand de Saussure . . . it achieved maturity only when it was consolidated with psychoanalysis" by the work of Lacan (p. 3). The subject which assumes priority in this "history" of semiotics is the subject as psychoanalysis defines it. And in such perspective Silverman is obliged to say: "We will endeavor to create a space for the female subject within these pages, even if that space is only a negative one" (p. 131).

14. Catharine A. MacKinnon, "Feminism, Marxism, Method, and the State: An Agenda for Theory," *Signs* 7, no. 3 (Spring 1982): 531. All further references to this work will be cited in the text.

15. Umberto Eco, *A Theory of Semiotics* (Bloomington and London: Indiana University Press, 1976), p. 314. All further references to this work will be cited in the text, preceded by the abbreviation *TS*.

16. Julia Kristeva, "The System and the Speaking Subject," *The Times Literary Supplement,* October 12, 1973, p. 1249, quoted by Eco, *A Theory of Semiotics,* p. 317. Kristeva's works most recently translated into English are *Desire in Language: A Semiotic Approach to Literature and Art,* trans. Thomas Gora, Alice Jardine, and Leon S. Roudiez, ed. Leon S. Roudiez (New York: Columbia University Press, 1980), containing essays from *Semeiotiké: Recherches pour une sémanalyse* (Paris: Seuil, 1969) and *Polylogue* (Paris: Seuil, 1977); and *Powers of Horror: An Essay on Abjection,* trans. Leon S. Roudiez (New York: Columbia University Press, 1982).

17. In the last footnote of Eco's *Theory,* the possibility is admitted that semiotics will overcome this "natural" boundary and, from a theory of codes and sign production, semiotics will develop (as he puts it) "a theory of the 'deep' individual origins of any 'wish to produce signs.'" In this sense "a threshold-trespassing semiotics could be conceived, which the present book does not dare to take into account" (p. 318). In his subsequent book, however, the concession will be effectively withdrawn.

18. "Peirce and the Semiotic Foundations of Openness," in Umberto Eco, *The Role of the Reader: Explorations in the Semiotics of Texts* (Bloomington and London: Indiana University Press, 1979), pp. 193–94. All further references to this work will be cited in the text, preceded by the abbreviation *RR*. The essay was first published, with minor variations, as "Peirce and Contemporary Semantics," *Versus*, no. 15 (1976).

19. Charles Sanders Peirce, *Collected Papers*, vols. 1–8 (Cambridge, Mass.: Harvard University Press, 1931–1958). All further references to this work will be cited in the text by the volume number followed by the paragraph number. This passage is in 2.228 (cited by Eco, *RR*, p. 180).

20. "A practical belief may, therefore, be described as a habit of deliberate behavior. The word 'deliberate' is hardly completely defined by saying that it implies attention to memories of past experience and to one's present purpose, together with self-control" (5.538). As for the term *habit*, Peirce uses it in a much wider sense than natural disposition or acquired habit, to include "associations" and even "dissociations." "Let us use the word 'habit', throughout this book . . . in its wider and perhaps still more usual sense, in which it denotes such a specialization, original or acquired, of the nature of a man, or an animal, or a vine, or a crystallizable chemical substance, or anything else, that he or it will behave, or always tend to behave, in a way describable in general terms upon every occasion (or upon a considerable proportion of the occasions) that may present itself of a generally describable character" (5.538).

21. The formulation is apparently very close to Althusser's view of the relation of the subject to ideology: the "concrete individual" (which we understand to mean an already constituted individual) is interpellated or "recruited" by ideology—which exists and works through the material practices of the ideological state apparatuses—and is thus "transformed" into a subject. At the same time, because ideology "is eternal" (a-temporal, or structural, like the Lacanian symbolic), individuals are "always-already interpellated by ideology as subjects." See Louis Althusser, *Lenin and Philosophy*, trans. Ben Brewster (New York and London: Monthly Review Press, 1971), p. 176. For a well-argued comparison of Eco's and Althusser's theories and their congruence with regard to, especially, aesthetic production, see Thomas. E. Lewis, "Notes toward a Theory of the Referent," *PMLA* 94 (May 1979): 459–75. In defending Althusser from the accusation of theoreticism often leveled against him, Lewis states: "Although Althusser unfortunately does not make this point clearly enough, *his notion of open-ended scientific knowledge implies precisely the intervention of practice* and the presence of cultural determination in the production of scientific knowledge" (p. 474; my emphasis). The same objection, and the same defense could be raised for Eco's theory of textuality as put forth in *Lector in fabula* (Milan: Bompiani, 1979), but the defense is rather weak. Merely to *imply* a relation of the subject to practices is not enough when the weight of the argument is otherwise on the structures.

22. I cannot do justice to Eco by developing my critique of *Lector in fabula* in this context, and must therefore refer the reader to my *Umberto Eco* (Firenze: La Nuova Italia, 1981).

23. See chapter 1, p. 35 and chapter 2, p. 55 above.

24. Peirce takes full credit for establishing pragmatism as a theory of meaning (or better, "a method of determining the meaning of intellectual

concepts, that is, of those upon which reasoning may turn," [5.8]), and even resorts to changing its name to "pragmaticism" ("which is ugly enough to be safe from kidnappers," [5.414]) after William James and F. C. S. Schiller have appropriated "pragmatism" for their own respective interests. But as far as semiotics is concerned, he declares himself to be "a pioneer, or rather a backwoodsman, in the work of clearing and opening up what I call *semiotic*, that is the doctrine of the essential nature and fundamental varieties of possible semiosis; and I find the field too vast, the labor too great, for a first-comer" (5.488). In Peirce's view, then, the semiotic domain is not coextensive with pragmaticism, a theory of meaning which addresses "intellectual concepts," but much broader; it encompasses all *possible* varieties of semiosis.

25. On Peirce's understanding of the self as a product of inference rather than intuition, and hence as a sign, see Walter Benn Michaels, "The Interpreter's Self: Peirce on the Cartesian 'Subject'," in *Reader-Response Criticism*, ed. Jane P. Tompkins (Baltimore and London: The Johns Hopkins University Press, 1980), pp. 185–200. Briefly, Michaels argues that Peirce's view develops out of his critique of the Cartesian *cogito* and the primacy, autonomy or transcendence which it confers upon the ego. "For Descartes, the self is primary—it can be known directly, and its existence is the single privileged certainty; for Peirce the self is derived—it can only be known by inference from the existence of ignorance and error" (p. 194). As a sign, the self is embedded in the larger system of signs Peirce calls "reality," and therefore subject to its "constitutive effects."

26. "Le registre du signifiant s'institue de ce qu'un signifiant représente un sujet pour un autre signifiant. C'est la structure, rêve, lapsus et mot d'esprit, de toutes les formations de l'inconscient. Et c'est aussi celle qui explique la division originaire du sujet." Jacques Lacan, *Écrits* (Paris: Seuil, 1966), p. 840. This essay, not selected for the English translation of *Écrits* (New York: W. W. Norton, 1977), is discussed in Anika Lamaire, *Jacques Lacan*, trans. David Macey (London: Routledge & Kegan Paul, 1977), pp. 72–77.

27. "Les signes sont plurivalents: *ils représentent sans doute quelque chose pour quelqu'un*; mais ce quelqu'un, son statut est incertain . . ." Lacan (*Écrits*, p. 840; my emphasis).

28. While he does not conceive of the subject quite as Lacan does, still Peirce's subject is a subject in language and, in its fashion, divided: "Two things here are all-important to assure oneself of and to remember. The first is that a person is not absolutely an individual. His thoughts are what he is 'saying to himself,' that is, is saying to that other self that is just coming into life in the flow of time. When one reasons, it is that critical self that one is trying to persuade; and all thought whatsoever is a sign, and is mostly of the nature of language. The second thing to remember is that the man's circle of society (however widely or narrowly this phrase may be understood), is a sort of loosely compacted person, in some respects of higher rank than the person of an individual organism" (5.421).

29. A more balanced and critically useful elaboration of the notion of suture is given by Stephen Heath, "Notes on Suture" in *Questions of Cinema* (Bloomington: Indiana University Press, 1981), pp. 106–107: "Suture names the relation of the subject in the symbolic which is its join in the chain, its representation from signifier to signifier ('a signifier represents a subject for another signifier') and its identification as one in the fiction of the sign ('a sign

represents something for someone'). The division-separation causation of the subject describes this process, the subject always returning in its implication in the desire of the Other . . . in which the subject always fails . . . and is always found again . . . taken up immediately in meanings and their production in discursive formations. A theory of ideology must then begin not from the subject but as an account of suturing effects, the effecting of the join of the subject in structures of meaning; which account would thus involve an attention to the whole history of the subject, the interminable movement of that history, and not its simple equation with ideology." It is this attention to the "whole history" of the subject—marking an important departure from the received definition of the relation (the "simple equation") of subject and ideology—that I wish to convey by the term "experience" (see note 2 above). But "experience" in its turn lends itself, because of its popular usage, to a "simple equation" of subject with individual, without social or semiotic mediation. Hence the necessity for a theoretical elaboration of the notion of experience, particularly within the feminist discourse.

30. J. Laplanche and J.-B. Pontalis, *The Language of Psycho-Analysis,* trans. Donald Nicholson-Smith (New York: W. W. Norton, 1973), pp. 481–82.

31. Though Peirce was well aware that his notion of habit extended far beyond consciousness and thus exceeded the boundaries of positivistic psychology (see, for example, his remarks about his contemporaries' "delusion that Mind is just Consciousness" and Von Hartmann's studies of the unconscious mind, in 7.364 ff.), he did not have the advantage of a developed theory of the unconscious with which his theory of habit might be confronted. We, however, do. That Peirce and Freud are even stranger bedfellows than Marx and Freud, and certainly no less reluctant to mutual "integration," need not discourage a rereading aimed at, not the integration but the possible articulation of one theory of meaning to the other.

32. See chapter 5, note 65.

33. Manuela Fraire, "La politica del femminismo," *Quaderni piacentini,* no. 62–63 (1977), p. 195. Fraire is reviewing a volume of materials and documents—articles, position papers, editorials, manifestos, press releases and other statements issued by various feminist groups and women's collectives in Italy between 1973 and 1976—edited by Biancamaria Frabotta, *La politica del femminismo* (Rome: Savelli, 1976).

34. Mary Russo, "Notes on 'Post-Feminism'," in *The Politics of Theory,* ed. Francis Barker et al. (Colchester: University of Essex, 1983), p. 27. Russo is discussing the recent work of Julia Kristeva and Maria Antonietta Macciocchi, the two intellectual figures principally associated with this latest "ism," and their attempts to bring feminism in line with antihumanist philosophy.

INDEX OF NAMES

INDEX OF FILMS